PRAISE FOR DAVID KRELL'S
1962: BASEBALL AND AMERICA IN THE TIME OF JFK

"Krell should be commended for presenting so many aspects of 1962 in an interesting and understanding way. His writing and research are impeccable. This is a book you will want to pick up and read again and again."
—Mark McGee, *Nine: A Journal of Baseball History and Culture*

"For those of us who remember 1962, we think of it as Camelot, the last year in which America was mostly at peace with itself. For those too young to remember, David Krell brings it back to life in an informative and entertaining way. Among other aspects of American culture, Krell vividly describes a baseball season that featured two new teams in the National League, a thrilling pennant race, and a World Series with a memorable ending; a year of wonderful Hollywood movies and not-so-wonderful TV shows; and the ups and downs of our popular young president."
—Lyle Spatz, author of *1921: The Yankees, the Giants, and the Battle for Baseball Supremacy in New York*

"Cultural historian Krell weaves a gripping account of a momentous baseball season, five no-hitters, an exceptional [National League] playoff between the Giants and Dodgers, and a seven-game World Series showcasing Mantle and Mays. All this and more against the backdrop of the Cuban Missile Crisis, the Space Race, and the Civil Rights movement."
—John Vorperian, SABR *Newsletter*

"Krell's look at 1962 hits the mark on a less-recognized year that in retrospect had as many twists and turns as did the pennant races and World Series and, like McCovey's drive, might have ended very differently."
—Jerry Milani, *Sports Media Report*

"Cracking the spine of David Krell's literary journey back to 1962 is like opening a time capsule on the bookshelf. Chapter by chapter, NASA, *The Flintstones*, Maury Wills, Bo Belinsky, and so much more are carefully unwrapped before your very eyes and exposed to twenty-first-century sunlight for what feels like the first time. In Krell's capable hands, everything old feels new again."
—Mitchell Nathanson, author of *Bouton: The Life of a Baseball Original*

"David Krell has done prodigious research to bring you the events, the issues, and the famous personalities of 1962. Not only will you encounter JFK, the seven Mercury astronauts, civil rights figures, and Marilyn Monroe, but you'll reconnect with Buddy Ebsen and the *Beverly Hillbillies*, the cast of *Car 54, Where Are You?*, and Edd 'Kookie' Byrnes. And yes, the Yankees won the World Series."
—Peter Golenbock, author of *The Bronx Zoo* and *Bums*

1978

1978

BASEBALL AND AMERICA IN THE DISCO ERA

DAVID KRELL

UNIVERSITY OF NEBRASKA PRESS

Lincoln

© 2025 by David Krell

All rights reserved
Manufactured in the United States of America

The University of Nebraska Press is part of a land-grant institution with campuses and programs on the past, present, and future homelands of the Pawnee, Ponca, Otoe-Missouria, Omaha, Dakota, Lakota, Kaw, Cheyenne, and Arapaho Peoples, as well as those of the relocated Ho-Chunk, Sac and Fox, and Iowa Peoples.

LIBRARY OF CONGRESS CATALOGING-IN-PUBLICATION DATA
Names: Krell, David, 1967– author.
Title: 1978: baseball and America in the disco era / David Krell.
Other titles: Nineteen seventy-eight
Description: Lincoln: University of Nebraska Press, [2025] | Includes bibliographical references and index.
Identifiers: LCCN 2024035550
ISBN 9781496239600 (hardback)
ISBN 9781496243669 (epub)
ISBN 9781496243676 (pdf)
Subjects: LCSH: Baseball—United States—History—20th century. | Baseball—United States—History—Chronology. | United States—Civilization—1970—Anecdotes.
Classification: LCC GV863.A1 K74 2025 | DDC 796.357/640973—dc23/eng/20241107
LC record available at https://lccn.loc.gov/2024035550

Designed and set in Adobe Jenson Pro by Katrina Noble.

This book is dedicated to the first responders, snowplow drivers, and snow shovelers during the blizzards of 1978.

CONTENTS

Acknowledgments ix

1. The Best Interests of Baseball: January   1
2. "A Chance to Be Absolutely Unbelievable": February   17
3. Goodbye Dark, My Old Friend: March   32
4. Move Over, Baby Ruth, Here Comes Reggie: April   44
5. Kingman's Performance and Lasorda's Outrage: May   54
6. Louisiana Lightning and Greased Lightning: June   66
7. Melodrama in the Bronx: July   79
8. A Rose by Any Other Game: August   95
9. The Boston Massacre: September   110
10. The World Series: October   127
11. A Tale of Two Sparkys: November   143
12. It's a Bird . . . It's a Plane . . . It's a Blockbuster: December   157

Notes   171

Bibliography   193

Index   195

ACKNOWLEDGMENTS

There were many people who participated in this journey to 1978. The staff at the New York Public Library was invaluable in fulfilling requests for its archives of New York City newspapers from 1978 on microfilm. Additionally, the NYPL's Inter-Library Loan program procured the *Los Angeles Herald Examiner* on microfilm.

Cassidy Lent, director of the library at the National Baseball Hall of Fame and Museum's Giamatti Research Center, answered questions and provided information with her usual patience, aplomb, and context. Kristen Reichenbach, manuscript reference librarian at the Library of Congress, accessed speeches of Herman Wouk, author of the best-selling book *War and Remembrance*, which debuted in 1978. Thanks to Art Carine for his input on the manuscript.

My indebtedness to those who shared their insights about 1978: Andy Abel, Rebecca Alpert, Chris Butts, Lisa (Katz) Gruber, Rock Hoffman, Allen Katz, Rhoda Katz, Gary Kroeger, Mike Miller, James Pietras, Greg Prince, Jory Schunick, Lacey Schunick, Victor Sloan, and Charlie Vascellaro.

This is the third book for which I've teamed with Maureen Creamer Bemko, who provided exemplary contributions in her role as copy editor.

Rob Taylor and his team at the University of Nebraska Press gave the green light for this idea backed by enthusiasm, feedback, and confidence.

My deepest appreciation to everyone!

1978

1

THE BEST INTERESTS OF BASEBALL

JANUARY

Ellicott Creek Park look like it jumped off a Currier and Ives Christmas card.

Snow blanketed the Buffalo area, a typical occurrence during winter in western New York. Saint Christopher Parish stood adjacent to the park under gray skies, fulfilling its duty on this mid-January day in 1978 as a gathering place to honor the life of a person who had recently passed.

Joseph Vincent McCarthy, Baseball Hall of Fame, class of 1957.

His death from pneumonia at the age of ninety triggered an outpouring of nostalgia for eras when newspapers had evening editions, baseball teams leaving their cities was a forbidden idea, and the designated hitter did not exist. As mourners scouted for seating opportunities among the pews in the brick-faced church on Niagara Falls Boulevard in Tonawanda, their thoughts turned to bygone years, when the world seemed simpler, slower, and less crowded for time.

Baseball notables were among the attendees. Hall of Famer Monte Irvin, New York–Pennsylvania League president Vincent McNamara, Hall of Fame director Ken Smith, New York Yankees vice president Marshall Samuel, and former Yankees PR director Bob Fishel filed into Saint Chris along with others paying their respects and preparing to take the legendary manager to his final resting place at Mount Olivet Cemetery.

Unlike fiery Leo Durocher or colorful Casey Stengel, McCarthy had a quieter way about him. "Joe McCarthy understood what good players could do for a manager and never pushed too many buttons to inhibit the best results," *Buffalo News* sportswriter Franklyn Buell reminded readers.[1]

His management style led to seven World Series titles in his eight Fall Classic appearances with the Yankees, between 1932 and the early part of May 1946, when he stepped down. McCarthy, a Philadelphia native, might not have chosen baseball as an outlet when he was a kid except for a fateful shopping trip for a new suit with his mother. There was an added incentive for ten-year-old Joe—a bat and ball were part of the purchase at Snellenburg's Department Store on the corner of Twelfth and Market Streets. "Mother argued against buying it," recalled McCarthy in 1937. "I coaxed and finally won." The New York Giants were in town to play the Phillies; they walked by the store as Mrs. McCarthy and her son walked out. "From that minute baseball became my life," he said. "I started to dream about the game—and have never stopped."[2]

McCarthy began his baseball journey in adulthood when he spent two years at Niagara University—courtesy of a baseball scholarship—and then joined the Minor Leagues.[3] From 1907 to 1921 he played in the Minors for the Wilmington Peaches, Franklin Millionaires, Toledo Mud Hens, Indianapolis Indians, Wilkes-Barre Barons, Buffalo Bisons, and Louisville Colonels.

A .260 career hitter, McCarthy never reached the Major Leagues. But managing is where he made his mark, starting with Wilkes-Barre in 1913 and Louisville from 1919 to 1925. McCarthy's first game at the Louisville helm was a 6–2 victory against the Kansas City Blues, after Patsy Flaherty resigned. The *Courier-Journal* called McCarthy "one of the brainiest players cavorting in the minors." Further plaudits indicated the manager's bright future: "McCarthy is popular with the players as well as the fans, and he should prove a big success with the club."[4] The Colonels twice won American Association pennants under McCarthy's leadership—1921 and 1925.

McCarthy went to Chicago and faced his idol, Connie Mack, when the Cubs played the Philadelphia A's in the 1929 World Series. Philadelphia won in five games. In late September during the following season, Cubs owner William Wrigley Jr. fired McCarthy. Bitterness was absent. "There has been no specific trouble between the business office and myself," said McCarthy. "The only official criticism I have heard is that I haven't made certain changes."[5] Wrigley said as much in his statement: "There has been no misunderstanding with McCarthy."[6]

Chicago had a 442-321 record under McCarthy; Cubs management made good on the contract that provided him with a bonus if the team reached second place in the National League. At the time, they were three games behind the first-place Cardinals.[7] The Cubs finished the season in second place, trailing by two games. St. Louis faced Philadelphia in the World Series and lost in six games.

After transplanting to the South Bronx in 1931, McCarthy became a cornerstone of the storied Yankees with Bill Dickey, Babe Ruth, Earle Combs, Lou Gehrig, Frankie Crosetti, Red Ruffing, and Lefty Gomez. In July of that year, Harold C. Burr warned readers of the *Brooklyn Daily Eagle*, "But the last story hasn't been written yet about Joe McCarthy, manager of the Yankees. He knows his own shortcomings and the shortcomings of his players."[8] Indeed, his time with the Yankees yielded terrific success—including being the first manager to win four World Series titles in a row—and coincided with some of baseball's landmark moments.

McCarthy was there when Ruth made his "called shot" and hit a home run at Wrigley Field in the 1932 World Series.

McCarthy was there when Gehrig proclaimed himself to be the luckiest man on the face of the earth between games of a Yankees-Senators doubleheader at Yankee Stadium in 1939, despite a disease that would claim his life two years later.

McCarthy was there when Joe DiMaggio led the Major Leagues in triples during his rookie season, won two of his three Most Valuable Player Awards, and set a record of hitting safely in fifty-six consecutive games in 1941. Four years later, there were inconsistent press reports regarding McCarthy's future at the Yankees helm. On July 31, 1945, Arch Murray of the *New York Post* cited a "highly reliable source" that a conflict, albeit amiable, with Yankees general manager Larry MacPhail influenced McCarthy's imminent departure. They simply had two differing styles—deliberate versus impulsive.[9]

Health was a prominent issue, though McCarthy's physician, Dr. Arthur Burkel, dismissed the idea of imminent retirement. "I would discredit the story entirely," stated Burkel as his patient recovered at home from "a stomach disorder." Mrs. Elizabeth McCarthy concurred, saying that her husband would return to the Yankees "when he's well again."[10]

It took another week and a half; McCarthy resumed his duties on August 9. The following May, he quit after a gall bladder attack.[11] Yankees catcher Bill Dickey replaced him.[12] A month later, the Yankees hired McCarthy as a scout, though a story circulated that Indians owner Bill Veeck wanted him to replace Lou Boudreau as manager.[13]

There was another rumor the following February that McCarthy would take over the 1947 Red Sox.[14] But his hiatus from the dugout lasted through the season, until baseball's sirens lured him to sign a two-year contract with Boston's American League club.[15] "Because I knew I'd been away from it long enough," said McCarthy. "I just couldn't forget it."[16]

McCarthy led a rebound, improving the Fenway fellas' record from 83-71 in 1947 to 96-59. That tally tied the Cleveland Indians, who won the one-game American League playoff 8–3 and beat the Boston Braves in six games to win the World Series.

In 1949 McCarthy's Bosox battled the Yankees to the end of the season in another hallmark of the epic rivalry between the clubs. New York won the pennant by one game, then captured the first of five consecutive World Series titles under Casey Stengel. During the season, McCarthy recapped a major point for baseball helmsmen with a caveat that can apply to leaders in any industry: "However, a manager should know the limitations of his material. I learned early in my managerial experience one never gains anything by kidding himself."[17] Another credo: "Play smart baseball on every pitch . . . every play. Don't beat yourself."[18]

McCarthy ended his managerial career a couple of months into the 1950 season. Weary from influenza and pleurisy, the sixty-three-year-old manager walked into his colonial house at 459 South Ellicott Creek Road in Amherst, a Buffalo suburb, on the evening of June 22. Reporters wanted to know if the venerable but worn-out McCarthy had resigned during the team's current road trip to play the Chicago White Sox. Red Sox management spiced the issue by labeling the time of McCarthy's return as indefinite.

The trip was difficult enough without the press questioning his job security. Frustration overwhelmed patience when, after touching down at Buffalo Municipal Airport at 5:20 p.m., McCarthy "rushed through the gate swinging at a photographer's camera" while looking for his wife, Elizabeth. A native of the Buffalo area, she navigated the airport trip with ease and deflected speculation about her husband resigning. "There's no truth to that report," she said. "He's just sick and I'm waiting for the doctor now. It is nothing to be alarmed about. Joe probably will be up and around tomorrow afternoon, and maybe he can answer any questions at that time. Joe will have a complete rest and a physical check-up here."[19]

The following day, McCarthy resigned.

Upon the suggestion, or perhaps insistence, of Dr. Burkel, McCarthy put his baseball career in the rearview mirror and stated that he was "physically tired, physically exhausted."[20] With baseball no longer consuming his days, McCarthy anticipated more time for his hobbies of fishing and hunting during his sunset years in western New York.

Like termites chomping on wood, the pressures of managing had chipped away at McCarthy. He did not feel valuable. "When it became more and more apparent that I just couldn't seem to do anything right for the ball club, I finally reached the decision that I had considered many times in the past," he told the *Boston Post*. "And maybe it will turn out the best for all concerned."[21]

McCarthy told Red Sox general manager Joe Cronin, "I'm tired even now after two good night's [sic] sleep. It may take me a long while to get fully rested. So I think you had better name a new manager right away." Despite Cronin's cajoling for more time, McCarthy held firm and alerted Red Sox owner Tom Yawkey as well: "Traveling has left me too physically exhausted to give the proper leadership to your team. So I think it would be best for all concerned if I stepped out now."[22]

Seven years passed before McCarthy got certified for Cooperstown in 1957, with Sam Crawford also receiving induction honors.[23]

Elizabeth died in 1971; McCarthy outlived her by more than six years. While the Yankees sought to clinch the 1977 AL pennant—their second of three consecutive league titles in the 1970s—McCarthy wrote a first-person account of his career for the *New York Times* in late September and noted that he still got letters. "And a lot of them from kids."[24]

The obituaries and eulogies for McCarthy recalled a life singularly dedicated to baseball. Fans knew the achievements. His approach, less so. Others may have been knowledgeable, proficient, and successful in their leadership, but McCarthy connected with those under his command by adhering to basic psychology. "In handling ballplayers you always have to remember that there are no two alike," explained McCarthy in a 1973 interview. "They come to you with different religions, different temperaments, at different salary levels, and various levels of intelligence. I always believed in taking a player aside when I wanted to talk to him. And I always tried to be around the hotel lobby so the players would see me and know I was available. You might say I was a mother hen."25

Two days after McCarthy's death on January 13, America's baseball fans could find a slice of his Yankees tenure depicted in NBC's TV movie *A Love Affair: The Eleanor and Lou Gehrig Story*, starring Blythe Danner and Edward Herrmann in the title roles along with Ramon Bieri as Babe Ruth and Gerald S. O'Loughlin as McCarthy.

Nearly nine months later, history repeated itself. The 1978 Red Sox fought in a one-game playoff just as McCarthy's Red Sox team did in 1948.

In section 28, lot 25 of Toledo's Woodlawn Cemetery, the Joss family headstone indicates the burial places for Adrian "Addie" Joss and five kin. Their individual headstones have their names, birth years, and death years. No famous quotes. No descriptions of the deceased. No expressions of affection.

Joss had been dead for nearly seventy years when the Veterans Committee elected him for membership in the Baseball Hall of Fame in January 1978. Octogenarians and nonagenarians recalled the Major Leaguer who pitched for Cleveland from 1902 to 1910 and died of tuberculous meningitis at the age of thirty-one. During his rookie season, the ball club used the name Bronchos. It changed to Naps the following year, reflecting the stardom, respect, and impact of the team's star, Nap Lajoie; Indians became the moniker in 1915, lasting more than a hundred years until Guardians replaced it in 2022.

The decision to place Joss alongside contemporaries Cy Young, Walter Johnson, Tim Keefe, and Jack Chesbro in the Cooperstown shrine highlighted his fantastic exploits, including winning at least twenty games for four consecutive seasons, two no-hitters, a perfect game, forty-five career shutouts, being a two-time Major League leader in ERA, and the second-lowest career ERA—1.89. He tallied an ERA below 2.00 five times and never went above 2.77.

Joss's perfect game, a 1–0 victory, happened against the Chicago White Sox at the end of the 1908 season on October 2. Ed Walsh—whose career 1.82 ERA is the lowest ever—had a powerful display with fifteen strikeouts and four hits allowed. Speed and spitballs were a formidable combination for him.

But Joss reigned with the fourth perfect game in the Majors. In 1910 Joss had a shortened season, though he racked up his second no-hitter—another 1–0 decision against the White Sox. He played in his last game on July 25, ending with a 5-5 record.

In addition to his playing, Joss used his baseball knowledge to write about the World Series from 1907 to 1909 for the *Toledo News-Bee* and the *Cleveland Press*.

To Joss, strikeouts were about as useful as pouring a jug of water into Lake Erie. He saw pitching as a face-off with the goal of outthinking the batter; success diminishes the threat. "The chances are twenty to one that if he does connect he will be an easy out," said Joss. "Now when that fellow strikes and misses don't you see that the pitcher must start all over again? The last strike is just as hard to get as the first one. When a man misses a ball on which he has been fooled it is just like having an entirely new turn at bat."[26]

Spring training was on Joss's agenda for 1911, but he collapsed during an April 3 game in Chattanooga. His doctor in Toledo thought he had pleurisy, but the diagnosis ultimately shifted to tuberculous meningitis. Joss died on April 14.

Three months after his death, the Naps raised money for the Joss clan with a benefit game against a group of stars from the American League: Tris Speaker, Clyde Milan, Eddie Collins, Ty Cobb, Home Run Baker, Sam Crawford, Hal Chase, Bobby Wallace, Gabby Street, Paddy Livingston, plus a troika of pitchers—Smoky Joe Wood, Walter Johnson, Russ Ford.

More than fifteen thousand people saw the game at Somers Park, which raised nearly $13,000 in ticket sales. The All Stars won, 5–3.

Larry MacPhail radiated energy in the way that a volcano does when it erupts.

Nicknamed the "Roaring Redhead" for his somewhat tempestuous persona, MacPhail also got tapped posthumously by the Veterans Committee in January for induction into the Hall of Fame. A visionary, MacPhail had transformed the game, and even though some may have looked askance at his ideas, they became common features. Whether his bluster irritated or inspired, he made a highly significant contribution to the national pastime.

MacPhail's baseball career began in 1931 when he became a part-owner of the Columbus Red Birds in the American Association. Branch Rickey, the

Cardinals' GM, endorsed MacPhail for an executive position with the Cincinnati Reds in 1933. After Powel Crosley Jr. bought the Reds a year later, MacPhail hired Red Barber to be the play-by-play radio announcer on WLW and WSAI. Barber broadcast the first nighttime game in Major League baseball; MacPhail inaugurated the innovation, having seen the positive impact in Columbus.

With less than two weeks to go in the 1936 season, MacPhail announced his resignation, effective November 1, and pointed to the strength of the Cincinnati operation under his leadership, particularly the overhaul of personnel. "I believe that my work here is about ended and can point with pride to the financial statements of the club over the last three years," he said. "Of the forty ball players under contract to the Cincinnati club only three were here when I came."[27]

MacPhail returned to baseball in 1938, becoming the Brooklyn Dodgers' general manager. A year later, he took over the team presidency after Stephen McKeever died. He brought Barber to Brooklyn; Barber became the vocal background of the Borough of Churches on WOR until owner Walter O'Malley moved the Dodgers to Los Angeles after the 1957 season.

MacPhail, an artillery captain in World War I, served his country during World War II by working for the War Department in public relations with the rank of colonel. "And I've never been happier in a job than I was here in Brooklyn," said Brooklyn's top baseball executive as he cried during his resignation announcement in late September 1942.[28] MacPhail partnered with Dan Topping and Del Webb to buy the Yankees after Jacob Ruppert died in 1943. Two years later, New York governor Thomas Dewey signed the Ives-Quinn antidiscrimination bill and Mayor Fiorello La Guardia created the Committee on Baseball to examine the topic of integration. MacPhail wrote a memorandum to the committee outlining his reasons against the idea.

He argued that integration would cost the Yankees an estimated $100,000 of lost revenue in rent and concessions without a Negro League team renting Yankee Stadium or other ballparks the Yankees owned in Kansas City, Newark, and Norfolk. Additionally, there was an issue of contract interference with the Negro League teams. Signing their best players would leave the Negro League games with inferior product on the field, leading to the demise of the Negro Leagues. Which is exactly what happened.

MacPhail theorized that if the Negro Leagues improved their efficiency as a business, then "Organized Baseball" would bring them into the fold—but as a distinct entity, with "a limited number of negro players, who [if they] first establish ability, character, and aptitude in their own leagues, might advance to the majors or big minors of Organized Baseball."[29]

Separate but equal. Mostly.

Branch Rickey, MacPhail's successor, stood against this type of segregationist advocacy aiming to keep the racial barrier unchanged. Jackie Robinson, after serving as an army lieutenant at Fort Hood in Texas, played with the Kansas City Monarchs in the Negro Leagues in 1945, then signed a contract with the Dodgers organization on October 23, and got orders from Rickey to play with the Triple-A Montreal Royals in 1946.

It was a wonderful year. Robinson thrived. The UCLA alumnus—who had lettered in baseball, football, basketball, and track—led the International League in batting average and runs scored; Montreal beat the Louisville Colonels in six games to win the Junior World Series. On April 15, 1947, Robinson played in his first Major League game, though this achievement discounts spring training games, including a three-game exhibition against the Yankees right before Opening Day.

The Dodgers met the Yankees in the '47 World Series, their first of six match-ups over the next ten years. When the Yankees bested the Dodgers in seven games, MacPhail reveled like it was Mardi Gras, New Year's Eve, and Christmas morning combined into one loud event. The bombastic executive had a bittersweet celebration that began in the Yankees clubhouse when he revealed his latest resignation, and the revelry continued at the Hotel Biltmore in midtown Manhattan, where "a three-room salon on the 19th floor" might have been mistaken for the site of a boxing undercard at Madison Square Garden.[30]

MacPhail punched his former protégé with the Brooklyn Dodgers, John McDonald, now a journalist, after the latter defended Branch Rickey, MacPhail's sworn enemy. "I wouldn't hit him back," said McDonald. "He's 20 years older than I am and besides he's a sick man. That's why he's quitting."[31] MacPhail later insulted his fellow owners, reportedly prompting Topping to assault him. The scuffle got broken up; Topping tried again in the press room, only to be restrained by reporters and players.

But there may have been an underlying reason for Topping's anger. MacPhail tried to leverage his share of Yankees stock into a public offering before agreeing that Topping and Webb could buy him out. It had been presumed that any friction between the parties had dissipated. Either it didn't or MacPhail's assault on McDonald had revived it.[32]

MacPhail resigned on the spot, selling his interest to Webb and Topping for $2 million and then focusing his energy on horse breeding. He died on October 1, 1975, at the age of eighty-five, suffering from dementia.[33] But the MacPhail name continued in baseball's executive ranks with his son Lee. Another son, Bill, became a sports TV executive. Andy MacPhail, Larry's grandson, has the presidency of three teams—Cubs, Orioles, and Phillies—on his résumé, in addition to a stint as the Twins' general manager. Great-grandson Lee MacPhail IV went the scouting route for several MLB teams.

The Baseball Writers' Association of America had one electee for the Hall of Fame in 1978—Eddie Mathews. He bashed 512 home runs in his career, prompting curiosity regarding why the BBWAA didn't elect him in his first year of eligibility, in 1974—or 1975, or 1976, or 1977. While some may have seen his lifetime batting average of .271 as a liability for inclusion, the homers should have been more than sufficient for the nine-time All-Star to get accepted.

Born in 1931, Mathews was a native of Texarkana, Texas. But Santa Barbara, California, lays a valid claim to his childhood, as the Mathews clan moved there when the future slugger was six years old. Visitors to this California city in the environs of the Santa Ynez Mountains, nearly one hundred miles from the suburban sprawl of Los Angeles, have an abundance of sights to see. History buffs can visit Mission Santa Barbara, a Spanish colonial church dating back to 1820. Stearns Wharf, built in 1872, is a spectacular destination where all-work, no-play, Type-A tourists can find peace through majestic sunsets and the Pacific Ocean waves. Exercise-minded folks can walk, run, or bicycle on the four-and-a-half-mile Cabrillo Bike Path along the beach.

Fans of the national pastime can check out Eddie Mathews Field, home of the Santa Barbara High School Dons baseball team. Mathews, a 1949 SBHS graduate, excelled in the California Interscholastic Federation. During his senior year, he bashed a home run that reportedly went 360 feet.[34] He went yard twice in a playoff game, knocking in five runs in an 8–2 victory.[35]

Signing with the Boston Braves organization in 1949 after high school, Mathews headed to North Carolina, where he joined the High-Point Thomasville Hi-Toms in the Class D North Carolina State League.[36] He batted .363; High-Point Thomasville led the NCSL with an eighteen-game margin over the second-place Mooresville Moors at the end of the season.

The Braves promoted Mathews to Double-A ball with the Atlanta Crackers in the Southern Association in 1950. He hit .286. Staying with Atlanta for thirty-seven games the following year, he had a .289 average when the front office bumped him to the Triple-A Milwaukee Brewers in the American Association. Mathews saw action in twelve games, hit .333, and left the Minor Leagues behind for good in 1952.

During spring training, he did well enough for *Boston Post* scribe Howell Stevens to opine that Mathews would make the team, if not as a third baseman, then an outfielder.[37] Braves manager John Quinn proved Stevens correct when he decreed Mathews to be on the roster and put him at third base.

Mathews played in 145 games during his rookie season, crushed twenty-five home runs, led the Major Leagues in strikeouts, and notched third place in Rookie of the Year voting. His sophomore year yielded forty-seven homers, tops in both leagues; the first of nine All-Star selections; and second place for the National League's MVP. His batting average jumped 60 points, from .242 to .302.

Toward the end of the 1953 season, Mathews noted the passion of the fans who embraced their new team that had been transplanted from Boston to Milwaukee in the spring; some fans even dressed up as Indians. "It's out of this world," he said. "If it weren't for those fans, we might still be in next-to-last place."[38]

After his second year in the Major Leagues, the twenty-two-year-old slugger prompted some comparisons to Babe Ruth. Mathews's power resided in his wrists. "More ballplayers talk about Mathews' wrists than about Marilyn Monroe's legs," wrote Tom Meany in the beginning of the 1954 season.[39] Later that year, Milwaukeeans swelled with pride when their slugger had the distinction of being on the cover of the first issue of *Sports Illustrated*.

Mathews secured the seventh game of the 1957 World Series for Milwaukee when the Yankees had two outs and the bases loaded in the bottom of the ninth. Moose Skowron hit a ball down the third base line; Mathews snared it backhanded and stepped on third base for the last out. They repeated as NL champs but lost to the Yankees in 1958.

During his first five seasons, Mathews had 190 home runs. He topped the Majors in homers twice during his seventeen-year career. A keen batting eye gave him the National League lead in walks four times; he led the Majors in walks and the NL in on-base percentage in 1963. Before the '63 season, it had been reported that the Indians offered $500,000 for Mathews. Braves general manager John McHale turned it down.[40]

His offensive value was unquestionable. Defense, another story. Braves skipper Bobby Bragan moved Mathews to the outfield in 1963, an experiment that lasted about as long as it took The Beatles to dominate the music industry after their appearance on *The Ed Sullivan Show* the following February. In forty-two games, he made 6 errors in 63 opportunities for a 91.4 percent fielding efficiency, the fourth lowest in the NL. However, his patrol of third base resulted in 13 errors in 389 opportunities, which topped the Senior Circuit with a 96.8 percent efficiency.[41]

The Braves moved to Atlanta in 1966 and traded their slugger—who had clocked 493 home runs—to the Houston Astros along with Arnold Umbach and a player to be named later for Dave Nicholson and Bob Bruce on New Year's Eve 1966. Sandy Alomar went to Houston at the end of the following February. But what stung Mathews more than the trade was how it was conducted. A sportswriter got to Mathews before the front office, which tried to correct the blunder but instead committed another one. Braves chairman Bill Bartholomay signed a letter addressed to "Edward" Mathews, instead of the proper moniker "Edwin."[42]

Phillies manager Gene Mauch praised the veteran, saying that "he'll at least add some class to your club." The word "leadership" also got tossed around, though the thirty-five-year-old Mathews demurred: "It is either something that comes naturally or not at all. And the more you try to force it, the more certain it is that it won't happen."[43]

Mathews reached the 500-homer level on July 14, 1967, against Juan Marichal during an Astros road trip to San Francisco, becoming the seventh player to reach the five-century mark. But his stay in Houston didn't last the '67 season; Mathews went to the Detroit Tigers in an August trade for a player to be named later.

There was a touch of glory involved. Mathews played in two games in the 1968 World Series and got another ring to match 1957's as Detroit beat St. Louis in seven games. "I can't think of anybody on the team who was more respected than Eddie," said Tigers icon Al Kaline, a 1980 Hall of Fame electee, upon Mathews's induction during the summer of 1978. "I don't know exactly what it was about him, but everybody respected him. You could see it from the first day he joined the club. He was a bear-down, no-nonsense type guy. He had a great knack for talking to kids. And he couldn't stand anyone who didn't give 100 percent. He'd get on the guys and no one would talk to him."[44]

The Tigers released Mathews after the World Series; he became a scout for the team.[45]

Mathews returned to the Braves and began coaching with his former tribe in 1971, then became the manager on August 7, 1972. His tenure included former teammate Hank Aaron breaking Babe Ruth's career home run record, but Atlanta's front office fired him on July 21, 1974, with a 50-49 record for the season. He then became a scout for the Braves. On September 10, 1975, the Milwaukee Brewers announced that Mathews would join the organization as a scout and Minor League instructor.[46] He later worked as a scout and coach for the Oakland A's and Texas Rangers.

Managing was in the past. "It's a 24-hour-a-day job," said Mathews during the events surrounding his Hall of Fame induction in 1978. "You get involved in much more than just bunting, hitting and running. It's family affairs; it's curfews; it's attitude; it's a whole bunch of things with 25 and 30 people involved." He also endorsed the theory that inferior or mediocre ballplayers are better helmsmen because they have to work harder at learning the intricacies of the game.[47]

When he learned about the Hall of Fame election, Mathews got nostalgic for the past. "We used to have fun playing," lamented Mathews. "We'd get to the park early and hang around an hour or two after the game talking baseball. Now, guys seem to have a contest on who can get out of the clubhouse first. That's not true of all players, but there are enough of them to make it obvious."[48]

The business side of baseball manifested in late January.

Vida Blue was stuck like a car in the mud after a rainstorm in his home state of Louisiana. On January 30, 1978, Major League Baseball commissioner Bowie Kuhn vetoed the deal that would send the three-time All-Star from the Oakland A's to the Cincinnati Reds for a reported $1.75 million and Minor Leaguer Dave Revering.

It was déjà vu all over again, to borrow Yogi Berra's famous phrase. The New York Yankees had an agreement with Oakland in the middle of the 1976 baseball season, but Kuhn had blocked that as well. In addition to the proposed deal with the Yankees, A's owner Charlie Finley agreed to send Joe Rudi and Rollie Fingers to the Boston Red Sox in exchange for $2 million. Kuhn thwarted that opportunity.

Yankees owner George Steinbrenner sent a letter to the commissioner two days before Christmas of 1977, outlining his dismay at the proposed A's-Reds trade and acknowledging that the $1.75 million figure exceeded the Yankees' proposed deal by more than $200,000.

But Steinbrenner believed that allowing Blue to go to Cincinnati would be unfair. He reasoned that the Yankees refrained from further pursuit of Blue after the commissioner's office said that a deal involving an amount of more than $400,000 would be examined in great detail and "with a clear inference that such a transaction would not meet with your approval."[49]

In both cases, Kuhn exercised his powers using the "best interests of baseball" rationale but admitted that his authority in this area stemmed from less than precise language. "This term is of constitutional generality, and necessarily so," said the commissioner, who had been a lawyer at the powerhouse firm Willkie Farr & Gallagher in New York City representing the National League before succeeding Commissioner William Eckert in 1968. "It cannot be defined comprehensively in three or four words or three or four pages in any rigid fashion."[50]

Kuhn's January 30 veto of the A's-Reds deal also addressed the "buying of success" strategy favoring teams with deeper pockets. The commissioner stated that he could not persuade himself that "the spectacle of the Yankees and Red Sox buying contracts of star players in the prime of their careers for cash sums totaling $3.5 million is anything but devastating to Baseball's reputation for integrity and to the public confidence in the game, even though I can well understand that their motive is a good faith effort to strengthen their clubs."[51]

He further justified his position by stating that "the proposed assignment promises a material adverse effect upon competitive balance. It would make a very strong Club even stronger, and would further separate that Club from most of its competitors; it also promises to make a weak Club even weaker."[52]

To a certain extent, he made sense.

Cincinnati had been to the World Series four times so far in the 1970s. They lost in '70 and '72, then won in '75 and '76. The championship seasons were particularly resonant for the Reds, who finished 1975 with a 108-54 record, twenty games ahead of the second-place Dodgers. Their margin was ten games in 1976. Still significant.

In the past five seasons, Blue had compiled an 81-67 record. Adding him to a Reds lineup already stocked with strength would likely diminish the NL West's competitive factor and, it stood to reason, negatively impact ticket sales. But the restraint had no definable forecast on the impact. How many other players would be subject to a ruling that was vague in its source and far-reaching in its effect?

During the previous year's spring training, U.S. District Court judge Frank McGarr ruled in favor of the commissioner. He addressed the "best interests in baseball" powers and boundaries in his legal analysis. "The questionable wisdom of this broad delegation of power is not before the court," explained McGarr in his 1977 ruling. "What the parties intended is. And what the parties clearly intended was that the commissioner was to have jurisdiction to prevent any conduct destructive of the confidence of the public in integrity of baseball.

"So broad and unfettered was this discretion intended to be that they provided no right of appeal and even took the extreme step of foreclosing their own access to the courts."[53]

The A's had already begun to wane. Oaklanders were mystified and miserable because Finley dismantled his stellar squad after it had won three consecutive World Series from 1972 to 1974 and brought another AL West flag to the Bay Area in 1975. Oakland lost the '75 AL playoffs to Boston.

After the season, Finley traded Reggie Jackson, Ken Holtzman, and Bill Van Bommel, a Minor Leaguer, to the Baltimore Orioles for Don Baylor, Paul

Mitchell, and Mike Torrez. Jackson signed with the Yankees after a year in Baltimore and joined his former teammate, Catfish Hunter, whom Steinbrenner had signed as a free agent after the 1974 season. The slugger proved to be the boost needed in the South Bronx, culminating with three homers off Dodgers pitchers Elías Sosa, Burt Hooton, and Charlie Hough in Game Six of the 1977 World Series to secure the title for the Yankees, their first since beating the Giants in 1962. They had lost to Cincinnati in 1976, to St. Louis in 1964, and to Los Angeles in 1963.

Oakland baseball was unrecognizable in 1977. Just three years after winning a third consecutive World Series, the A's finished in last place in the AL West—thirty-eight and a half games behind the Royals. Despondency governed A's fans as they saw their once favorite players who had worn green and gold now playing with other teams. Jackson and Hunter compounded the misery for Oakland with their success as Yankees. Sal Bando joined the Brewers. Joe Rudi, the Angels. Gene Tenace and Rollie Fingers stayed in California, finding places with the Padres. Bert Campaneris played for the Rangers.

But Finley refused to stay prone regarding Kuhn's interference, appealing the district court's decision for any kind of traction on his authority to conduct the business of the Oakland Athletics—specifically, trading players. The U.S. Court of Appeals would hear arguments in February.

As Vida Blue received the bad news about his future, the Ohio Valley and Great Lakes regions dealt with the aftermath of winter's fury—a blizzard dropping more than two feet of snow in some areas. The storm reportedly knocked out power to 150,000 homes in Ohio.[54] Winds reached 60 miles per hour in Michigan; the Lower Peninsula got more than twenty inches of snow.[55]

Winter's assault continued with an early February blizzard in the Northeast and New England. Epic doesn't even begin to describe it.

2

"A CHANCE TO BE ABSOLUTELY UNBELIEVABLE"

FEBRUARY

Snowstorms are boons to children.

Living in a region vulnerable to snow presents the possibility of school cancellations depending on the severity of the snowfall. Kids suddenly become interested in meteorology and watch the weather reports on local TV news programs with great anticipation.

They pray. They hope. They wait.

In the first week of February, students across the New York City metropolitan area and New England braced for a possible reprieve from the education system as they perched on the edges of their beds and waited for an early morning telephone call, like a prisoner waiting for a pardon from the governor. Calls regarding school cancellations usually came around 7:00 a.m. Parents who signed up to be in the telephone chain for other parents in the school answered the phone, informed their offspring, and called the next group of people on their lists.

An announcement of "no school today" prompted shouts of joy preceding an array of possibilities. Stay in pajamas and watch TV. Stay in pajamas and read comic books. Stay in pajamas and play board games. Teenagers have the chore of shoveling the driveway and sidewalk, then sprinkling rock salt to melt ice. Parents work from home, trying to ignore the noise of their children's celebration.

For the children of Springfield, New Jersey, a snow day meant a voyage to Baltusrol Golf Course, where a massive hill welcomed brave souls who wanted the thrill of sledding down it. Baltusrol had held the U.S. Open three times; it would host the tournament in 1980 and 1993 as well. But for Springfield's youth enjoying the snowfall, Baltusrol might as well have been a Winter Olympics site.

It was a familiar scene across suburbia. But the storm on February 6–7, 1978, could hardly be termed ordinary. It was a bona fide blizzard that shut down businesses, put airport travelers in limbo, severely restricted or canceled mass transit, created health hazards, and forced people to stay inside unless necessary. Initial cost projections for Newark exceeded $500,000.[1]

Already wobbly from a mid-January storm, northern New Jersey had suffered nearly a foot and a half of snow by the late evening of February 6. Getting snow off the highways and roads was a Sisyphean task but mandated to minimize risk for emergency vehicles. "We have all our snow trucks out and they are plowing the roads clear, but as soon as they clear the streets they are covered again," said Metuchen mayor Donald Wernik. "All we can try to do is keep the streets open. It looks like a losing battle."[2]

On the home front, it felt the same way as suburbanites shoveled their walkways, driveways, and sidewalks. With the storm approaching, those who got caught shorthanded regarding food and supplies last time would not let that happen again. Or so they believed. Kenvil Power Mower in Kenvil reported that its inventory of snowblowers had already been depleted. "The manufacturers ran out of them, and they haven't been producing them because the last few winters haven't been that bad," said a bookkeeper in another store that sold out its snowblowers in mid-January. "Next year, they'll probably overproduce. You have to guess in this business."[3]

American Royal Hardware described rising sales of kitty litter as a substitute for the increasingly scarce salt and calcium chloride. Around 90 percent of the snow melt material in this Upper Montclair store had already been purchased; it had started with four thousand pounds and got down to four hundred.

A day later, Governor Brendan Byrne toured the beaten state by helicopter for three hours to survey the damage at the famed Jersey Shore. Awestruck, the Garden State's forty-seventh governor described it as the "worst storm I've ever seen along the coast."[4] Flooding was a major consequence. In Bradley Beach, a popular Monmouth County shore town during the summer, the storm caused an estimated $2.5 million in damage.[5] Ocean County offered a preliminary estimate of $10 million in damage.[6] Even stalwart mail carriers were prevented from making their rounds for two days. That had reportedly never happened before this blizzard.[7]

To be stranded in a house can be claustrophobic, albeit with creature comforts. To be stranded on the road can be isolating, frightening, and dangerous. The battering boosted the tire business, amplified by customers worried about another storm after suffering in mid-January and looking to improve their safety on the road. A tire store owner in Union revealed that his sales amounted to "more than 1,000 tires" above his previous year's total for the mid-January to mid-February period. Ignoring the weather had given way to preparing for it. "We've also gotten a lot of people who didn't bother with snow tires because we haven't had much snow in the last few winters. There are always those people who are going to hold out."[8]

Homebound by the blizzard, people watched TV for updates from the local news teams. New York's WCBS got hoorays and huzzahs from TV critic Jerry Krupnick in the *Star-Ledger*—based in Newark—particularly for remembering an impact on New Jersey, which often gets lesser coverage. "The other channels occasionally hinted at the fact that this side of the river was getting clobbered along with the rest, but mostly gave the impression that this was strictly a New York happening," stated Krupnick.[9]

As cabin fever set in, New Jerseyans could thumb through the *Star-Ledger's* DAY section—which provided information about a roster of valuable entertainment opportunities—and start planning their postblizzard calendars. They didn't have to cross a bridge or go through a tunnel into Manhattan for stellar entertainment options. James Darren had been a teen idol in the late 1950s and 1960s with a thriving singing career, had a guest appearance as his Stone Age avatar Jimmy Darrock on *The Flintstones*, and appeared in starring roles in three movies in the *Gidget* series. Baby boomers could find the gracefully aging, still youthful-looking forty-one-year-old Darren crooning and telling stories at Club Bené in South Amboy while their children saved their allowances and afterschool job money to buy tickets for Elvis Costello, performing at the Paramount on the boardwalk in Asbury Park.

Sandy Dennis and Jean Marsh starred in *Fallen Angels* at the Paper Mill Playhouse in Millburn. Sports fans looking for an addition to hockey and basketball as a void filler between the Super Bowl and spring training could head to Seton Hall University, where tennis star Ilie Nastase would take on Vitas Gerulaitis in an exhibition later in the month.

Bargain hunters received a jolt when they saw an ad for the Rockford furniture chain covering nearly a full page in the *Star-Ledger*. Declaring an emergency sale because the storm had "slowed business," Rockford offered multiple living room arrangements, including a set with a grandfather clock, sofa, love seat, chair, cocktail table, and end table for under $500.[10]

Indeed, the 1970s was a paradisiacal era for retail stores in New Jersey. With Lincoln's Birthday approaching, newspaper advertisements enticed readers to bring their wallets to Bamberger's, Huffman Koos, Dover Furniture, Korvettes, Two Guys, Herman's World of Sporting Goods, Channel Home Centers, Hahne's, Stern's, Levitz, Abraham and Straus, Prince, BFO, Brick Church Appliance, Allen Carpet, and Rickel Do It Yourself Home Centers. But a trip to a retail store for holiday discounts seemed like a distant event as the Mid-Atlantic and northeastern regions of the United States got assaulted for the second time in a few weeks.

Folks snowed in by Mother Nature's latest example of power and fury might have envisioned a trip to a warmer climate as soon as possible. Getting away from this winter pummeling with a couple of best-selling novels, an ocean, and temperatures hovering around 77 degrees in the shade with a cool breeze seemed like the perfect antidote to the miserable weather that had begun 1978. But higher costs resulted from the impact of a supply-and-demand economy. Travel agencies fielded phone calls from interested, sometimes desperate, people who needed a break. Soon.[11]

When informed about the costs, they probably got hopeful from an American Airlines ad for a 40 percent discount on fares. Unfortunately, it wouldn't start until March 23, when most, if not all, of the snow would be melted, provided that another storm did not occur.[12]

United had a similar ad, giving a 45 percent discount for trips to LA, San Francisco, and San Diego. But that didn't kick in until March 27. National Airlines offered a fare of $55 to Miami or Fort Lauderdale if you traveled Monday through Wednesday; they kicked it up to $75 for the rest of the week. There was a catch: no meals. National called it a Super No Frills Fare.

In Central Park, the National Weather Service reported that the snow depth measured 17.7 inches, marking the highest total for New York City in the thirty years since the post-Christmas blizzard of 1947.[13] More than a thousand cars and other vehicles made the famed Long Island Expressway into a parking lot for ten miles "between Melville and Huntington."[14] Before the storm began on February 6, commuters who decided to seek refuge in the city, instead of heading to the suburbs and risking getting stuck in traffic, found no luck at the New York Hilton, which stated that it had no vacancies among its array of more than 2,100 rooms.

It was a common story. Although companies closed early, some improvised, letting their employees stay in their buildings because of the dearth of hotel rooms. The Federal Reserve Bank and Chase Manhattan were two examples reported in the *New York Times*, with the latter "setting up cots for employees in its auditorium."[15]

New England's hammering included winds near 100 miles per hour hitting Plum Island. Logan Airport measured over 60 miles per hour; Chatham exceeded 90.[16] Mount Washington, a town in the extreme western part of Massachusetts, got nearly two feet of snow in a twenty-four-hour stretch, with gusts up to 125 miles per hour. Governor Michael Dukakis, who would run unsuccessfully for president ten years later, declared, "The weather situation that now exists in the state of Massachusetts is the worst in its history."[17]

In 2003 WCVB-TV aired a retrospective for the twenty-fifth anniversary of the blizzard and reminded Bostonians of the timeline. On the evening of February 6, 1978, all seemed quiet, with light snow falling on Boston. WCVB meteorologist Harvey Leonard had predicted a "classic" nor'easter, but that forecast seemed in jeopardy. "And then just as darkness started to fall on Monday the sixth in Boston, that was it," said Leonard in the anniversary special. "It settled in, and there was no looking back. In fact, I was working with John Henning at the time. We went outside and I think that's about the time the 75-mile-per-hour wind gust occurred. John's hat—gone. Lord knows where that is. Decided 'that's a bad idea, we'll go back into the station.'"[18]

Boston got struck. Snowfall exceeded two feet, fifty-four people died, and approximately two thousand homes were destroyed. Route 128 had an estimated 3,500 cars stranded. Snowdrifts reached up to fifteen feet in some areas. Winds reached nearly 80 miles per hour in Boston; financial damage in the area was projected to be $1 billion.[19]

As the snow and ice melted during the rest of February and life in the storm-ravaged regions crawled back to normalcy, TV remained a mainstay of the American lifestyle, with fare ranging from silly to serious in 1978. *Happy Days* ranked at the top of the Nielsen ratings, which represented the number of viewers watching TV. Anchoring ABC's prime-time lineup on Tuesday nights, this show that had begun as a single-camera comedy about life in the mid-1950s had morphed into an enormously successful sitcom filmed in front of a live audience.

The show's genesis began in a segment for a 1972 episode of *Love, American Style*, a comedy anthology series on ABC. "Love and the Happy Days" highlighted Richie and Potsie, 1950s teenagers played by Ron Howard and Anson Williams. After the box office success of 1962-set *American Graffiti* in 1973—also starring Howard—ABC saw potential in a nostalgia-based show and commissioned a series. *Happy Days* first aired on January 15, 1974, as a midseason replacement for *Temperatures Rising*, a sitcom starring Cleavon Little as a surgeon.

Happy Days, which ran for eleven seasons, is initially set in Milwaukee during the mid-1950s, as evidenced by cultural references. A salient example with a specificity of time is a season 2 episode focusing on Richie Cunningham, Howard's character, using the Stevenson-Eisenhower 1956 presidential contest as a romantic springboard to get close to a Stevenson supporter.

But like other TV shows—and movies—set in the past, *Happy Days* did not adhere strictly to chronology; Hollywood's storytellers sometimes alter timelines, scenarios, and characters for the sake of the story. Arthur "Fonzie" Fonzarelli is the show's ultimate cool character with his leather jacket, motorcycle, and ability to attract women by snapping his fingers. The Lone Ranger is his hero, and John Hart, who played the Lone Ranger on TV in the 1950s after Clayton Moore got into a contract dispute with the show's producer, made a guest appearance as the famous cowboy. A Lone Ranger lunch box is a prop in the episode, but it's a contemporary one from the early 1980s.

Happy Days is in good company regarding chronological inaccuracies. An episode of *The Marvelous Mrs. Maisel* features Britain's Princess Margaret appearing on *The Gordon Ford Show* during her visit to America. *Mrs. Maisel* has the royal appearance taking place in 1961; Princess Margaret's American trip happened in 1965.[20] Ad man Don Draper improvises the slogan "It's

Toasted" during a meeting with Lucky Strike executives in the first episode of *Mad Men*, which is set in 1960; Lucky Strike first used that slogan during World War I.[21] Bob Cerv starts the 1961 season with the Yankees in the TV movie *61** when in fact he did not come to New York in a trade with the Kansas City Athletics until May.[22]

Aaron Sorkin condensed real-life events involving Lucille Ball and Desi Arnaz into 2021's *Being the Ricardos*, which uses the week-long production of an *I Love Lucy* episode as the setting. Mark Wahlberg starred as a Boston police officer in *Patriots Day*, a 2016 film about the 2013 Boston Marathon bombing; his character is fictional, representing the hundreds of city police officers who participated in the investigation, manhunt, and capture of the two bombers.

On February 28, 1978, the *Happy Days* episode "My Favorite Orkan" catapulted Robin Williams into the stratosphere of stardom with his portrayal of the alien Mork from the planet Ork. But the idea didn't originate with the show's creator, Garry Marshall, or his writing staff. *Star Wars* had been a blockbuster movie during the previous summer, and some movie theaters still featured it in the beginning of 1978. Scott Marshall, Garry's eight-year-old son and a huge *Star Wars* fan, asked if there could be an alien on *Happy Days*. When the noted showrunner explained that it would be unrealistic, Scott showed his creative chops by countering, "Well, Richie could have a dream."[23]

Casting became a snafu. Usually, a sitcom production starts with the cast gathering around a table and reading the script on Monday. They spend the rest of the week rehearsing, rewriting, and blocking (figuring where the cast should be in the scene). Then it's filmed or videotaped in front of a live audience on Friday night.

By Wednesday, they didn't have an actor for Mork. Then, Marshall met Williams. To say that his performance overwhelmed the studio audience and the millions watching at home is to say that Farrah Fawcett had a nice smile. Anson Williams recalls, "The script that he guest starred was the worst script ever in the history of *Happy Days*. Ever. At the end of Wednesday rehearsal—we shoot on Fridays—the guest actor quit because he was really bad. It really wasn't his fault. The script was really bad and he didn't improve it. He just quit. And there we were Wednesday night without a Mork. Al Molinaro recommended to Garry Marshall this young guy named Robin Williams who was in his Harvey Lembeck improvisational class. He said he's really funny.

"It was camera blocking day. So, it's mechanical. There's no writers down there. You're just getting the shots with cameras because we shoot on Friday. Well, the door opens and Jerry Paris comes running after me. 'He's a genius! He's a genius! He's a genius!'

"And every writer on staff is on the set just writing like crazy. And there's Robin Williams [improvising] the entire show. Nanu nanu. Sitting on his head. Creating it on the spot. Just this light was on this young man. I had never seen that kind of talent, and that kind of genius, and that kind of spontaneity. And the connection with everybody. The next night, Friday night, twenty-four hours later, it was the best show of the year. And the audience was screaming, they wouldn't stop stomping. They were so entertained. They were so blown away by this new talent. I'll never forget the feeling of that evening."[24]

From schoolyards in Sebastopol to delis in Delaware, whoever watched *Happy Days* talked about this guest star whose career trajectory went from inching along to turbocharged speed. "My Favorite Orkan" starts with Richie claiming to his friends at Arnold's—the hamburger joint that serves as a hangout for the characters—that he saw a flying saucer. When they go outside, whatever Richie saw in the sky is gone. They tease him and then confirm that it may be a subconscious compensation for his boring, humdrum life.

Richie goes home and falls asleep on his couch only to be awakened by Mork, who explains that he's on Earth to collect just such a humdrum specimen to take back to Ork; he demonstrates his unearthly powers, such as pointing his finger and shorting out the TV. Escaping to Arnold's, Richie finds refuge until Mork tracks him down. Enter Fonzie, the leather-jacket-wearing tough guy with a heart of gold who always stands by his best friend, Richie.

Played by Henry Winkler, Fonzie has powers of his own, including being able to hit a jukebox and have a song start playing. Mork and Fonzie engage in a contest of skills, known as a "tallywacker" to the Orkan. If Fonzie wins, Richie stays on Earth. One match-up features Mork pointing at the door to the women's restroom and taking it off its hinges. Fonzie locates a place on the wall next to the men's room door and hits it with his fist, causing that door to fall.

The contest is basically a draw, causing Mork to forget about the average earthling and take the champion back to Ork. They enter the time warp in slow motion. In a BBC interview, Winkler recalled his education at Yale Drama

School and how it helped him with that scene. "I used the slow motion training that I used with a Polish teacher, who studies [Jerzy] Grotowski, who was a famous director. And we used slow motion and learned how to use our bodies. I used that in the Fonz."[25]

When Richie's parents and sister wake him up, they convey the news that the light in the sky was a weather balloon. Richie is then left alone in the living room when the doorbell rings. It's Williams playing a truck driver who's lost. The whole thing was a dream. Or was it?

ABC saw great spin-off potential, so Marshall, Dale McRaven, and Joe Glauberg created *Mork & Mindy* for ABC's fall schedule. For continuity, *Happy Days* producers expanded the last scene with an additional take of Williams outside the Cunningham household to air in a rerun and in syndication. Mork communicates with his overseer, Orson, whom the audience never sees or hears; it's explained that Mork's next assignment is go to Earth in 1978 and observe. The Orkan informs the boss that he arranged his visit so that the 1950s folks do not know whether his appearance was real or a dream. Robin Williams reprised his role in a 1979 episode of *Happy Days*.

Building a résumé to complement his stand-up career, which had attracted notice in San Francisco and Los Angeles, Williams found two opportunities in sketch comedy before *Happy Days*. George Schlatter hired him for NBC's reboot of *Laugh-In*, which lasted only six episodes. Williams also appeared in *The Richard Pryor Show*, an innovative and provocative show starring the comedian whom Jerry Seinfeld would later call the "Picasso of our profession."[26] NBC canceled it after four episodes; Williams appeared in two.

San Francisco was, for all intents and purposes, his home base. But success at the clubs combined with the *Happy Days* appearance did not inflate Williams's ego, not even by a scintilla. Indeed, he recognized the challenge of performing in comedy clubs, especially late in the evening after several comedians have already performed. But the city known for the Golden Gate Bridge, Candlestick Park, and Sam Spade held special appeal as a launching pad. "The audiences are intelligent yet not cruel, so you can develop a certain style," explained Williams. "It's a great incubator for a comedian; they love madcap, wonderful things."[27]

Williams's portrayal of Mork showcased his boundless energy. During a month in which a significant percentage of the U.S. population got pounded by vicious weather, his performance with features like eating flowers and sitting on his head—in addition to funny voices and made-up words that he used in the episode—gave the TV audience a true break for a half hour.

At Juilliard, Williams had been known to be a deeply talented fellow. It's an urban legend that when Williams left the storied New York institution, he did so because John Houseman, the director of the Drama Division, believed the school had no more value for him and gave him a personal edict to conquer the world with his talent. Williams's biographer Dave Itzkoff calls that tale into question. Juilliard assessed its students yearly to decide who should stay and who should go. A lack of discipline did not outweigh Williams's obvious skills, emphasized by his entering Juilliard with advanced student status, but Williams was no longer in the advanced program by his second year. "And after the third year, the sort of discipline problems really did not improve," says Itzkoff. "And even though he was learning and benefiting from the training, you know, he was just felt not to be the right fit for what they taught. And he was one of the students that got cut sort of by mutual decision."[28]

His legacy is astounding, though, including an Academy Award for *Good Will Hunting*, six Golden Globe Awards, and five Grammy Awards for his comedy albums. Williams's movie career began in 1980 with the lead role in *Popeye*, based on the comic strip character. It was a flop. But he rebounded later in the decade with *Moscow on the Hudson*, *Dead Poets Society*, and *Good Morning, Vietnam*, followed by *Mrs. Doubtfire*, *One Hour Photo*, and the *Night at the Museum* trilogy.

Suffering from Lewy body dementia, the comedian who rose to fame as the alien Mork committed suicide at the age of sixty-three in 2014. That night, Winkler phoned *The Rachel Maddow Show* on MSNBC and shared his memories of Williams: "I'm telling you, Rachel. No hyperbole. You knew you were in the presence of somebody very special. Of greatness. Somebody said earlier in the show that he had chutzpah. And it was not chutzpah. It was not nerve. He needed . . . it was his soul, the way he was put on the Earth, you said something to him, he sucked it in, and he blew it out. And it came out so with originality and so powerfully and so funny that your jaw dropped.

"How he was off the set, he was boundlessly filled with energy. He never stopped working. He would go to the clubs at night and do his act and work on his act. He'd act all day and do the show with us or then, eventually, his own show. And then we saw that he was limitless, that he could do great drama, he could do drama with comedy, he could do comedy. He was a miracle. I'm not kidding. It took your breath away.

"And how was he when he was just talking to you? He was as quiet and as gentle as the breeze. No matter when you saw him, how long it was between the times you saw him, you were first met with a hug. He talked to you like you were the only human being in the world at the moment."[29]

Williams's appearance on the February 28, 1978, broadcast of *Happy Days* garnered immediate plaudits from the audience populating Stage 19 at Paramount Television, the production company for the show. "When Robin came out to take his curtain call that night after the filming of *Happy Days*, all three hundred people in the studio audience gave him a standing ovation," said Marshall. "There was no doubt in their minds that he had the potential to become a star."[30]

The episode punctuated the show's magic in capturing America's hearts during an uncertain time, procuring around forty million viewers per episode at its height. *Happy Days* provided an antidote for the malaise, pressure, and volatility affecting the American psyche ever since the John F. Kennedy assassination, followed by the assassinations of Martin Luther King Jr., Medgar Evers, and Robert F. Kennedy; escalation of America's involvement in the Vietnam War, resulting in more than fifty-eight thousand servicemen dying and countless others suffering physical and mental wounds; riots in Los Angeles, Newark, Washington DC, Detroit, Philadelphia, Chicago, and Cleveland; political clashes over civil rights; two oil crises; inflation; and the Watergate scandal leading to the resignation of President Richard M. Nixon and several of his aides going to prison.

America needed something to hold on to, something recalling a time that was simpler, benign, and slower paced. *Happy Days* formed a powerful entry in the category of nostalgia that created a baseline in popular culture throughout 1978. But America also needed a hero.

A former gang member with the Falcons, Fonzie was a high school dropout and an expert mechanic who had the toughness of a street hood but the heart of a lion; he later got his high school diploma and inspired kids to read when he brandished his library card. In the early episodes, Fonzie lived by himself in a small apartment. His living arrangements changed when *Happy*

Days started being filmed before a live audience—the producers put Fonzie in a room with a bathroom above the Cunninghams' garage, thereby allowing more interactions with the family.

Fonzie stood by his friends and considered them his family, largely because he had no family of his own. His parents had abandoned him; "Grandma Nussbaum" is referenced in early episodes as the parental figure in his childhood. Besides attracting women with a finger snap and powering a jukebox with his fist, Fonzie had a hero status with a variety of skills.

When a performer known as the Amazing Randi accidentally gets drunk before a fundraiser, Fonzie replaces him and performs the milk can trick.[31]

When Richie's sister Joanie needs a dance partner for a marathon, Fonzie steps in and caves to exhaustion, only to rally with the Russian dance known as the Kazatsky with the Jewish celebratory song "Hava Nagila" as his musical accompaniment.[32]

When Fonzie is in a slump with women and work, he asks Richie to write to the TV show *You Wanted to See It* and ask for "Fearless" Fonzarelli to jump over fourteen garbage cans on a motorcycle; the record is twelve.[33]

When Mrs. Cunningham's uncle is on the precipice of losing his dude ranch in Colorado, Fonzie saves it by riding a killer bull named Diablo and winning a prize of $1,000.[34]

Then, there's the shark.

A three-part episode set in Hollywood inspired a phrase indicating when a show is either desperate for viewers or begins to lose quality—Fonzie faces the challenge of a smart-mouthed beach lover named the California Kid and does a water-ski jump over a shark. "Jump the shark" is now part of the popular culture lexicon, though arguably incorrect in its provenance. The Hollywood storyline kicked off the 1977–78 season; *Happy Days* went off the air in 1984. Had the show really deteriorated in a significant manner regarding quality and viewership, it would not have been able to survive for seven more seasons.[35]

Marshall had his sister, Penny Marshall, and Cindy Williams guest star in a 1975 episode as Laverne DeFazio and Shirley Feeney, two streetwise girls whom Fonzie arranges to double date together with Richie. It reunited Howard with Williams, who had played his girlfriend in *American Graffiti*. ABC okayed a spin-off for the characters in the following season—*Happy Days* and

Laverne & Shirley delivered a one-two punch for the network, outpacing the competition and forming a cornerstone of its successful prime-time lineup in the late 1970s, which included *The Love Boat, Fantasy Island, Three's Company, Eight Is Enough, Soap, Vega$, Hart to Hart,* and *Barney Miller.*

ABC tried to leverage the show's success with another spinoff: *Potsie & Ralph.* It launched in November 1977 with a backdoor pilot, which takes an established show and uses secondary characters or introduces new characters as the crux of an episode to see if there's spin-off potential. ABC balked at elevating it to a series.[36]

During "My Favorite Orkan," Richie asks whether Mork is on Earth to take Hank Aaron, a star player with the Milwaukee Braves in the 1950s. Mork says that Aaron's too famous, before revealing the assignment to find someone "humdrum." The mention of Aaron not only recalled the show's time period but also reminded the audience that baseball had begun its yearly emergence from slumber after the "hot stove" period, which starts the day after the World Series and ends when pitchers and catchers report to spring training in mid-February.

In early 1978 the New York Yankees headed south to Fort Lauderdale with a World Series title, their twenty-first since the team's establishment in 1903. To add power, they wanted Dave Winfield on the roster. Playing for the San Diego Padres since his rookie year of 1973, Winfield racked up impressive stats, including ninety-two RBIS across 157 games in 1977. He later joined the Yankees in 1981 for an astonishing ten-year deal worth $23 million, but he was an acquisition target as early as February 1978.

One glitch—San Diego wanted Yankees third baseman Graig Nettles as part of a deal; Nettles was an unavailable asset. Yankees president Al Rosen, a former third baseman with the Cleveland Indians and the American League Most Valuable Player in 1953, clarified the issue for doubters and naysayers: "Winfield has a chance to be a fine ballplayer. He's a potential superstar and anybody would like to have a player like that. But not if it meant trading Nettles."

Rosen also described the pitching roster in glowing terms, claiming "a chance to be absolutely unbelievable."[37] His prophecy would be fulfilled in 1978.

The leader of the Yankees' World Series nemesis from 1977 refused to discuss the recent past, instead focusing on the 1978 season with the usual positivity and vagueness exhibited by managers during spring training. "The only thing we're talking about is getting ready for the National League," said Los Angeles Dodgers manager Tommy Lasorda. "We'll get ready the same way we did last year and hope we can start just as fast."[38]

Lasorda led the Dodgers to a 30-10 start in the first forty games of 1977. After a hundred games, they were 62-38 and on the way to a 98-64 finish. It was the first season for Lasorda at the helm after succeeding Walter Alston—who had managed the club since 1954—though he had managed four games in 1976.

Controversy hovered over baseball in the 1978 preseason like a dark cloud waiting to unleash a torrent. With the A's and Giants drawing poorly in 1977—less than five hundred thousand and approximately seven hundred thousand, respectively—it didn't seem that the Bay Area teams could coexist any longer in the same region. Oil mogul Marvin Davis had offered to buy the A's and move them to Denver, but the team had a contract with the city for the Oakland–Alameda County Coliseum.

Still reeling from the trade that had sent Tom Seaver to the Cincinnati Reds in exchange for Pat Zachry, Doug Flynn, Dan Norman, and Steve Henderson the previous June, New York Mets fans learned that Lenny Randle had new requirements regarding his five-year contract. Randle had come to the Mets from the Texas Rangers about six weeks before the Seaver trade, an egress triggered by the ballplayer attacking his manager during 1977's spring training, getting suspended, and facing an assault charge.

With the Mets, Randle became a fan favorite. In 136 games, he batted .304, drew sixty-five walks, hit twenty-two doubles, and knocked in twenty-seven runs. On July 9, 1977, he ended a marathon game approaching four and a half hours when he broke a 5–5 tie in the bottom of the seventeenth inning with a two-run homer off Montreal Expos left-hander Will McEnaney. "I got a lot of verbal promise of more money after the great season I had last year," claimed the twenty-nine-year-old. "But so far I've been offered nothing more than a token raise."[39]

The Boston Red Sox had their own malcontent. In Winter Haven, Florida, Rick Wise expressed displeasure, the source of his complaint being time instead of money. Starting twenty games and pitching relief in six, Wise compiled an 11-5 record in 1977 but felt that Boston skipper Don Zimmer did not use him enough as a starter. The bullpen was a punishment in the right-hander's view. "The man has no confidence or respect for me," said Wise of his manager.[40]

Wise had done well since coming from the St. Louis Cardinals along with Bernie Carbo for Reggie Smith and Ken Tatum after the 1973 season. Wise started only nine games, for a 3-4 record in 1974, but his combined record over the next two seasons was 33-23. "I've had the first or second best record on this club three of the four years here," said the right-hander. "Last year, I had the best percentage. Nobody took my job last year. It was given away."[41]

Wise's friction wasn't the only drama that the Red Sox would face in 1978.

3

GOODBYE DARK, MY OLD FRIEND

MARCH

Baseball is a game of milestones.

During 1978 spring training, four teams approached a tenth season since the expansion in 1969—the San Diego Padres, Montreal Expos, Kansas City Royals, and Milwaukee Brewers (originally the Seattle Pilots). Not once had the Padres finished above .500, so reaching the ten-year mark provided one of the few reasons for San Diegans to celebrate their ball club.

Randy Jones had a 16-3 record in the middle of the 1976 season, prompting a *Sports Illustrated* cover story touting him as potentially the first thirty-game winner since Denny McLain went 31-6 in 1968. Tapering, Jones finished with a 22-14 record; he led the Major Leagues in wins, games started, and complete games. The San Diego Chicken, while not an official mascot of the team, became a national sensation after Ted Giannoulas first donned his costume in 1974 and paraded around San Diego Stadium.

Padres owner and McDonald's mogul Ray Kroc had given Padres fans a jolt of hope by closing high-profile deals with Rollie Fingers and Gene Tenace before the '77 season, but the team's 20-28 record by the end of May gave him pause about continuing with John McNamara managing. Alvin Dark got tapped to be the Padres' fifth manager; team president Buzzie Bavasi described him as "a proven winner."[1]

Dark had quite an introduction. The Padres swept the Giants in a Candlestick Park doubleheader. Using twenty players in the first game, a 12–8 victory, and putting twenty-one players on the field for the second game, a 9–8 squeaker, gave San Diego the team record for players in an NL twin bill;

San Francisco used thirty-three players, giving the teams a combined Major League record of seventy-four.

Mike Ivie was the star of the day, batting third against the Giants rather than his usual place in the middle of the order. His five doubles in the doubleheader tied a record; he went 5 for 5 in the second game. Dark revealed that he sourced his strategy for the batting order from a previous stint managing Chicago's NL squad. "The Cubs always respected Ivie and I always thought he'd be a good No. 3 hitter because he makes good contact," said San Diego's new manager. "He's not too fast, but when he hits the ball like that, he doesn't have to be."[2]

Volatility continued for the Padres in 1978 when Dark got fired in the middle of spring training. As Padres president Ballard Smith—Bavasi's successor and Kroc's son-in-law—disclosed, "Alvin wanted to know the reasons. I explained it had nothing to do with his baseball ability but with his ability to communicate."[3]

Vague but concise. Dark said that he saw the writing on the wall when Padres general manager Buzzie Bavasi stepped down and Bob Fontaine— Bavasi's assistant—replaced him. Dark knew that Kroc had wanted him to manage the Padres, but Bavasi and Fontaine didn't. "In case you're wondering what a manager's chances are in a situation like that, I'll tell you: None," wrote Dark in his autobiography. "He's a dead duck. If the general manager doesn't back the manager with the players, the press, and the owner, the manager might as well head for the bus station."[4]

Dark was part of baseball royalty, which gave the Padres a note of prestige. He had won two American League West pennants and a World Series title as manager of the Oakland A's in 1974 and 1975. But his ballplaying career, dating back to the late 1940s, also had terrific ballast. Playing in fifteen games for the 1946 Boston Braves gave Dark a taste of the Major Leagues, and the following year with the Milwaukee Brewers, Boston's Triple-A team in the American Association, provided some needed seasoning for the twenty-five-year-old. It was a worthwhile investment. Dark attained a .303 average with 186 hits, 121 runs scored, 49 doubles, 7 triples, and 10 home runs with Milwaukee, which won the Double-A title.

He exploded during his official rookie season with the Braves in 1948, winning a Rookie of the Year Award for his achievements, including a .322 batting average and thirty-nine doubles. Dark placed third for National League MVP; Stan Musial got the award for leading the Majors in hits and slugging percentage while also topping the National League in batting average, on-base percentage, and RBIs. Dark's fellow Boston Brave Johnny Sain received second place for eclipsing Major League hurlers in wins, games started, complete games, and innings pitched.

Boston won the NL pennant but lost the World Series to the Cleveland Indians in six games. Dark played in every game of the 1948 Series, offering an anemic output. Batting .167 belied his career batting average of .289, higher than fellow shortstops Phil Rizzuto and Pee Wee Reese achieved. But those two are in the Hall of Fame while Dark remains an argument starter regarding Cooperstown. He had some amazing performances. On May 13, 1949, he went 4 for 5, knocked in two runs, and scored twice in a 6–5 victory against the Brooklyn Dodgers. It was part of an eighteen-hit barrage also highlighted by Eddie Stanky scoring three times and notching five hits, complemented by Bob Elliott's three-RBI and four-hit performance.

After the 1949 season ended, the Braves traded Dark and Stanky to the New York Giants; Boston got Red Webb, Willard Marshall, Buddy Kerr, and Sid Gordon. "I am now set at second base with a combination that can make the double play and now can concentrate on selecting the best third baseman from the fine young talent we have," said Giants manager Leo Durocher.[5] Further, the Giants' skipper recognized Dark's leadership abilities and dubbed his new import the team captain.[6]

In the Giants' storied year of 1951, Dark was a standout—he led the Major Leagues in doubles and hit .303 for the first of a series of three straight seasons at or above the .300 mark. On June 9 he participated in the 10–1 clobbering of the Cubs with two home runs—a three-run clout and a solo bash—joined by Wes Westrum, Bill Rigney, and Stanky also going yard. He went 4 for 5 against the Phillies on August 17, scoring three times in the Giants' 8–5 win.

In the second game of a September 5 doubleheader against the Braves, Durocher's team added a decisive 9–1 entry to the win column; Dark notched four hits and scored three times. Another doubleheader showcased Dark's offensive skills, but he wasn't alone as New York tallied seventeen hits in the second game against the Pirates on September 16. Dark smacked four hits at Forbes Field, got an RBI, and scored a run in the 6–4 victory.

Dark's 1951 offense put him among elite National Leaguers—fourth place in runs scored; fourth in singles; eighth in batting average; tied for fifth in total bases with Duke Snider; and tied for sixth for hit by pitch with Stanky, Wally Westlake, and Billy Johnson. The princes of the Polo Grounds forced a three-game NL playoff against the Brooklyn Dodgers after trailing by thirteen games in August. Decades later, journalist Joshua Prager uncovered a sign stealing scheme that the Giants had used in the second half of the season. Ralph Branca alleged that Bobby Thomson had the sign for his pitch, which allowed him to hit the ninth-inning, game-winning home run in game three, also known as the Shot Heard 'Round the World. In the World Series, the Yankees beat the Giants in six games.

Surpassing his postseason performance in 1948 with outstanding offense in the 1951 and 1954 World Series, Dark played in every game of both contests with batting averages of .417 in '51 and .412 in '54, when the Giants swept the Indians. A nine-player deal sent Dark to the Cardinals in 1956. He was batting .252 in 48 games but fared better with St. Louis—.286 in 100 games that season, following it with .290 in 140 games for 1957. A year later, Dark got traded to the Cubs after batting .297 in 18 games. He played in 114 more games, ending '58 at .295. His 1959 stats: .264 in 136 games. Dark last played with the Phillies and Braves in 1960.

Before he joined the Padres as a manager, Dark had a substantive body of work helming teams. In 1961 he replaced Bill Rigney with the Giants. His four seasons with the team resulted in winning records each season and a World Series berth after a three-game playoff against the Dodgers in 1962. Facing the Yankees, Dark's squad battled valiantly but lost in seven games.

Dark managed the Kansas City A's in 1966 and most of 1967; A's owner Charlie Finley fired him after 121 games. Players issued a statement criticizing Finley—who claimed that Dark had lost control of the team—and pointed to conflicting information. According to Finley, Dark claimed he didn't know about the statement before it became public, but A's hurler Jack Aker stated otherwise. Then, Aker contradicted Finley: "I read the statement to Alvin after our meeting but he had no comment."[7]

Dark joined the Indians, which he piloted for three full seasons, then got fired after 103 games in 1971. Two years with the A's, now in Oakland, yielded a World Series title and two AL West pennants.

Dark's personal life rested on Christianity, but he violated his religious precepts during a Giants-Cardinals game in 1962. Protesting a called strike on Orlando Cepeda, Dark strode to umpire Shag Crawford and offered a different type of testimony, one full of shouted expletives. Anger and impulse replaced patience and tolerance. There was neither excuse nor explanation other than Dark claiming, "It was Satan's work. The devil was in me. Never before have I so addressed any man—and, with the Lord's help, I hope to have the strength never to do so again." Of his target, Dark noted, "Crawford is a fine man and a fine umpire. It was doubly wrong to say to him what I wouldn't willfully say to the worst of men."[8]

Religion took another hit when Dark, a married man, had an ongoing affair with a flight attendant, Jackie Troy, whom he ultimately married eight years after meeting her in 1962. Dark had known his first wife, Adrienne, since high school. His extramarital relationship, though obviously significant and grounded in love, contravened the religious values that Dark had publicly espoused. He acknowledged the apparent hypocrisy, noting his imperfections as a Christian and a man. "The truth is, of course, we all measure short of what God wants us to be," he wrote in 1974. "But if being a Christian also implies doing a better job handling your life, then it's an obligation worth striving for. Just don't ever think you can do it without Christ's help."[9]

While the 1978 Padres braced for pitching coach Roger Craig to be the team's sixth skipper, their LA brethren entered a new era—Dodgers manager Tommy Lasorda dubbed second baseman Davey Lopes to be the fifth captain in team history, joining Pee Wee Reese, Duke Snider, Maury Wills, and Willie Davis in this honor. Quiet determination brought Lopes from a poor upbringing in East Providence, Rhode Island, to the Major Leagues in sun-soaked Los Angeles. Lasorda knew that being a leader of peers requires more than prodigiousness on the field and friendliness in the clubhouse. A team leader needs to connect with his squad.

Lopes had earned respect, marked by leading the NL in stolen bases in 1975 and 1976; his seventy-seven steals also led the Majors in 1975. But the fiery Dodgers manager changed Lopes in other ways. "Lasorda pushed me toward being even more aggressive, more extroverted," revealed Lopes. "He instilled a lot of his own personality in me, both in my approach to baseball and in my personal life." Moreover, Lopes had the endorsement of fellow infielder Ron Cey, LA's third baseman. "He tried to do a lot of things last year but was restricted by not having the official title," said Cey. "This will give him the weight he needs, will give an impact to his suggestions."[10]

Lopes began his professional career in Single-A ball with the Daytona Beach Dodgers of the Florida League, where he batted .247 and .280 in 1968 and 1969 while also emerging as an impressive base runner, with twenty-six stolen bases in his first year and thirty-two the following season. He caught Lasorda's attention in 1970 spring training while working out at the team's storied facility in Vero Beach.

After hearing a batter smack the ball hard, Lasorda—then the manager of the Dodgers' Triple-A Spokane Indians in the Pacific Coast League—peered toward the base paths, where he saw Lopes sprinting around the bases and winding up on third with a "head-first slide." Lasorda was hooked on the player whom he described as "a bona fide, blue-chip, big league prospect" and brought him to the Pacific Northwest.[11]

Lasorda persuaded Lopes to change his position from outfielder to infielder, a move that eventually established him as a Dodgers fixture at second base. He had a respectable start in Spokane, achieving a .262 average, eleven steals, and one hundred games. Improvement in '71 manifested in batting .306; his thefts more than doubled, with twenty-seven. After the season, the team moved to Albuquerque. Lopes batted .317 and nearly doubled his base steals again with forty-eight in 1972. The Dodgers elevated him to Chavez Ravine at the end of the season. In '73 he placed sixth in Rookie of the Year voting.

The Dodgers had been Lasorda's employer continuously since 1960, when he joined as a scout. Before then, he played in eight games with the team in 1954 and 1955, when it called Brooklyn home. A leadership track began in 1965, when he managed the Pocatello Chiefs in the four-team, Idaho-based Pioneer League for rookies. They played sixty-six games in a June–August schedule; Pocatello tied for second place with a 33-33 record. The other PL teams were Idaho Falls Angels, Magic Valley Cowboys, and Treasure Valley Cubs. Ogden, Utah, replaced Pocatello in 1966, procuring Lasorda's services for three seasons.

When Dodgers general manager Buzzie Bavasi outlined Lasorda's main responsibility as developing and educating talent rather than winning ball games, the new manager looked at that modus operandi as ineffective at best and insulting at worst. "Telling me I didn't have to win was like telling the Wright Brothers to take a train," Lasorda wrote in his autobiography. "I'd spent my entire life striving to win, fighting to win, I didn't know any other way. I understood that my primary job was to introduce young players to professional baseball in the most positive way, but I believed that creating a winning atmosphere was the most positive way. I intended to teach, just as Buzzy [sic] wanted me to do, and what I intended to teach was how to win."[12]

It was clear back then and remained so throughout his managerial career—which he spent entirely with the Dodgers before retiring in 1996—that Lasorda embraced a hard-nosed, tough-minded, joy-creating approach to baseball. For Thomas Charles Lasorda, only one team embraced his philosophy. Of his players, he stated, "We teach them the Dodger way, not only in playing tactics but in how they conduct themselves in everyday life. We teach aggressive baseball, how to be gentlemen when not in uniform, the meaning of winning."[13]

Lasorda took his approach to Spokane in 1969. The following year, he led the Indians to the PCL championship, where they swept the Hawaii Islanders. In 1972 the Albuquerque Dukes—formerly the Spokane Indians—added another PCL title for the LA Dodgers organization. A stint managing the Tigres del Licey in the 1973 Dominican Winter Baseball League yielded the Caribbean World Series title. Then, he got his wish—a third base coaching job with Los Angeles and a path to one day replace Walter Alston, who had been the Dodgers' manager since 1954. Alston stepped down after the 1976 season; Lasorda led LA to the NL pennant and the World Series in 1977, where the Yankees defeated them in six games.

An imprimatur of supremacy surrounded the Dodgers when spring training began. The *Street and Smith Official 1978 Yearbook* declared, "The Dodgers clearly are the team to beat."[14]

Their NL competition undoubtedly agreed, remembering the highlights of '77. Reggie Smith led the league in on-base percentage, placed third in slugging percentage, and tied with the Padres' Dave Winfield for sixth in runs scored. Steve Garvey notched fifth place for hits in the Senior Circuit; Bill Russell tied for eighth with Enos Cabell of the Astros.

LA had terrific pitching as well. Burt Hooton notched the fourth-lowest ERA in the Major Leagues. Tommy John's twenty wins put the southpaw in a seven-way tie for third place with John Candelaria, Jim Palmer, Dennis Leonard, Dave Goltz, Rick Reuschel, and Bob Forsch behind Steve Carlton and Tom Seaver.

Dodgers vice president Al Campanis committed what even the team's most diehard fan might have called an example of sacrilege when he put the '78 Dodgers above previous incarnations. Campanis claimed, "We will have the best-rounded team in the 21 years that we have been in Los Angeles."[15] Bravado? Analysis? Somewhere in between? It was quite a statement considering that the Dodgers swept the 1963 Yankees team that won the AL pennant by ten and a half games over the second-place White Sox.

The year before, Don Drysdale had topped the Majors with twenty-five wins and won the Cy Young Award; Maury Wills set a new Major League record for stealing bases, with 104 thefts; and Sandy Koufax had the lowest ERA in the NL. Additionally, Tommy Davis had the highest batting average and the most RBIS in the Major Leagues in 1962. It was an exemplary season, even though the Dodgers lost to the Giants in a three-game National League playoff.

Besides the positive forecasts for Los Angeles during 1978 spring training, one player received a distinct honor off the field in Lindsay, California—Lindsay Junior High School got renamed Steve Garvey Junior High School.[16]

Los Angeles was 0 for 2 in the World Series during the 1970s, losing to the A's in 1974 and the Yankees in 1977. Cincinnati Reds manager Sparky Anderson praised the rival squad as being better than the Yankees but not as good as the Reds, who had four World Series appearances and two titles since Anderson's first year piloting the team in 1970. Anderson figured that 1978 could result in another World Series berth for the Big Red Machine. "Maybe I'm wrong, but on an overall basis I think we have more players who have performed more consistently than the Dodgers," opined Anderson. "If you put the teams next to each other and had every player perform up to his capability, to his career statistics, we would win."[17]

Anderson also pointed to Cincinnati's record of excellence, which would have boasted a World Series opportunity in 1973 had the Mets not beaten the Reds in the NL championship series, three games to two. "In my opinion, the Dodgers still have to play catch-up with us," said Anderson. "They may be wearing rings that the organization gave them as a token for making the playoffs, but the big stone isn't there, it still isn't a World Series ring."[18]

Commissioner Kuhn had twice prevented Charlie Finley from trading Vida Blue—first to the Yankees and then to the Reds—but the A's owner rebounded with a trade to another NL West squad during spring training. The San Francisco Giants procured Blue for six players, a player to be named later, and $395,000, which came close to Kuhn's limit of $400,000.[19]

In New York, Mets followers readied for the Lenny Randle situation to be settled. Randle began March by talking to the team about his salary conflict in an effort of reassurance: "When I step out on that field and walk across the white lines, everything else is out of my mind . . . troubles at home, financial worries, any feelings I might have about someone."[20]

The Mets' front office pushed back on allegations about unfulfilled promises, emphasizing a raise of $8,000 in the middle of 1977 and Randle's refusal of an additional $5,000 as '77 ended because the ballplayer felt he deserved a higher figure. Randle continued to play for the team, but his '78 performance fell dramatically: 132 games and .233 batting average. Spring training in 1978 was a strange, painful time for the Mets, given Tom Seaver's absence from the team and an Associated Press article touting him as a potential thirty-game winner with the Reds.[21] A different challenge existed for their Bronx-based American League counterparts. Recent success plus a legacy of excellence made the Yankees a target. Fathers told their sons about Mickey Mantle; grandfathers piped up with tales of Lou Gehrig. On WPIX-TV, former Yankees shortstop and 1950 MVP Phil Rizzuto joined Frank Messer and Bill White for broadcasts, always ready with a tale about the team's glory years of the late 1940s and early 1950s underlined by his famed exclamation for a terrific defensive play or at bat: "Holy cow!"

Were the Yankees on the verge of another dynasty? Two AL pennants and one World Series title in the previous two years formed a pretty good foundation, but conflict behind closed doors proved to be a weak point for the ball club. Or so the competition thought. "I have the greatest respect for Billy Martin," said Orioles chief scout Jim Russo. "But there's already dissention [sic] on the Yankees, and there will be."[22]

When asked about it, Reggie Jackson emphasized the team's strength, bonds, and endurance created by the white-hot spotlight. "Listen, this team has somehow transcended all the hoopla, media attention and BS. You take a group of grown men who went through what we went through last year and still won, and it makes them something special."[23]

Further, the Yankees were proficient in '77 but not dominant. They won the AL East by two and a half games over the Orioles and Red Sox—who tied for second place—but the AL pennant took the full five games to capture in the AL championship series against the Kansas City Royals. "Dissension tore 'em up last year, but they overcame it," said Royals outfielder Amos Otis. "I don't think they can overcome it again. In fact, I think they'll be torn apart by dissension. And that's one reason we'll win the World Series."

Otis also pointed to pride and money being factors in the conflict, one example being Jackson's salary surpassing that of every other Yankee. When all is said and done, the folks patrolling the dugout on any other team would cheer their brothers. One for all and all for one. Not so for the fellas who wear pinstriped uniforms with no names on the backs. "Over at the Yankees, there are guys on the bench who know they can play out there and they're not going to pull for each other," said Otis.[24]

It began with Jackson's five-year deal exceeding $3 million and a 1977 *Sport* magazine article featuring the quote, "Munson's tough, too. He *is* a winner, but there is just nobody who can do for a club what I can do. . . . There is nobody who can put meat in the seats [fans in the stands] the way I can. That's just the way it is. . . . Munson thinks he can be the straw that stirs the drink, but he can only stir it bad."[25]

From the barbershops in Harlem to the country clubs in Westchester County to the community pools in northern New Jersey to the summer camps in Connecticut, Reggie Jackson was the subject of conversation. Not in a good way. All was forgiven, but maybe not forgotten, by the end of the season, when Jackson hit a home run three times in Game Six. It had only happened twice before in a World Series game, when Babe Ruth did it in 1926 and 1928.

More irritation occurred when Yankees owner George Steinbrenner amplified his pitching staff with Rawly Eastwick, Andy Messersmith, and Goose Gossage in the off-season for the '78 roster. Their résumés were impressive. Eastwick led the NL in saves in 1975 and topped the Major Leagues in

1976, contributions that helped lead Cincinnati to World Series titles. Messersmith had topped the NL with twenty wins for the Dodgers in 1974, and he led the Senior Circuit in 1975 for games started, complete games, and shutouts. Gossage had joined the White Sox in 1972, quickly becoming a stalwart member of the bullpen; he led the Majors in saves in 1975.

Adding two stellar relievers did not sit well with ace reliever Sparky Lyle, the 1977 Cy Young Award winner and American League leader in game appearances and games finished. Lyle feared, and rightfully so, that his playing time would diminish. Complaints were public, which led to Eastwick trying to clarify the situation—he believed that Yankees manager Billy Martin would use him in long relief, not as a closer. Lyle was not in jeopardy.[26]

One member of that '77 squad no longer wore pinstripes, a cause for melancholy. Mike Torrez had been with the Cardinals, Expos, and A's before landing in the South Bronx in a trade for Dock Ellis, Marty Perez, and Larry Murray at the end of April 1977. He went 14-12 during the regular season. In the AL playoffs against Kansas City, Torrez started one game and appeared in another, resulting in an 0-1 record. But he shone in the World Series with two starts and two victories against the Dodgers.

Practicing quietude regarding his Yankees tenure, Torrez did not indulge curious minds thirsty for gossip about the behind-the-scenes conflicts, underscored by the clash between Jackson and Martin on June 18, 1977, at Fenway Park, when Martin pulled the right fielder because he perceived a half-hearted effort in fielding a base hit. A shouting match neared fisticuffs in the visitors' dugout; Yogi Berra and Elston Howard kept the two separated. Torrez recounted that event during spring training in 1978. "Reggie is hard to get to know," said the hurler. "You can be his best friend one minute and the next, he'll look at you as if to say, 'Who the hell are you?'"[27]

Granted free agency after the 1977 season, Torrez signed with the Red Sox at the end of November. Coming off a second-place finish in 1977, Boston had an arsenal of offensive talent ready to take on the Yankees: Carlton Fisk, Carl Yastrzemski, Jim Rice, and Butch Hobson, each tallying more than a hundred RBIs in 1977, though the squad lacked speed. Only Rick Burleson and Yastrzemski reached double digits in steals, with thirteen and eleven, respectively. Pitchers had solid but not overpowering outings; Luis Tiant led the staff with twelve wins.

Red Sox Nation hoped that Torrez could enhance the efforts of Tiant et al. After all, he had solid numbers, including a winning percentage of at least .567 in five of the past six seasons. In 1977 he placed seventh for complete games and tied for seventh in wins for the American League. Two years earlier, he tied for fourth in wins.

On June 25, 1977—a week after the Jackson-Martin brouhaha—Torrez threw a complete-game, 5–1 victory against Boston. The Yankees front office sensed Torrez's value at $750,000 across five years and bumped his salary to twice that amount at the end of the season, giving Torrez a substantive dilemma—stay with a proven winner or seek a new opportunity, hopefully with a pennant contender. Boston's management waved its checkbook, inking a contract worth $2.65 million over seven years, which comes to nearly $380,000 per season. Boston also guaranteed that a trade wouldn't occur until year six, presuming it happened at all.

During 1978 spring training, Torrez revealed that the Yankees' second offer was untimely: "If they had made the same offer to [my agent] in June, I would have signed." Regarding the team's prospects, Torrez balanced his new teammates' experience against the competition's notable talent. "We have the best chance to beat out the Yankees," he said. "Detroit can be tough. They have some good young hitters, but they haven't been in a pennant drive yet. That counts for something."[28]

Torrez's analysis proved correct. At least initially.

4

MOVE OVER, BABY RUTH, HERE COMES REGGIE

APRIL

If Reggie Jackson were a piece of music, he would be a symphony full of blaring horns, compelling violins, and emphatic timpani.

Swagger personified, Jackson swatted 281 home runs in eleven seasons before coming to New York with a curriculum vitae creating anticipation for a new era of Yankees excellence—an MVP Award, membership on six All-Star teams, three league slugging percentage titles, two league home run titles, and three World Series rings. Fans rejoiced at the team's new acquisition about five weeks after the Reds swept the Yankees in the 1976 World Series.

Jackson's career began in the Minor Leagues with the A's organization in 1966, escalating to the parent club in 1967—their first season in Oakland—and taking a one-season detour to Baltimore in 1976 before Yankees owner George Steinbrenner convinced him that New York should be his new base of operations. Detractors indicated a downside: Jackson had twice led the Major Leagues in strikeouts and four times led the American League. Those stats provided an interesting talking point, but Jackson had good company for whiffing. Babe Ruth topped the Majors in strikeouts four times and headed the American League five times. Mickey Mantle became a three-time strikeout leader in the Major Leagues, surpassing the other AL batters in two additional seasons. As far as Yankees fans were concerned, risking a strikeout on the scorecard fell far short of the reward.

Behind the scenes, Jackson had a rocky start in his transition to pinstripes. Appreciation of his formidable talents may have been present in the Yankees' clubhouse, but it did not translate to acceptance. There was a culture clash.

Jimmy Wynn, formerly of the Atlanta Braves and Houston Astros (the team once known as the Colt .45s), played thirty games with the '77 Yankees and observed, "The players on this team like to get on one another. Reggie didn't understand that at first. I said if he laughed with them and took part, he'd get along better." Jackson blamed news coverage for the friction. "When the press started aggravating the situation, I thought it would have been better for everybody if I had not come at all. I knew this team didn't need the controversy. Besides, this was a great team before I got here. They don't need Reggie Jackson to win."[1]

True. The Yankees won the 1976 American League East by ten and a half games over the second-place Orioles with an offense complemented by formidable pitching. Dock Ellis, Catfish Hunter, and Ed Figueroa placed in the top ten among AL pitchers for wins in 1976; Figueroa and Ellis achieved that status for winning percentage as well. Sparky Lyle led the league in saves.

The Yankees offense performed with aplomb, underscored by Thurman Munson batting .302, playing in his fifth All-Star Game, and winning the league's MVP Award. Mickey Rivers batted .312. Both were in the top ten for batting average in the American League. Chris Chambliss hit .293 and Roy White trailed with a .286 average. Willie Randolph tied for ninth in stolen bases while Rivers ended 1976 in seventh place. Jackson's power bolstered the batting even further, emphasized when he secured his place in Yankees lore with three blasts off Dodgers pitchers Burt Hooton, Elías Sosa, and Charlie Hough in Game Six of the 1977 World Series.

The Yankees held their home opener on April 13, after a five-game road trip yielding a 1-4 record; they took one of three games from the Texas Rangers and lost the next two to the Milwaukee Brewers before Ron Guidry had the honors of christening Yankee Stadium for 1978.

Guidry's performance in 1977 had given Yankees fans another excuse to savor the upcoming season during the hot stove months—he tied for ninth in American League wins with Figueroa, Tom Johnson, and Paul Splittorff. Additionally, Guidry tied for second place in shutouts with Bert Blyleven and Dennis Leonard, earned ninth place in strikeouts, and tied for fourth place in winning percentage with Johnson—each had a 16-7 record.

More than forty-four thousand fans went through the Yankee Stadium turnstiles to see the World Series champs inaugurate their 1978 home schedule with a 4–2 win over the Chicago White Sox. Reginald Martinez Jackson owned the day. New York's World Series hero crushed a three-run homer in the bottom of the first inning after Randolph led off with a walk and Rivers singled; Thurman Munson struck out. Jackson's bash invigorated Yankees fans despondent over him striking out four times against Milwaukee in the previous game.

Chicago rebounded with two runs in the top of the second. Eric Soderholm hit a one-out double; Wayne Nordhagen sent him home with a base hit. After Guidry struck out Bill Nahorodny, Nordhagen moved to second base on Don Kessinger's single and scored on Junior Moore's single.

New York got an insurance run in the bottom of the eighth. Bucky Dent's sacrifice fly scored Roy White, who had led off with a walk and then scampered to third on Graig Nettles's double. Guidry threw a complete game, got tagged for ten hits by the Chicagoans, struck out four, and walked two. Skilled but not overpowering, Guidry admitted, "I was lacking speed on my fastball. I didn't feel as strong as I usually do."[2]

But the home opener against the White Sox on April 13 offered attractions beyond the game. Standard Brands unveiled the Reggie bar—a one-and-a-half-ounce, circle-shaped combination of chocolate, caramel, and peanuts—fulfilling a prophecy that Jackson had declared during his tenure with the A's dynasty: "If I played in New York, they'd name a candy bar for me." There were seventy-two thousand samples distributed, an abundance suitable for the superstar's presence, production, and ego.[3]

After the home run, Yankees fans hurled Reggie bars to the field. They considered it a tribute. Others, an insult. White Sox manager Bob Lemon threatened to bring his team to the dugout if it happened again. "Let them throw them when he's in right field," said Lemon, who had been inducted into the Baseball Hall of Fame in 1976 for his pitching career with the Cleveland Indians. "See how he feels. People are starving all over the world and 30 billion calories are laying on the field. So he has a candy bar and he'll make another $100,000 and somebody else will get hurt."[4]

A pregame ceremony honored Roger Maris and Mickey Mantle, who battled in 1961 to break Babe Ruth's single-season home run record. Ruth clocked sixty round-trippers in 1927, breaking his record of fifty-nine set in 1921. Maris eclipsed him with his sixty-first homer on the last day of the 1961 season, which introduced a 162-game schedule; Ruth had 154 games. Mantle got sidelined with an injury in September, ending his home run tally at fifty-four.

A beloved Yankee who had started with the organization in 1951, Mantle received the favored status among Yankees fans to break the record in this battle of the titans. Maris came in a trade from Kansas City after the 1959 season. Even though Maris had won the 1960 American League MVP Award—and would do so again in 1961—it wasn't enough to let him coexist in the hearts of fans.

Plus, Maris endured a controversy over the record's authenticity because of the extra eight games. In turn, sportswriters placed an asterisk on the achievement or had separate entries for the 1927 and 1961 home run totals in lists of baseball records after Major League Baseball commissioner Ford Frick endorsed a distinction.

A 1965 episode of *The Dick Van Dyke Show* had illustrated this qualification in a scene with Rob Petrie and his son, Ritchie. Curious about Ritchie's knowledge regarding where babies come from, Rob tells Ritchie to ask him anything that he doesn't learn about in school. Ritchie asks if Babe Ruth really hit more home runs than anyone else. Rob responds, "Except Roger Maris, I guess, except that he's got an asterisk by his name."[5]

The film *61**, directed by comedian, actor, and famed Yankees fan Billy Crystal, premiered on HBO forty years after Maris broke Ruth's record. In addition to the debate about keeping separate records, the TV movie—which starred Barry Pepper as Maris and Thomas Jane as Mantle—showcased the personal toll on Maris, including his hair falling out from the stress.

So, Maris rebuffed previous invitations to come back to the stadium nicknamed The House That Ruth Built. Even with his pal Mantle present, the opening pitch of the first home game of 1978 was bittersweet for the ballplayer who had won five American League pennants and two World Series titles with the Yankees, plus two National League pennants and a World Series title with the Cardinals. Maris hoped that it would be a source of clarification for his loved ones regarding his career. "Why did I finally decide to do it? Because I have six kids, from 12 to 20 years old, and they ask questions," said the forty-three-year-old. "They read through the boxes of stuff, all those clippings that say how awful I was as a ballplayer, and I've got to tell them something."[6]

Maris had been a recluse regarding these types of events because of the media onslaught, which further intensified the year after he broke Ruth's record. He could do nothing right. His value, ignored. "They got on me for hitting only 33 home runs, they wrote how I was jealous of Mickey, how we didn't get along, and it mushroomed. The more they wrote, the more I went into my shell."[7]

In 1962 Maris led the Yankees in home runs with thirty-three. Mantle clocked thirty. Jackson identified with Maris's plight. "You bet I can relate to Roger Maris and his pressures," explained the Yankees' No. 44, who said that he discussed it with Maris in spring training. "So I know what he went through, I appreciate it," Jackson said. "The press, the public, the whole pressure. And even after he was voted most valuable player for the second time, he couldn't get a raise. I had it myself—I led the league in home runs in 1975, didn't sign and got cut $30,000."[8]

After the 1966 season the Yankees traded Maris to the Cardinals for Charley Smith, who spent two years in pinstripes before ending his career in 1969 with a .239 average and 69 home runs for his career. Maris retired after the 1968 season with 275 career homers, a .260 batting average, and the distinction of being a subject of ongoing debate among baseball historians, scholars, journalists, and fans.

He returned for the home opener in 1985, bringing a baseball to the pitching mound for the other half of the M&M boys to use for the first pitch ceremony. Six years later, Commissioner Fay Vincent and the MLB committee on statistical accuracy okayed Maris's count of sixty-one homers as the official record for a single season. It affirmed a decision that had been made—and perhaps forgotten—in 1968, when another committee ruled that single-season records should not have a distinction based on the number of games in the schedule.[9]

While the debut of the Reggie candy bar excited Yankees fans, a character's unveiling in Philadelphia surprised the crowd at Veterans Stadium on April 25, 1978, before a Phillies-Cubs game: the Phillie Phanatic. This creation with green fur, a long nose, and a Phillies jersey quickly became an icon.

Phillies fans share their insights on the Phillie Phanatic's cultural impact. Allen and Rhoda Katz have long-standing ties to the Philadelphia area and its NL ball club. Allen praises the Phillie Phanatic's interaction with the fans:

"He's good with kids. He spends his time wandering all through the stadium. He makes an honest effort to have people be with him and engage with him."[10] Rhoda grew up as a Phillies fan in northeast Philadelphia. She remembers, "My first cousin was the president of the Eddie Waitkus Fan Club. I was vice president. I think he lived somewhere near where she lived. We just liked when the Phanatic danced on top of the Phillies' dugout because we had seats on the third base line."[11]

Their daughter, Lisa (Katz) Gruber, recalls, "When I was in third grade at Red Lion Elementary School, the school was sponsoring a bike-a-thon around the neighborhood in Huntington Valley. My neighbors sponsored a dollar a mile. I went thirty miles. The winner got a Phillie Phanatic doll. It was six inches high. My greatest sporting achievement."[12]

Chris Butts points to several reasons that the Phillie Phanatic is a great mascot. "The San Diego Chicken came before him. It was more of a showman, a wiseass. Not as interactive as the Phanatic, who's a cheerleader, engaging with the fans. The Phanatic is a showman in the Max Patkin sense in how he mimed. He would do all the mannerisms during the lineup announcements, like Joe Morgan's arm flap. Kids gravitate toward him. His ability to make people laugh is important."[13]

Rebecca Alpert says, "I first met the Phanatic in 1978 preseason. The Phillies were trying to draw attention to their new mascot and sent him to events around the city. My husband at the time worked at a local synagogue as the assistant rabbi and school principal and invited the Phanatic to an event they were holding, so I got to meet him at close range. He clearly had a way with people; adults and children were treated the same. He connected to us, clowning around with us, dancing, joking, embracing."[14]

Victor Sloan, a native of Wilmington, Delaware, believes the Phanatic's appeal comes from being different: "I think he's great because it's so bizarre and not an obvious connection with the team. The Swinging Friar is obvious. To me, it's just so out there. Others are riffs on the team name. And then, the other mascot may be a cute animal, like a dog. The Somerset Patriots have a dog."[15]

James Pietras grew up in Hamilton, New Jersey, and played Little League for six years before joining the Lou Gehrig League, where he played from ages twelve to fifteen. He points to the universal quality of the Phillie Phanatic and uses the phrase "unbridled passion" to describe why Philadelphia is a great sports city: "He's a great mascot primarily because he brings people of all ages together in a comical way to enjoy the downtime. I greatly enjoy his helmet-stomping activity when they change bases in the middle of the game. He gets one of the plastic helmets from the opposing team and smashes it all over the field. With other mascots, there really isn't the level of interaction, especially with younger fans. He'll find a guy with a bald head and do a spit shine. He always gets involved in the different areas of the stadium and does things outside the stadium."[16]

Rock Hoffman aligns the Phillie Phanatic with comedic giants: "He is classically funny like the Three Stooges or the Harlem Globetrotters. You know the routine but still laugh. My favorite Phanatic moment was when he was the guest picker on ESPN's College Game Day produced in Philadelphia on October 31, 2015. He made his picks of who he thought was going to win that day's college football games without saying a word and it was brilliant."[17]

Cherry Hill, New Jersey, native Mike Miller's favorite moment in Phillies history is Tug McGraw striking out Willie Wilson to win the 1980 World Series. He concurs regarding the Phillie Phanatic's energy: "He engages the fans with his sense of humor, his dancing, and of course, the hot dog gun. He is great at pantomime, whether mimicking the umpires, casting spells on the opposing pitchers, or recreating the action on the field. We used to share a ticket plan in section 118 at Citizens Bank Park and the Phanatic would run down our aisle in the seventh inning every game. The kids—ours and others'—would excitedly come toward the aisle for a run of high fives."[18]

TV viewers taking a break from baseball found a new offering every Sunday night in April 1978, with a five-part miniseries on CBS described as "enervating," "a clattering mess," "tacky, trashy potboiler," "second-rate contemporary 'Giant,'" and "one of the most exploitive, repugnant hours on television."[19] CBS ignored the noise, developed it for the prime-time lineup in the fall, and created a popular culture icon. *Dallas* ran for thirteen seasons.

The show revolved around the Ewing clan, led by oil mogul John Ross "Jock" Ewing and his wife, Ellie Southworth Ewing, also known as Miss Ellie. A wildcatter and a drifter in his younger days, Jock partnered with his brother, Jason, and Willard "Digger" Barnes, a drunk who could sense where oil lay underneath the ground. Jason also liked to drink. When Jock held on to their shares of an oil well to prevent them being thrown away on booze and gambling, Digger saw it as theft and a rift formed between the two friends. Jason eventually moved to Alaska.

Jock also began dating Ellie, whose family owned the Southfork Ranch but could no longer afford it because of the Great Depression's painful economy. Ellie married Jock to save Southfork; they had three sons—J.R., Gary, and Bobby. Because Ellie was Digger's sweetheart, the enmity between the two friends intensified.

Greatly respected among his peers in the cartel—a group of Texas oil barons running independent companies—Jock ascended to the top of the oil industry in Dallas. Digger continued his drinking, wallowed in misery, and whined to fellow barflies about his downturn. His grudge lasted for the rest of his life.

In the first episode, Bobby, the youngest Ewing son, brings home a surprise—a wife. But what's more shocking than their elopement is her identity. She's Digger Barnes's daughter, Pamela. Her brother, Cliff, carries the burden of his father's ill will. As a government lawyer and later an oil executive, he targets the Ewings for destruction. It's a running theme throughout the series, but his raison d'être is continually thwarted, usually by John Ross Ewing Jr., the oldest son, also known as J.R.

The Ewings' middle son, Gary, left Southfork before the events of the miniseries began. Gary and his wife, Valene, had married and had Lucy when they were teenagers themselves. After Gary abandoned them, Valene took her baby daughter to stay with her mother in Tennessee; J.R. arranged for Lucy to be taken from Valene and transported back to Southfork.

A teenaged Lucy has a sexual relationship with Southfork's foreman—Ray Krebbs—predating the events of the miniseries but ending by the end of the second episode because Pam interferes. Ray is Pam's former boyfriend, but Lucy's new aunt has no residual feelings for him. She's just looking out for Lucy. It's discovered a few years later that Ray is the illegitimate son of Jock, a result of an affair in England when he served in World War II. The previous Ray-Lucy relationship was not addressed and probably ignored because of the family lineage making him her uncle by blood.

Dallas was a cornerstone of CBS's Friday night lineup through the late 1970s oil crisis, early 1980s recession, and the extravagance that defined the rest of the 1980s. Ewing Oil is worth $200 million when the show begins.

Toward the end, the company is valued at $2 billion. Created by David Jacobs, *Dallas* encompassed a fictional universe with recurring characters, including cartel members Jordan Lee and Punk Anderson, doing business with Ewing Oil; Harv Smithfield, serving as Jock's attorney; WestStar CEO Jeremy Wendell, battling J.R.; and Dallas Police Department detective Harry McSween, consulting with J.R. on various investigations.

Jim Davis and Barbara Bel Geddes played Jock and Miss Ellie. Patrick Duffy and Victoria Principal played Bobby and Pam, a pairing that appeared to be the initial foundation of the show's storytelling. Larry Hagman and Linda Gray played J.R. and his wife, Sue Ellen, a former Miss Texas. Charlene Tilton played Lucy; Ken Kercheval played Cliff. Credits for Hagman had included guest starring roles on *Barnaby Jones*, *McCloud*, and *Dan August*.

Hagman's best-known role before the 1978 miniseries was as NASA astronaut Captain (later Major) Anthony Nelson on *I Dream of Jeannie*, an NBC sitcom airing from 1965 to 1971 and coinciding with the space race that yielded terrific bounty in popular culture, including *Star Trek*, *My Favorite Martian*, and *Lost in Space*. He found "Jeannie" in a bottle on an island beach after his spacecraft splashed down nearby; Jeannie's desire to help her "master" with his career conflicted with his efforts to conceal Jeannie's powers as a genie, leading to humorous situations often involving slapstick.

In the *Dallas* series, Hagman showed the incredible range of his acting. Although it was an ensemble, J.R. emerged as the breakout character. He manipulated lovers, rivals, business partners, and family members with the finesse of a pianist giving a performance at Carnegie Hall and the patience of a wartime general devising a battle plan. His roster of bedroom companions included Sue Ellen's sister, Kristin Shepard. Cartel members were allies one minute, targets the next. J.R.'s scheming caught up with him in the last episode of season 3, when somebody shot him while he worked in his office in the Ewing Building late at night.

"Who Shot J.R.?" became a worldwide query during the summer of 1980, intensified by the Screen Actors Guild and American Federation of Television and Radio Artists going on strike in July. The work stoppage extended into the fall, which prolonged and increased the curiosity. When Hagman went to the London Palladium for the Queen Mother's eightieth birthday,

England's matriarch asked, "I don't suppose you could tell me who shot J.R.?" Hagman responded, "No, ma'am. Not even for you."[20]

After the strike ended, the TV networks resumed their schedules of original programming with a delayed start of the 1980–81 season. The third season of *Dallas* premiered on November 7, 1980, though J.R.'s assailant would not be discovered until the end of the fourth episode: Kristin shot J.R. Three months after the world learned of Kristin's deed, the storyline inspired a running theme on an episode of *Saturday Night Live* hosted by Tilton. "Who Shot C.R.?" referred to cast member Charles Rocket, who appeared at the end of the show and declared, "I'd like to know who the fuck did it." Tilton and the cast were visibly shocked at the utterance of this expletive.[21]

Dallas spun off *Knots Landing*, with Gary and Valene settled in the suburbs of Southern California. It premiered in 1979 and lasted fourteen seasons; a two-part miniseries aired in 1997.

CBS aired a three-hour *Dallas* prequel in 1986. *Dallas: The Early Years* showed the genesis, success, and fallout of the Jock-Jason-Digger relationship; Ellie and Jock's coupling; and a Ewing barbecue at Southfork, which was a staple in the series. CBS brought back the *Dallas* banner for two TV movies in the 1990s—*Dallas: J.R. Returns* and *Dallas: War of the Ewings*. TNT revived the premise in 2012 with actors from the original series reprising their roles and a new generation of Ewings and Barneses, but this incarnation ignored the storylines of the TV movies. It lasted three seasons, for a total of forty episodes.

While J.R. Ewing's enemies licked their wounds in the *Dallas* miniseries, Charlie Finley did the same when the U.S. Court of Appeals for the Seventh Circuit sided against the A's owner in his lawsuit challenging the commissioner. Finley's argument proved insufficient to overcome Bowie Kuhn's bar on selling Vida Blue, Joe Rudi, and Rollie Fingers for millions of dollars.

5

KINGMAN'S PERFORMANCE AND LASORDA'S OUTRAGE

MAY

There is rudeness. There is temper. There is vulgarity.

Then there is Tommy Lasorda on May 14, 1978.

The Chicago Cubs beat the Los Angeles Dodgers 10–7 in a fifteen-inning game at Dodger Stadium, but the time span of five hours and two minutes did not set off Lasorda's eruption on this Mother's Day. Dave Kingman's three home runs fueled the ire, which became evident when the Dodgers' manager gave a raw, florid, and expletive-filled response to a seemingly simple query from reporter Paul Olden: "What's your opinion of Kingman's performance?"

Lasorda ranted, "What's my opinion of Kingman's performance? What the fuck do you think is my opinion of it? I think it was fucking horseshit! Put that in, I don't fucking—opinion of his performance? Jesus Christ, he beat us with three fucking home runs!

"What the fuck do you mean 'what is my opinion of his performance?' How can you ask me a question like that, 'what is my opinion of his performance?' Jesus Christ, he hit three home runs! Jesus Christ! I'm fucking pissed off to lose the fucking game, and you ask me my opinion of his performance? Jesus Christ! That's a tough question to ask me, isn't it? What is my opinion of his performance? . . . Well, I didn't give you a good answer because I'm mad, but I mean, that's a tough question to ask me right now, 'what is my opinion of his performance?' I mean, you want me to tell you what my opinion of his performance is. . . . That's right! Jesus Christ! Guy hits three home runs against us. Shit, I mean I don't want to, I don't mean to get pissed off or anything like that, but, you know, you ask me my opinion.

"I mean, he put on a hell of a show, he hit three home runs, he drove in, what, seven runs? . . . Eight runs! So what the hell more can you say about it? I didn't mean to get mad or anything like that but god damn, you ask me my opinion of his performance."[1]

Los Angeles tallied the game's first run when Davey Lopes scored on Ron Cey's two-out double in the bottom of the first. Lopes had led off with a walk, then took second base when Chicago's starting pitcher, Dennis Lamp, balked. Two more runs for the home team came in a third-inning sequence.

Scoreless through five innings, the Cubs ended the blanking with Kingman's first homer—a two-run blast—in the top of the sixth.

A seesaw type of scoring began when Chicago went ahead 4–3 in the top of the seventh and LA scored two runs in the bottom half of the inning. Bobby Murcer's solo shot led off the Cubs' eighth, tying the game at 5–5. Reggie Smith put the Dodgers ahead with a single, scoring two base runners, only to be matched by another two-run round-tripper from the slugger nicknamed "Kong" in the ninth.

Both teams battled in this 7–7 stalemate until Kong Kingman smacked his third home run, a three-run effort in the top of the fifteenth. In addition to the seven RBIs from the homers, Kingman's ground ball with the bases loaded in the seventh inning resulted in a force out and a run scored.

Kingman had clout but not capacity, tallying 442 wallops over the outfield fences while batting .236 in his career, which he spent with the Giants, Mets, Padres, Angels, Yankees, Cubs, and A's. His roster of home runs—many of which were towering shots forcing fans to crane their necks for a glimpse of the baseball—included 36 in 1975 and 37 in 1976 for the Mets.

On June 15, 1977, Kingman went to the Padres in a trade for Bobby Valentine and Paul Siebert. It was the same day that the Mets sent Tom Seaver to the Reds for Dan Norman, Pat Zachry, Doug Flynn, and Steve Henderson. "Before Dave Kingman arrived at Shea Stadium, no New York Met in the 1970s had hit more than 24 home runs in a season," recalls Greg Prince, New York Mets author and historian. "Kingman showed up and shattered that decade's standard by a dozen. For two seasons, 1975 and 1976, Kingman was as popular an everyday Met as there ever was. By 1977 he was ready to move on, unsatisfied with his contractual status now that free agency had kicked in. The 1970s made a young fan grow up fast. It wasn't personal, kids. It was business. Kingman, like Tom Seaver, felt the market had left him behind, and they both wanted the Mets to make them whole. The Mets, falling apart from every angle, weren't so inclined."[2]

Baseball historian and Kingman aficionado Charlie Vascellaro notes, "As if it wasn't bad enough losing 'The Franchise'—the greatest pitcher and all-time fan favorite, the Mets dealt the team's all-time home run leader on the same night in exchange for six almost anonymous players. The whole thing felt like one big punch to the gut and completely deflated whatever air was left in the Mets balloon."[3]

Bouncing around the Major Leagues like a pinball at a Coney Island arcade, Kingman wore four team uniforms in 1977, including a ten-game stint with the Angels, who claimed the slugger on waivers in early September and traded him to the Yankees nine days later. Kingman played eight games for Steinbrenner's crew. "I played on so many teams last year it was hard to know where I fit in," shared the six-foot-six-inch ballplayer during spring training in 1978. "It's a little harder to do your job when you're putting so many uniforms on."[4]

The Cubs had signed Kingman to a five-year contract for $1.3 million in the off-season, giving him financial and employment stability. He batted .221 in 1978 coming into the Mother's Day game. "I consider the first month of the season a disaster," said Kingman, who had broken into the Major Leagues in 1971. "But you can only go so long before something snaps. It started to come around the other night [Wednesday] in San Diego against Randy Jones."[5]

Kingman hit three home runs in a game five times during his career. Achieving this power at Chavez Ravine in 1978 also happened before—he had enjoyed a triple-homer day for the Mets against the Dodgers two years earlier. "It's always a great feeling to come back to Dodger Stadium," Kingman revealed after the Mother's Day game. "I can't put it into words. It's one of the most beautiful parks in either league. The whole atmosphere is pure baseball."[6]

Accomplishing the feat twice in 1979, when he led the Majors with forty-eight home runs and the NL in slugging percentage, Kingman also swung and missed often. His 131 strikeouts topped the National League. He dropped to eighteen homers in 1980, but he only played in eighty-one games. Back with the Mets in the strike-shortened season of 1981, Kingman went yard twenty-two times and tied for third place in the Major Leagues with Eddie Murray,

Dwight Evans, Bobby Grich, George Foster, and Tony Armas. Strikeouts were plentiful again; Kingman whiffed 105 times, to lead his NL peers.

His thirty-seven homers led the NL in 1982 and tied him for third place again in the Majors, this time with Dave Winfield. But he also tied with Reggie Jackson to lead the Majors in strikeouts. Kingman's homer count fell to thirteen in 1983. So did his playing time—100 games. Finishing his career with the Oakland A's, Kong delighted fans of the green and gold as an everyday player with no fewer than 144 games a season from 1984 to 1986. He put the ball into the bleachers thirty-five, thirty, and thirty-five times, respectively, and hit another trio of home runs in a 1984 game.

Kingman placed second in home runs for the 1986 American League behind Toronto's Jesse Barfield and ended his professional career in 1987, batting .203 and hitting two home runs across twenty games with the 1987 Phoenix Firebirds—the Giants' Triple-A team in the Pacific Coast League.

LA's Mother's Day loss in 1978 came in the middle of a twelve-game home stand against the Cardinals, Cubs, Pirates, and Giants, ending in a 7-5 record. In the NL West, San Francisco occupied first place followed by Cincinnati at one and a half games behind; Los Angeles trailed by two games. At this point in 1977, the Dodgers had a 25-7 record and an eleven-game lead over the second-place Giants. The 1978 season was shaping up to be a challenging journey for them. Likewise for the Yankees.

A couple of days before Kingman's awesome display, the Yankees lost a game against their AL playoff rivals from the past two years because of an at bat that should have been the last out for a victory. Instead, Kansas City Royals slugger Amos Otis hit an inside-the-park home run to defeat the pinstriped visitors 4–3. A threat every time he stepped in the batter's box, Otis placed fourth in the 1978 American League for slugging percentage, seventh for batting average, and tied for eighth in RBIs. If he got on base, the defense prepared for his prodigiousness on the base paths—Otis placed ninth in stolen bases.

But the star center fielder who had two seasons leading the American League in doubles and one league title for stolen bases, played on five All-Star teams, plus owned a World Series ring from his NL tenure with the Mets at the beginning of his career did not win the game because of his slugging ability or base-running instincts. The responsibility belonged to the fellas from the South Bronx.

It was a good match-up. New York had been on a decent track, winning ten of their last twelve games. The Royals dominated at the beginning of the season with an 11-2 record but were 1-7 so far in May. Now they enjoyed the home field advantage against the Yankees, who had embarked on an eleven-game road trip that also included stops in Chicago, Cleveland, and Toronto.

Ed Figueroa took the hill for the visitors, sporting a 4-1 record so far in 1978. The Royals tagged him for two runs in the bottom of the third when Frank White hit a single, stole second base, and scored on a triple by Summit, New Jersey, native Willie Wilson followed by Tom Poquette's sacrifice fly scoring Wilson.

Paul Splittorff started for the Royals and kept the Yankees scoreless until the top of the fifth, when they scored one run. In the seventh, Chris Chambliss led off with a single and Graig Nettles hit a two-run homer to make the score 3–2. Roy White popped out to Royals second baseman Frank White, and Bucky Dent grounded out to third baseman Al Cowens, but the New Yorkers rebounded by loading the bases on three straight singles and putting their prized slugger in a prime situation to pad the score.

First, Mickey Rivers got on base with his second hit of the night, but Paul Blair replaced him as a pinch runner and then in center field. Willie Randolph's base hit prompted Royals manager Whitey Herzog to replace Splittorff with Marty Pattin; Munson singled, which sent Steve Mingori from the bullpen to face Reggie Jackson. A grand slam—or even a hit—was not to be. Jackson flew out to Otis in center field.

When the Royals came to bat in the ninth, Figueroa retired the first two batters—Hal McRae and Cowens—on flyouts to the outfield and walked Darrell Porter on four pitches. Yankees manager Billy Martin called on ace reliever Goose Gossage to face Otis, who was 1 for 3 against Figueroa with a two-out double in the bottom of the seventh.

Otis met Gossage's pitch with a powerful swing that sent the ball to the warning track in right-center field, and Blair ran to catch it. Jackson, the same. They collided, sending the ball that had been in Blair's glove onto the ground and far enough away to prevent the center fielder from snatching it in time to get Otis out. Jackson said, "When the ball is hit, my thought is to let him get it. But as he and I were getting to the ball, I wasn't absolutely sure he could get it, and he couldn't call, and there just wasn't anything to do but try to catch it. He did.

"I think I could have if he hadn't been there."[7]

Blair revealed that he didn't know the incident's effects beyond the accidental clash with his teammate. For him, the Yankees won the game. "I thought I still had the ball," said the thirty-four-year-old veteran ballplayer. "Then I saw I didn't even have my glove. He kicked everything off. The glove, the ball."[8]

An eight-time Gold Glove recipient, Blair had the speed, range, and judgment to snare the ball for a Yankees victory. He also had Otis's respect. "You're goddamn straight I got lucky," stated the Royals slugger. "If you had to pick one outfielder to go and get it, it would be Blair. He's the best one there is. I'm good but that goddamn Blair can play outfield."[9]

Games where a player hits three home runs or a mishap causes a reversal of fortunes in the bottom of the ninth inning are anomalies that entertain, making great fodder for the sports segment on local TV news shows. Milestones, on the other hand, are celebrated at the time and etched with permanence into baseball's chronicles as marks of excellence to which ballplayers can aspire. Pete Rose had many in his career. He joined an exclusive club on May 5 when he notched his 3,000th hit, an achievement delighting Reds fans at Riverfront Stadium seeing the home team take on the Montreal Expos.

Rose got No. 2,999 on a "high-chop base hit" to Expos pitcher Steve Rogers in the third inning, for which Rogers blamed himself. "My hand got in between the ball and the glove," stated the right-hander, who had reached second place in NL Rookie of the Year voting in 1973 and made his second All-Star team in 1978. "It would have been bang, bang and I would have had to have made the best play of the night to get him."[10]

Rogers had a solid output: striking out the side in the second inning, tallying a strikeout in the third, and whiffing the first two batters in the fifth. With a 3–1 lead—Johnny Bench's fourth-inning solo home run providing the sole Cincinnati run—Rogers faced Rose. A switch hitter, the man nicknamed "Charlie Hustle" for his enthusiasm batted left against the right-handed Rogers and sent a line drive to the left-field turf for No. 3,000, setting off a moment of celebration for Cincinnatians ranking with the unveiling of Union Terminal, the dedication of *The Genius of Water* statue and fountain, and the inauguration of native William Howard Taft as the twenty-seventh president.

Rose had been a fan favorite for his aggressive style of play, which some baseball followers found to be unnecessary. In the 1970 All-Star Game, an exhibition match-up with no impact on the regular season or postseason, Rose pummeled catcher Ray Fosse at home plate like he was a linebacker charging a running back. "I started to slide headfirst, but Ray had the plate blocked and I'm not gonna break both my collarbones," said Rose in a 2017 interview. "And you never slide if you can't reach the plate. And I went over him and I tagged the plate with my right hand. This is the God's honest truth. I guess my knee hit his shoulder. I missed the next three games, he didn't miss any."[11]

Three years later, Rose took a lead off first base in game three of the NL championship series when Joe Morgan grounded to Mets first baseman John Milner, who threw to Bud Harrelson for a 1–6–1 double play. Rose ignited a brawl with a hard slide into Harrelson.

But Rose's controversial exploits were forgotten, or at least ignored, on this chilly May night as he entered a club boasting only a dozen other members: Hank Aaron, Cap Anson, Ty Cobb, Eddie Collins, Roberto Clemente, Al Kaline, Nap Lajoie, Willie Mays, Stan Musial, Tris Speaker, Honus Wagner, and Paul Waner.

Montreal scored again in the top of the eighth; Dan Driessen went yard with George Foster on base to make the score 4–3, which was the final count. Reds devotees rejoiced at Rose's postgame statement about the 3,000-hit milestone: "If I would dedicate the hit to anybody it would be to the fans in Cincinnati. Imagine, over 37,000 here in 35-degree weather."[12]

May would not be the last time in 1978 that Pete Rose caused a celebration, Tommy Lasorda vocalized his outrage, or Reggie Jackson received a spotlight for his ballplaying. Meanwhile, summer beckoned with the kickoff to Memorial Day weekend. Vacationers had an expanded opportunity in the city where Miss America got crowned, Jerry Lewis and Dean Martin made their professional debut as a comedy team, and Lyndon B. Johnson got nominated at the Democratic National Convention to be the party's candidate for president in 1964.

Atlantic City.

Since the 1960s, Al Stein had told relatives, friends, and customers at his antique store located at the corner of Missouri Avenue and Pacific Avenue that gambling was coming to Atlantic City. They looked at him askance.

Sure, casinos could benefit from the city's great entertainment lineage, including the 500 Club, which birthed the Martin-Lewis pairing.

Sure, it's geographically convenient for drawing customers from two major metropolitan areas—AC is a little more than a one-hour drive from Philadelphia and double that from New York City.

Sure, it has the allure of the boardwalk, beach, and Atlantic Ocean.

But skeptics didn't see the trajectory that Stein saw. Political challenges would be difficult to navigate, as they would ignite debates about the propriety of gambling. Plus, Atlantic City did not have a major airport, which made traveling from outside the Eastern Seaboard a frustrating trek—if not a harrowing one—usually requiring flying into New York City, Newark, or Philadelphia and driving to South Jersey. Traveling by car or bus meant suffering traffic jams on the Garden State Parkway and Atlantic City Expressway, especially on weekends in the summer. Train travel options were limited. Critics had additional concerns, beginning with the city's image. Long prized as a resort destination for families, Atlantic City risked becoming a lucrative site for a criminal element—whether through organized crime or independent operators—looking to satisfy visitors seeking recreation beyond the casino floor and entertainment venues. Prostitution was a possibility. Drugs, too.

On Friday, May 26, 1978, Stein's prognostication came true. Fears, concerns, and comments continued as New Jersey governor Brendan Byrne ushered in legalized gambling—and hopefully a healthy boost for the state's tax revenues—when he strode to a predetermined spot on the casino floor of Resorts International, cut a ceremonial ribbon, and revealed a paternal axiom regarding gambling: "My father told me never to bet on anything but Notre Dame and the Yankees, but for everyone who doesn't want to follow my father's advice the casino is now open."[13]

Resorts International counted more than twenty-five thousand visitors for the first day, which had less than optimal weather. But clouds and light rain mattered little to those scurrying for openings among the nearly nine hundred slot machines, in addition to about eighty tables featuring blackjack, craps, and other games. Atlantic City's only casino at that time, Resorts would ultimately be joined by other entities, including Bally's, Hilton, and Caesars Palace. New York City real estate mogul and future president Donald Trump also staked a beachside claim for a gambling and entertainment venue.[14]

Atlantic City later showcased high-level boxing events, most notably the Mike Tyson versus Michael Spinks heavyweight championship fight in 1988, which lasted ninety-one seconds, with Tyson winning by knockout. Commerce did not live up to expectations, though. Several casinos closed, either for business reasons or bankruptcy. Whatever the city's fate may be in the rest of the twenty-first century, the foundation of gambling can be traced back to a drizzly day in 1978 when optimism prevailed.

New Jersey had another reason to celebrate: less than thirty miles from Manhattan, the Cannon Ball House in Springfield got tagged as a national landmark. In 1780 the War for American Independence—otherwise known as the Revolutionary War—turned a corner at the Battle of Springfield, where this farmhouse served as a field hospital for wounded soldiers from the British and American armies. The British exempted the house from the burning and destruction other structures experienced as the troops retreated from a surprisingly solid defense by the American rebels. The house's nickname came from its being hit with a cannonball during the battle.[15]

Although it didn't happen as far back as the Revolutionary War, the birth of rock and roll may have seemed like it had been two hundred years ago given the cultural revolutions in the United States since the late 1950s. In addition to the Vietnam War, Americans had endured the assassinations of President John F. Kennedy, civil rights leaders Martin Luther King Jr. and Medgar Evers, Democratic presidential candidate Robert F. Kennedy, and two attempts on President Gerald Ford's life during his brief partial term in office following the Watergate scandal that forced Richard Nixon to resign the presidency.

Happy Days satisfied a nostalgic urge for the 1950s every Tuesday night for thirty minutes on ABC. In addition, Hollywood populated its film roster in 1978 with stories recalling a time when the country enjoyed peace and prosperity under President Eisenhower's governance but witnessed a transformation in popular music headed by a disc jockey from Cleveland who made his way to New York City. Alan Freed spearheaded the popularity of rock and roll through his radio shows, concerts, and films promoting a new type of music that critics lambasted as contributing to juvenile delinquency and teenagers embraced as a sonic emblem of joy, freedom, and love.

American Hot Wax gave a fictionalized account of Freed in a story set in 1959, climaxing with one of his famed rock-and-roll shows at the Paramount Theater in Brooklyn. Jerry Lee Lewis and Chuck Berry appear as themselves. *American Hot Wax* adheres to a precept mentioned in *Jolson Sings Again*, the 1949 sequel to 1946's *The Jolson Story*, both starring Larry Parks as entertainer Al Jolson. In the sequel, Parks as Jolson talks about the idea for the initial film and cautions the producers not to worry about the details, just the aura of his life.

One example of a factual inaccuracy in *American Hot Wax* is the radio station in New York City. It's WROL, a fictional station. Freed spun records at WINS. Another scene shows a group called The Planotones recording "Come Go with Me," but The Del Vikings made that hit record.

Still, it worked. "'American Hot Wax' is by turns romantic, touching, lighthearted and painful," wrote Bob Wisehart in the *Charlotte News*. "Its excesses—Freed's canonization, for example—are forgivable because the whole is so artfully put together and attractive." *Newsday* film critic Joseph Gelmis called the film "impressive moviemaking," while admitting that he "didn't care for '50s rock when it was the rage and who feels no nostalgia for it now." Furthermore, he wrote, "it looks terrific, the editing is dynamic, the acting is flawless, the music is masterfully integrated into the action."[16]

Tim McIntire played Freed, earning plaudits from the *Atlanta Constitution* for a "wonderful performance" and the *Fort Worth Star-Telegram*, which praised his "portrayal of the famous disc jockey" as a "masterful characterization which shouldn't be overlooked amid all the [musical] fury."[17]

An on-screen postscript explains that Freed got indicted and died penniless five years after the events of the movie. The specifics are absent but significant; Freed pleaded guilty to "payola"—receiving bribes from record companies for certain songs to get airtime. He also had a financial interest in songs that he played on his radio shows. Freed got a nod in 1978's *The Buddy Holly Story* when a radio station owner in Lubbock, Texas, describes Holly's new sound as part of rock and roll: "Disc jockey up in Cleveland made that one up and he's doing real fine with it, too."

Buddy Holly had a brief career with several hit songs between 1956, when the movie starts, and his death at twenty-two years old in 1959 from injuries sustained in a plane crash with fellow performers Ritchie Valens and J. P. "The Big Bopper" Richardson after a concert at the Surf Ballroom in Clear Lake, Iowa. Gary Busey's portrayal of the Lubbock-born songwriter and singer earned him an Oscar nomination for Best Actor. "His acting is not imitation; it is total immersion," wrote film critic Peter Travers. "From the start, we accept him as real."[18] A similar description appeared in the *Muncie Star*: "His mannerisms and singing style are so close to Holly's that it's as if he and Holly were one and the same. Seldom has an actor meshed so well with his on-screen character."[19]

Rex Reed of New York's *Daily News* lauded Busey in his rather acerbic dissection of Holly's music and the film's story depicting an easy, glide-like rise to rock-and-roll fame with very few stumbles or setbacks. "Busey's work is so rich, unaffected and captivating that most of the movie slips by before you realize how simple and thin the material is," wrote Reed, who filmed a cameo as himself in *Superman*, which premiered in December. "Buddy Holly's widow apparently had tight control over the script, so if there were any juicy scandals in her husband's life they've been discreetly eliminated. The portrait of wife Maria Elena is too sweet a cameo to be believed."[20]

Again, the paradigm of dramatic license emphasized in *Jolson Sings Again* is executed here. There was a Coral Records, but the character of Coral executive Ross Turner, played by Conrad Janis, was either a fictional creation for the movie or a composite character. There was a three-man band called Buddy Holly and the Crickets, but the names Jesse Charles and Ray Bob Simmons were created for the movie. Don Stroud played Jesse, the drummer. Charles Martin Smith played Ray Bob on bass. Niki Sullivan spent some time with Holly as a rhythm guitarist, making the band a quartet. That is not addressed. But there's a rather glaring omission of a major factor in Holly's success—record producer Norman Petty receives nary a mention, but the Turner character might represent him.

The final sequence takes place with Holly performing at Iowa's Clear Lake Auditorium accompanied by a full band, including a horn section, during the Winter Party '59 rock-and-roll tour of the Midwest. February 3 is the date on the marquee. None of this is correct. Holly's last performance took place at the Surf Ballroom in Clear Lake, Iowa, on February 2. There was not a band of the size portrayed in the movie.

Despite its inaccuracies, the film's depiction of Holly's ascendancy and the soundtrack, including "Peggy Sue," "True Love Ways," "Rave On," "It's So Easy," "Words of Love," and "That'll Be the Day"—all performed by Busey—gave 1978 moviegoers a taste of rock and roll's emergence through the eyes of a young, ambitious innovator with obvious but ultimately unfulfilled talent because of the plane crash less than six miles from its takeoff point at the Mason City airport. Richardson was twenty-nine years old. Valens, seventeen. The crash was determined to be a result of pilot error; eighteen-year-old Roger Peterson was not certified to fly using only instruments.[21]

In baseball a Yankees pitcher had compiled a 7-0 record for the Yankees by the end of May. An outstanding performance in June made him a legend. It would be quite a summer for the national pastime.

6

LOUISIANA LIGHTNING AND GREASED LIGHTNING

JUNE

They didn't call Ron Guidry "Louisiana Lightning" because he liked thunderstorms in the Pelican State.

On June 17 the pitcher who wore No. 49 in pinstripes and had yet to lose a game handled the California Angels with the skill of a surgeon as he recorded eighteen strikeouts, allowed four hits, and won a complete-game shutout at Yankee Stadium for his eleventh victory of 1978. The Yankees supported him with four runs.

Bobby Grich got the first hit off Guidry with a lead-off double in the first inning, but the lefty retired the next three batters; two struck out. New York got its first run in the bottom of the first when the first three batters hit singles: Roy White led off, moved to third base on Thurman Munson's base hit, and crossed the plate as Gary Thomasson followed suit.

The Yankees got their remaining runs on a terrific sequence in the bottom of the third. Munson banged a lead-off single and scored on Thomasson's triple. Reggie Jackson singled home Thomasson, then advanced one base when Paul Hartzell tossed a wild pitch; Graig Nettles's single scored Jackson for the Yankees' fourth run of the game.

Guidry's output nipped at the heels of Steve Carlton, Tom Seaver, and Nolan Ryan, who had all topped the Major Leagues with nineteen strikeouts in a game until Roger Clemens broke the twenty-strikeout barrier in 1986. Ryan, an Angels ace from 1972 to 1979 with five seasons leading the Majors in strikeouts—including the record of 383 in 1973—examined Guidry's dominance against his teammates and lauded him: "That kid was overpowering.

Anytime somebody can break that record, I'm all for it. It's just a matter of time. It's going to happen."[1]

But Ryan's pitching compadre Frank Tanana, who notched seventeen strikeouts in a 1975 Angels game against the Texas Rangers, did not give Guidry all the credit as he pointed out the need for California's offense to be strategic when facing the lanky pitcher with overpowering flings. "If hitters go up and just swing at everything he's throwing, he'll be unbeatable," said Tanana. "You gotta make him throw the ball over the plate. We swung at a lot of bad pitches."[2]

While Guidry's 10-0 record may have inspired confidence in Yankees fans before the June 17 game, the southpaw did not forecast a strong performance, or even a lengthy one, in front of the 33,162 people in attendance. Twenty years after the outstanding event, Guidry recalled that he approached Yankees relief pitcher Sparky Lyle with an inquiry and a disclosure: "What's the earliest you've ever come into a game? I feel like I don't have anything."[3]

His performance began a Yankees tradition that Guidry traced to the fourth inning; fans stood and applauded when the southpaw got two strikes on Don Baylor before notching his seventh strikeout of the game. Getting out of the seats and clapping continued in subsequent innings, soon becoming a fixture throughout baseball. "And that's not a credit to me but to the fans of the New York Yankees," said Guidry. "I didn't start it. Yankees fans did. Their passion that day changed the atmosphere at baseball games forever."[4]

The game started at 8:00 p.m. It took two hours and seven minutes to complete. Northern New Jerseyans who had arranged to go out for a late dinner at Spirito's in Elizabeth and return home around 10:00 p.m. to catch the last few innings on WPIX-TV found their plans thwarted, as were those of folks bowling at Echo Lanes in Mountainside, taking an evening stroll through the downtown section in Cranford, or going to the movies at the Rialto Theater in Westfield. They missed most or all of Guidry's epic effort and settled for highlights during the sports recap by Jerry Girard on WPIX's 10:00 p.m. *Action News* newscast—only slightly delayed by the game—or his counterparts on other stations.

Baseball insiders looked with admiration at Guidry's dominance but perhaps remembered that his tenure as a Yankee almost got cut short on two occasions, the first being a proposed deal with the Orioles ultimately involving ten players that happened almost two years to the date before the June 17 game. Orioles general manager Hank Peters said that the Yankees had also brainstormed deals involving Bobby Grich—who signed with the Angels after the 1976 season—and Graig Nettles. But they all stayed put, Guidry because of his southpaw status. "It wasn't that they were that high on Guidry," observed Peters in 1986. "He was left-handed and they didn't want to give up any more left-handed pitching."[5]

Yankees president and general manager Gabe Paul had strategized a deal with the Blue Jays during 1977 spring training to trade Guidry for Bill Singer, whom the nascent squad selected from the Twins in the expansion draft for their first season. Blue Jays general manager Peter Bavasi preferred Singer, whom he described as "the marketing face of the new Blue Jays."[6]

Effective but not overpowering in the early part of the 1978 season, Guidry had three no decisions and two wins in April, including the White Sox game in which the Reggie bar debuted; fans consumed the latest product from the chocolate industry while Guidry pitched a complete game and struck out four in the 4–2 victory. On April 30 the left-hander, also nicknamed "Gator," had a two-hitter with seven strikeouts and a 2–0 lead against Minnesota going into the seventh inning at Metropolitan Stadium. A walk, a batter reaching on a Bucky Dent error, and a single led to a run scored; Yankees skipper Billy Martin replaced Guidry with Goose Gossage after a sacrifice bunt put runners on second and third.

The Twins tied the game later in the inning, but the Yankees got their go-ahead run in the top of the ninth on Chris Chambliss's RBI single; Gossage got credit for the 3–2 win. All five starts in May resulted in victories for Guidry.

Three more followed in June before his eighteen-strikeout performance against the Angels, a team mired in a competitive AL West division led by the Royals with batting exemplars George Brett, Al Cowens, and Amos Otis. One and a half games separated the teams. Three others were close: Oakland and Texas both stood two games behind Kansas City; Chicago trailed by two and a half games.

Besides being a masterpiece of pitching, the 4–0 victory on June 17 underscored the resilience of the Yankees. After beginning June with a 3-6 road trip, they returned to the South Bronx and won two games each against the A's and

Mariners, then lost the first game of the three-game series against the Angels. Guidry's shutout was the second game. New York lost the next one, ending the home stand with a 5-2 record.

A seven-game road trip followed. The Yankees lost two of three at Fenway Park and took three of four at Tiger Stadium. After splitting a two-game set against the Red Sox at Yankee Stadium, they went to Milwaukee and lost both games of a doubleheader—7–2 and 5–0—followed by a decisive 10–2 win against the Tigers to close out June.

At the end of the month, Boston owned first place in the American League East. The Brewers trailed by eight games. The Yankees, nine. It presented a discouraging situation for rooters of the squad once known as the Highlanders, especially given the recent renaissance underlined by AL pennants and a World Series championship in the past two seasons.

New York's other Major League team, by comparison, faced depressing circumstances. The Mets had begun June with a 23-27 record and ended it at 33-45. Compounding their fans' misery was a sight that remained difficult, if not traumatic, to perceive even though they had had a year to process it: Tom Seaver wore another team's uniform.

In addition to a nineteen-strikeout game against the Padres in 1970—which included ten consecutive strikeouts—Seaver had underscored his excellence with plenty of examples during his ten and a half seasons with the Mets, counting among them Rookie of the Year, three Cy Young Awards, five seasons leading the NL in strikeouts, and winning ten of his last eleven games in the "miracle" season of 1969 plus one of the Mets' four victories against the Orioles in the World Series.

On the night before Guidry's execution of excellence, Seaver threw a no-hitter for the Cincinnati Reds against the St. Louis Cardinals at Riverfront Stadium. Mets fans had just marked the one-year anniversary of the June 15, 1977, trade sending the pitcher known as "The Franchise" and "Tom Terrific" to Cincinnati.

Seaver faced a dicey situation in the second inning after Keith Hernandez drew a walk with one out. Jerry Morales whiffed, then Hernandez stole second base and advanced to third because of an error by Reds catcher Don Werner. Ken Reitz walked but Seaver got Mike Phillips out on a ground ball to third baseman Pete Rose to end the threat.

For the next six innings, however, Seaver dispatched the visiting club in three-up, three-down fashion and further intrigued the 38,216 people in the stands as each inning ended. Jerry Mumphrey pinch-hit for Buddy Schultz to lead off the ninth; Schultz had replaced right-hander John Denny in the top of the seventh. At thirty-three years old, Seaver had the experience, discipline, and humility necessary to prevent the excitement from overtaking him when Mumphrey walked on five pitches. "After that walk, I told myself, 'Wait a minute pal, you can lose this game,'" revealed Seaver, who had a 4–0 lead.[7]

Seaver retired Lou Brock on a fly ball and Garry Templeton's grounder to shortstop Dave Concepción resulted in Mumphrey getting forced out at second base. Dan Driessen fielded George Hendrick's ground ball, stepped on first base, and secured the first no-hitter for the Reds since Jim Maloney's in 1969; Maloney also threw one in 1965. Although a no-hitter is an outstanding achievement, Seaver told sports journalist Dick Schaap that he did not classify his June 16 performance among his top ten games.[8]

Denny worked on a no-hitter through four innings, but the Reds compiled three runs in the bottom of the fifth thanks to Rose smacking a two-run double and scoring when Joe Morgan doubled. Driessen provided the Reds' fourth run with his solo homer leading off the bottom of the sixth. Rose also hit a single in the seventh. It was the second consecutive game in which the player called "Charlie Hustle" for his aggressive style hit safely; forty-two games followed, for a hitting streak that dominated sports headlines throughout the summer.

Don Werner recalls, "It was on a Friday. Normally, Johnny Bench would be starting but he had a bad back. I played for three weeks in a row. It was a great opportunity. Going on the stuff that Tom had that day, I didn't think a no-hitter was viable at all. In the sixth inning, I realized they didn't have any hits. He'd have a high fastball that would be 107 miles an hour on today's radar gun and a hard slider. He didn't have the fastball that night and the Cardinals hit a lot of ground balls. There were only three strikeouts. It wasn't a typical game. He threw 115 pitches. A week before, his stuff was unbelievable."

Werner played in fifty games in '78. That night, he witnessed history.

"After Lou Brock grounded out to lead off, Seaver called me out to the mound. I thought I did something wrong. He told me that whenever a pitcher has to cover first base, the catcher should come out to give the pitcher a breather. He'd also want to know if a batter was ahead of or behind a pitch. After my playing career was over, I coached for thirty-one years. As a teaching tool, I said he didn't have his good stuff but he found something that works. That's exactly what Seaver did that day. Around the seventh or eighth inning, his fastball came back.

"He learned the hitters. He knew them as good as anybody and learned from observation. He knew how his stuff related to getting hitters out. His work ethic was unbelievable. After the game he'd be riding the bicycle and he'd run in the outfield between starts. He was an incredible student of the game.

"He never wanted the catcher to move on the corners, just give a target down the middle on the knees. I never caught a pitcher like that before or after. I didn't catch on one knee; Seaver didn't like that. He was a teacher to the young pitchers. He'd be reading books on broadcasting before the game.

"Tom Seaver pitched to some great catchers. Jerry Grote, Carlton Fisk, Johnny Bench. But he never threw a no-hitter with any of them, so I had to do it!"[9]

It was the only no-hitter for Seaver in his career, though he got close in his tenure with the Mets—five one-hitters. But the feat had an impact besides glory. It reinforced an aura of superiority jeopardized by his performance early in the '78 season beginning with the Reds' Opening Day game: playing in Cincinnati against the Houston Astros, the home team won, 11–9.

Drubbed by two rain delays—each lasting more than a half hour—during the first three innings the teams were tied at 1–1 when César Cedeño led off the top of the fourth with a home run. Another rain delay interrupted the game; this one lasted nearly forty minutes. José Cruz doubled and scored on Bob Watson's single, Joe Ferguson's homer made the score 5–1, and Reds skipper Sparky Anderson replaced Seaver with Pedro Borbón.

Cincinnati bounced back with ten runs over the remainder of the game; Houston rallied for four runs in the top of the ninth.

Seaver didn't get a decision in his next two starts, lost the three games that followed, and went on a tear with an 8-1 record between May 6 and June 16. At the end of August, he had a 12-13 record for the season but finished strong with four wins and one loss in September.

Looking for his seventeenth victory of 1978 in an afternoon home game against the Atlanta Braves on the Reds' last day of the season, Seaver showcased his fireballer skills by notching eleven strikeouts in eight and a third innings. With an 8–3 lead and two outs in the bottom of the eighth, Anderson had a man on third base when he sent Champ Summers to pinch-hit for Seaver. Summers walked, but Ray Knight popped up to shortstop Darrel Chaney for the final out.

A Seaver victory seemed as likely as Cincinnatians raving about the famed reuben sandwiches at Izzy's, but Atlanta tied the game in the top of the ninth with a five-run rally and ruined his chance to end the season with a win. The score stayed 8–8 until the bottom of the fourteenth, when George Foster cracked a two-run homer giving him forty round-trippers for the season. For the second year in a row, Foster led the National League; his fifty-two homers in 1977 also topped the Majors.

June continued being a month of pitching milestones as Don Sutton, a Seaver peer whose rookie season of 1966 preceded Seaver's by a year, set a team strikeout record for the Los Angeles Dodgers. Facing the Braves at Fulton County Stadium on June 29 before a crowd barely exceeding 7,400, Sutton, a four-time All-Star and recurring panelist on the game shows *Match Game* and *Match Game pm*, began with the first two batters getting on base; Rod Gilbreath hit a lead-off double and Rowland Office singled. Then he struck out Gary Matthews for the first of three times that night, inching ahead of Don Drysdale with his 2,284th strikeout—a new record for the Dodgers dating back to 1958, their first season in LA after emigrating from Brooklyn.

Counting the Dodgers' National League history beginning with its debut season of 1890, Sutton occupied third place for strikeouts behind Drysdale and Sandy Koufax. But other categories held more importance for the alumnus who was All-State and voted Most Likely to Succeed at J. M. Tate High School in Cantonment, Florida, located in the state's panhandle region near Alabama. Sutton prized shutouts, innings pitched, games, and wins.

He threw a complete game, which the Dodgers won 7–3 for his 198th career victory. The Braves also figured in another milestone of Sutton's, which happened two summers before the record-breaking strikeout: the right-hander notched his 2,000th career strikeout against them on July 26, 1976.

Sutton traded Dodger blue for other colors, later playing with the Astros, Brewers, and Angels. He began his career in the Dodgers organization with the 1965 Santa Barbara Dodgers in the Class A California League, compiling an 8-1 record, 101 strikeouts, and a 1.50 ERA in ten games. His first game as a professional baseball player was an 8–2, five-hit victory against the San Jose Bees with eleven strikeouts.[10]

In mid-June 1965, while Gary Lewis sang about a diamond ring that lost its shine, the Righteous Brothers mourned about a girlfriend losing that loving feeling, and Roger Miller aligned metaphorical royalty with a simple life, the Dodgers sent their ace to the Albuquerque Dodgers in the Texas League. Although already formidable, Sutton acquired a new pitch for his repertoire by watching an installment of *Game of the Week*, featuring Jim Bouton starting for the Yankees and showing the mechanics of his changeup during a TV interview after the game. "It looked pretty good to me and I decided to try the change-up when I pitched the next day against the Bees," confessed Sutton. "It worked real well and I've used it ever since."[11]

Albuquerque and the Tulsa Oilers were the only Texas League teams not located in the Lone Star State, the others being the Amarillo Sonics, Austin Braves, Dallas–Fort Worth Spurs, and El Paso Sun Kings. Sutton comported himself nicely, ending the season with a 15-6 record, 138 strikeouts, and a 2.78 ERA in twenty-one games.

In 1966 Sutton joined the Los Angeles Dodgers. He started thirty-five games, pitched in two others, and ended the season with a 12-12 record and 2.99 ERA. Sutton impressed the baseball world with not only his ability but also the way he carried himself. Dodgers executive Fresco Thompson's statement is an example of the credit bestowed upon the twenty-one-year-old: "When Drysdale first came up, he gave the impression on the field of having been around a long time. But it was years before he could control his temper. Sutton is completely composed, both on and off the diamond."[12]

One of Sutton's best games resulted in a loss to the Montreal Expos at Jarry Park in 1972, when the righty threw a one-hitter for twelve innings until Montreal broke a scoreless tie. John Boccabella hit a lead-off single off Dodgers relief pitcher Pete Richert in the thirteenth, moved to second on Ron Hunt's single, got to third base on a passed ball credited to catcher Duke Sims, and crossed the plate when Richert had difficulty grasping Mike Jorgensen's ground ball.

Sutton pitched four other one-hitters and ten two-hitters in his career but never a no-hitter. As he neared the milestone of turning forty, Sutton had 279 victories. But it did not seem to many that he would reach 300, least of all to the pitcher himself. No longer the youngster with poise who perhaps didn't have the power of Drysdale or Koufax but plodded along with determination, consistency, and skill—plus a scuffed ball here and there, according to some opponents—Sutton revealed the toll of his efforts in September 1984. "What I have to put out far outweighs what the return would be," said Sutton, who had notched his 3,000th strikeout the year before. "It doesn't make sense. It's out of reach."[13]

Wrong. On June 18, 1986, the curly-haired pitcher joined Christy Mathewson, Warren Spahn, Steve Carlton, and Grover Cleveland Alexander—whom Sutton was once reported as having been cast to play in a remake of *The Winning Team*—along with fourteen other pitchers in the 300-win club.[14] Before an Anaheim Stadium crowd of 37,044, Sutton threw a complete game in the Angels' 5–1 victory over the Texas Rangers; it was a three-hitter.

Sutton played another season with the Angels before returning to the Dodgers in 1988, starting in sixteen games and going 3-6. But the relationship ended with friction. While still employed by the Dodgers, Sutton talked with the Houston Astros about an opening in the front office and reportedly talked to other teams about similar positions. These actions, if true, violated Major League Baseball's rule forbidding communications unless the team employing the player authorizes them.

Claiming that Dodgers executive vice president Fred Claire knew about the phone calls and okayed them because they were "informal," with the purpose of "gathering information," Sutton explained, "I went to Fred and talked to him about this. He said that it was no problem as long as it didn't jeopardize this season."[15]

The report appeared in the *Los Angeles Times* on August 10. A day later, *Times* readers learned that the Dodgers had released Sutton, though Claire underscored his belief that the pitcher hadn't broken any rules, guidelines, or confidences. "If there was any misunderstanding, I'd take the responsibility," said Claire. "I'm confident Don did not stray beyond the line. It didn't have a bearing on today's move."[16]

Furthermore, Claire emphasized Sutton's recent game—which turned out to be his last—against the Cincinnati Reds, a 6–0 loss at Riverfront Stadium. Sutton pitched seven innings.[17]

Sutton retired with a 324-256 win-loss record and 3,574 strikeouts headlining his accomplishments, which also include leading the Major Leagues in ERA in 1980, leading the National League in games started in 1974, and notching fifty-eight career shutouts. His Dodgers tenure ranks him at the top of the team's pitchers: first in wins, innings pitched, shutouts, batters faced, and games started. He's also given up more hits, earned runs, and home runs than any Dodgers pitcher but has second place for strikeouts behind Don Drysdale.

Ten years later, the Baseball Hall of Fame inducted Sutton with more than 81 percent of the Baseball Writers' Association of America voters' picks; 75 percent is required for admission. It did not surprise his former manager, Tommy Lasorda, who said, "When you gave him the ball, you knew one thing—your pitcher was going to give you everything he had."[18]

And so he did on a June night in 1978 when he battled the Braves and became the Dodgers' team leader for strikeouts. It was not an overpowering victory. Sutton racked up five strikeouts in the 7–3 win, but one batter accounted for three of them; Atlanta got nine hits off the righty.

The next afternoon, Willie McCovey took his turn reaching a milestone—500 home runs. It just happened to also take place at Fulton County Stadium. Nicknamed "Stretch," San Francisco's six-foot-four-inch first baseman had led the NL in home runs three times, slugging percentage three times, and RBIs twice. His slugging percentage in 1969 and 1970 also topped the Major Leagues.

McCovey's recent path to the 500 mark had been tougher than seeing Lime Point from Fort Point on a foggy day in the Bay Area. No. 498 had happened more than three weeks earlier, when he hit a solo bash during a Giants road trip against the Phillies' Steve Carlton to break a scoreless tie in the fourth inning; Philadelphia won, 4–3.

Dennis Kinney got tagged for the 499th homer, an unnecessary clout leading off the bottom of the eighth with the Giants ahead of the Padres 8–1 at San Diego Stadium on June 27. McCovey provided the ninth run for the Giants, who tallied sixteen hits in the 9–1 victory.

Three days later, McCovey got No. 500. Braves lefty Jamie Easterly had a 1–0 lead when McCovey began the top of the second inning with his third straight bases-empty home run to tie the score. Jeff Burroughs, the Braves' left fielder, ran for a possible snare but soon discovered that the ball had a different purpose. McCovey doubled to lead off the top of the fourth; Jim Dwyer replaced him on the base paths and then on defense at first base.

Reaching 500 home runs is a rarity. McCovey's achievement, which happened in the first game of a doubleheader, made him the twelfth player to accomplish it in the Major Leagues. But the visiting team faced a rather doleful picture on June 30, trailing 10–6 in the top of the ninth and mounting a powerful rally with two outs. Bill Madlock hit a solo homer with two outs, Darrell Evans singled, and Jack Clark went yard for the second time that afternoon to get the Giants within a run of tying. But Dwyer's flyout to Burroughs ended the game. Of his historic moment, McCovey put things in perspective by noting, "I'd have felt a lot better about the homer if we'd hung on to win."[19]

Atlanta won the second game, 10–5. Heading into July, San Francisco led the National League West by three games over LA and three and a half games over Cincinnati. San Diego was the next closest ball club, separated from the division leader by ten games. As the 1978 season approached its halfway mark, designated by the upcoming All-Star Game, a brief but significant scene in the year's biggest movie underscored baseball's prevalence in American culture. Premiering on the same night that Tom Seaver threw his no-hitter, *Grease* had become a sensation by the end of June.

Grease continued Hollywood's trend of using the late 1950s as a setting for stories in 1978. On the heels of 1977's disco-themed blockbuster *Saturday Night Fever*, John Travolta starred as Danny Zuko in *Grease*. Travolta had become a cultural icon, first as the dimwitted Vinnie Barbarino on ABC's *Welcome Back, Kotter* and then as Saturday night disco king Tony Manero.

Olivia Newton-John played Sandy to Travolta's Danny, a mismatched couple. He's a greaser. She's prim and proper. But producer Allan Carr had envisioned at least two other pairings—Elvis Presley and Ann-Margret, then Henry Winkler and Susan Dey. Winkler was the No. 1 star on TV in a show already set in the time period. Dey had starred in *The Partridge Family*, which aired from 1970 to 1974 but enjoyed a bountiful life in reruns in the late 1970s.[20]

Travolta noted the social nuances in playing a character from a different era. Drugs were not prevalent in the late 1950s, nor were social issues. "Also, there wasn't the urban sense of style or behavior that kids everywhere get from TV today," said the actor. "There had to be an innocence that nobody was really aware of, because they didn't have the sophistication to compare it with."[21]

Reviews were generally favorable. Chicago film critic Gene Siskel gave it three stars out of four because Travolta's performance outweighed "a fairly long list of faults," including solos by Newton-John and Stockard Channing being "visual disasters." In the *Corpus Christi Times*, Johnny Holmes critiqued Newton-John: "Her dancing is quite up to par, but her voice, though pleasant simply isn't forceful enough to carry her through some of the movie's more demanding tunes."[22]

The biting commentary did not acknowledge the appeal of "Hopelessly Devoted to You," Newton-John's deeply emotional exaltation of loving someone despite the other person's refusal, fear, or ignorance in reciprocating. Her rendition defined Sandy's appeal, vulnerability, and optimism, climbing to No. 3 on the *Billboard* rankings and gaining an Oscar nomination for Best Original Song. Moreover, the film's soundtrack is noted for being in the top ten best-selling soundtracks, though specific rankings differ.[23]

Los Angeles Times arts editor Charles Champlin offered a more cutting appraisal. "The editing in the musical sequences is frequently and nervously bizarre, cutting away constantly from any sense of emerging lines and patterns and even, often, away from the dancers' feet," wrote Champlin. He also categorized the portrayal of the 1950s as "played back through a grotesquely distorting 70s consciousness" and called the choreography "furiously energetic, which is not the same as exciting."[24]

Critics be damned! *Grease* topped the box office grosses in 1978, pulling in nearly $160 million.[25] *Grease's* genesis began more than seven years before Travolta and Newton-John graced the silver screen as Danny and Sandy. While astronauts landed on the moon in Project Apollo, the NBA went through a season of expansion with three new teams, and America's involvement in the Vietnam War showed no sign of slowing, much less ending, a stage production called *Grease* debuted at Chicago's Kingston Mines Community Theater on February 8, 1971, and got labeled "one of the most screamingly funny shows in town" by the *Tribune*.[26]

It went to Broadway a year later, underwent a transformation, and ran for eight years. Gone were the references to Chicago, the character names steeped in Polish lineage, and the breakdown of dialogue versus music. An attorney teaching at Northwestern Law School had seen the Kingston Mines Theatre performance and put up $50,000—compiled from "some friends in the securities business" and his own coffers—to be a producer of the show. When the film version premiered, Tony D'Amato recollected that his contribution to the initial Broadway incarnation went beyond money: "The show was 70 per cent dialog and 30 per cent music. I told them they should reverse the ratio. It turned out they had quite a folio of songs they hadn't put into the show."[27]

Clive Barnes penned a favorable review in the *New York Times*, the gold standard for the Broadway community: "The cast worked hard and well, with an almost manic enthusiasm." Of the leads, he offered this: "As the hero and heroine, Barry Bostwick and Carole Demas could not have been better."[28]

Ilene Graff played Sandy on Broadway, with eleven actors as Danny, including Bostwick, Jeff Conaway, Richard Gere, Treat Williams, and Greg Evigan. "Barry had that rare talent of making you believe you were the most important person in the scene as he bestowed all his attention on you," said Graff. "He was pure magic."[29]

Grease's box office success had a terrific foundation from the stage. Travolta and Newton-John singing about an affection-filled courtship in "Summer Nights," Sandy's makeover to become a leather-jacket-and-Lycra-pants-wearing sex bomb, and a drag race at the Los Angeles River—named Thunder Road for the story—are among the greatest moments in cinema history.

Enhancing the nostalgic allure were appearances by 1950s icons Frankie Avalon, Sid Caesar, Eve Arden, and Edd Byrnes as the lecherous host of *National Bandstand*—a takeoff on *American Bandstand*—who hits on one of the Pink Ladies, supposedly seventeen years old.

In 1978 nostalgia presented a salve for a country that had been emotionally pummeled since the late 1950s setting of *Grease*. America needed an outlet. But Hollywood didn't have a monopoly on comedy, tragedy, pathos, and catharsis. Baseball fans, journalists, and insiders knew that a ballpark located at East 161st Street and River Avenue in the South Bronx provided scenes that an Oscar-winning producer would envy.

7

MELODRAMA IN THE BRONX

JULY

Teams rely on chemistry. It's an undefinable quality that complements, enhances, and inspires performance. It can also be combustible. To wit, the New York Yankees of 1978.

A loss to the Royals at Yankee Stadium on July 17 completed a three-game sweep of the reigning World Series champions, but the eleven-inning event did more than register their forty-second entry in the "L" column against forty-seven wins. Once again, the fellas in pinstripes underlined their misfortunes with drama, pathos, and commotion. Yankees skipper Billy Martin suspended Reggie Jackson after the 9–7 defeat. Indefinitely.

With the score tied 5–5 in the bottom of the tenth, Thurman Munson banged a lead-off single off Al Hrabosky. Martin had wanted Jackson to bunt but told third base coach Dick Howser to remove the order; Jackson bunted anyway.

Defiance led to suspension, contributing another chapter to the Martin-Jackson saga, which rivaled daytime soap operas for interpersonal conflicts. Jackson explained the bunting strategy based on his recent performance: "I had not been playing regularly and I wasn't swinging the bat very well. I thought under the circumstances that bunting was the best thing I could do. Even after Howser spoke to me, I didn't realize exactly what the consequences would be. I didn't consider it an act of defiance, and I don't feel I did anything wrong. I would even do it again if I didn't know what the consequences would be. For that reason, it would have been better if I had struck out swinging and avoided the hassle."[1]

Ever since the slugger first donned a Yankees uniform during the previous year's spring training, there had been friction between the fiery, scrappy manager and the powerful, popular slugger. "The guy's been doing this to me for a year and a half now," explained a frustrated Jackson, whose 0-for-4 night dropped his batting average from .264 to .260. "Just yesterday, he called me over and asked me to sit next to him in the dugout, and said, 'You're a nice guy. You're a fine guy. I just wanted to tell you that.' I can't win. No matter what I do, I came off as a big, greedy moneymaker against a poor, little streetfighter."[2]

The Yankees didn't need conflict in their clubhouse, particularly after a hard-fought game resulting in a loss. Kansas City scored first thanks to Darrell Porter's solo homer leading off the top of the second inning. New York responded with Munson's two-RBI double an inning later and tacked on another three runs in the bottom of the fourth when Graig Nettles went yard after Lou Piniella and Chris Chambliss hit back-to-back singles.

The Royals closed the gap to 5–3 in the top of the fifth. Freddie Patek cracked a lead-off double and later scored on George Brett's single. Hal McRae's single put Brett on third base, leading to Martin replacing starting pitcher Catfish Hunter with Sparky Lyle. John Wathan's sacrifice fly allowed Brett to score.

Kansas City tied the game in the top of the ninth, and a four-run eleventh inning gave the visitors a seemingly comfortable 9–5 lead; controversy emerged for the Yankees during this barrage. Second base umpire Durwood Merrill tossed Goose Gossage—who had replaced Sparky Lyle in the seventh inning—"for swearing" after the three-time All-Star walked Willie Wilson on a full count with the bases loaded for the first of the quartet of runs and "stormed toward home plate umpire Larry Barnett, complaining that the fastball had been a strike."[3]

Despondency reigned. "You hate to lose a ballgame on one pitch when you think it's a strike," said Gossage, who would be the American League saves leader in 1978. "And everyone on the field thinks it's a strike, except one guy. It's a shame there isn't the pressure on them (the umpires) that's on us. I'm not gonna say anything (about the umpiring or about what he said to Merrill that prompted his ejection). You couldn't print it anyway."[4]

Naturally, Martin argued the call as well but avoided getting ejected. Rookie hurler Bob Kammeyer took over and gave up a two-run single to Patek; Frank White's single scored Wilson.

When the Yankees came to bat, Al Hrabosky dismissed the first two batters—Fred Stanley on a ground ball to Brett and Mike Heath on a pop-up to second baseman White. Willie Randolph's homer revived the home team's rooters hoping for a rebound; Mickey Rivers doubled, then scored on Munson's single. KC capped the Yankees at seven runs when Wilson caught a fly ball to left field by Cliff Johnson, pinch-hitting for Jackson.

Losing to the Royals—whom the Yankees had bested in the 1976 and 1977 AL playoffs—in addition to Gossage's ejection and Jackson's suspension, reflected a rather dreary story. New York's AL squad skidded. Badly. Including his July 17 effort, Jackson had put up zeroes in the hits column for seven out of the last seventeen games. A day later, Jackson's indefinite suspension got trimmed to five games, but Yankees owner George Steinbrenner sided with Martin regarding discipline. "Everybody knows that Reggie is close to me," said Steinbrenner, who had purchased the team in 1973 with a group of investors. "He's a good friend. But you've got to back the manager. If you don't, you get to the point where a player can listen [to] the manager and disregard what he says. Then you're done. You might as well hang it up."[5]

Jackson faced an uncertain future at best. *New York Times* sportswriter Dave Anderson opined that the slugger's disrespect would land him in an offseason trade, "probably to a National League team." Montreal led the contenders with a sweetener beyond money—Jackson had played for Expos manager Dick Williams when he helmed the mighty A's to World Series titles in 1972 and 1973.[6]

Catfish Hunter hadn't taken the mound in almost a month before Martin called on him to start against the Royals. The eight-time All-Star and 1974 Cy Young Award winner had endured a rough season all the way back to spring training, when doctors diagnosed him with diabetes and designed a treatment plan that included insulin shots, urine tests, and a strict three-thousand-calorie diet.[7]

Pitching a one-hitter through six innings against the Minnesota Twins on May 9 provided a high point for the Yankees in the spring. Lyle substituted with a 3–0 lead and gave up one run but secured the victory, the sixth in a seven-game home stand. Twelve days later, a warning sign sent chills through the South Bronx and other environs where Yankees fans resided; warm-ups for the second game of a Yankees–Blue Jays twin bill exacerbated a shoulder problem for Hunter. "I can't even throw the ball now," said Hunter, who explained that the source of his shoulder problem was in his back.[8]

Hunter's next appearance happened on June 21 in enemy territory: Fenway Park. Boston led 7–2 when the righty got tapped to relieve Dick Tidrow in the bottom of the eighth. Fred Lynn and George Scott welcomed him with back-to-back homers; Hunter retired Dwight Evans on a fly ball to the outfield before Butch Hobson singled and sprinted to third base on Rick Burleson's double.

Jerry Remy struck out, followed by Jim Rice drawing a walk to load the bases. But Hunter ceased Boston's offensive torrent by striking out Carl Yastrzemski. Dennis Eckersley kept the New Yorkers at bay in their half of the ninth, giving up a single to Chris Chambliss and a walk to Gary Thomasson. The 9–2 score gave Eckersley his seventh victory of the season—a six-hitter—against two losses.

Boston's ace had something else on his mind after the game as he revealed the fraternal respect among pitchers by explaining his concern. "I felt sorry for Hunter," said Eckersley. The Red Sox skipper agreed. "It's a sad thing to see such a great competitor pitch badly," said Don Zimmer. "I don't know whether he's hurting, but that's not the Catfish we've known."[9]

Hunter most definitely felt pain in his right arm. "It hurts from the shoulder all the way down to the finger," explained the hurler, who got sidelined until the Yankees-Royals game on July 17. "I thought it would come off on one damn pitch."[10]

During Jackson's sabbatical, the Yankees won five straight games. But anxiety hovered. Before tossing a six-hit, 2–0 shutout against the Twins, Ed Figueroa declared, "I feel like I like to get out of this club. Not next year, this year. Too much junk going on. I want to go play with a nice quiet ball club. If they not going to trade me, I not going to show up in spring training."[11]

Lyle chimed in regarding the aura of misery, remaining stoic about playing time and contractual issues. "Nothing I could say now would help me," explained the reliever. "I'll have plenty to say when I finally get out of here. Maybe that will be before the end of the year—when we see where we're going. If we're out of it, I might be gone."[12]

Paul Blair called the clubhouse atmosphere "strained" with Jackson's presence.[13] Chambliss also added, "I don't think he can come back and have things be rosy. If things don't change, something's going to happen. I just hope they do what's in the best interests of the team." Furthermore, the Yankees' first baseman explained, Jackson "didn't just hurt the manager; he hurt the team. The man's hitting fourth; we needed runs. He's always wanted to hit fourth and in that situation we needed him hitting away so we could score some runs. His point was not to do what the manager said. That's what I got from it."[14]

The Yankees won their first four games without Jackson being in the clubhouse or the dugout. He returned on Sunday, July 23, but didn't play in the 3–1 victory at Comiskey Park. If his fellow Yankees thought that Jackson would be immune from the effects of the drama, they thought wrong. "It's uncomfortable, it's miserable," he revealed.[15]

Perhaps he should have stayed home. At O'Hare International Airport, Martin underlined the five-game winning streak in a verbal barrage against the slugger who had received the 1977 World Series MVP Award: "We're winning without you. We don't need you coming in and making all these comments. If he doesn't shut his mouth, he won't play and I don't care what George says. He can replace me right now if he doesn't like it." Forty-five minutes later Martin declared, "The two of them deserve each other. One's a born liar, the other's convicted."[16] His statement referenced Steinbrenner's 1974 conviction regarding illegal contributions to President Richard Nixon's campaign; MLB commissioner Bowie Kuhn ordered a two-year suspension of the Yankees' owner and later shaved it to a year and three months.

A day after his tirade, Martin resigned. Steinbrenner then hired former White Sox manager Bob Lemon, whom the White Sox had fired three and a half weeks earlier. Lemon had street cred. Pitching for the Indians from 1946 to 1958, the seven-time All-Star led the Major Leagues in victories twice and the AL three times. In addition, he led the AL in complete games five times and topped the Majors in shutouts in 1948, the year that the Indians won the World Series.

In Kansas City, where the Yankees were getting ready for a two-game series to close out their road trip, Billy Martin shielded his eyes with sunglasses but couldn't hide his emotions as he choked up while delivering a prepared statement at the Yankees' hotel. It included a denial of the quote about Jackson being a liar and Steinbrenner being convicted.[17]

There was a familiar quality about the departure, though. Martin had played for the Yankees from 1950 to the middle of 1957, when a controversy inspired the front office to trade him to the Kansas City A's along with Ralph Terry, Woodie Held, and Bob Martyn; New York got Ryne Duren, Jim Pisoni, and Harry Simpson in return.

The Yankees' management in the late 1950s believed that Martin's behavior negatively influenced superstar Mickey Mantle, as evidenced in a brawl at the Copacabana nightclub in Manhattan. Several Yankees, accompanied by their wives, had been present during the fracas—Martin, Mantle, Hank Bauer, Yogi Berra, Johnny Kucks; they denied any wrongdoing but couldn't escape the bad publicity. A patron claimed that he got clobbered by the ballplayers.

Yankees manager Casey Stengel had used his clout on three occasions to keep Martin in pinstripes instead of being traded, but the Copacabana incident made the front page of the newspapers. There wasn't any card that Stengel could play to keep his second baseman, whom he had begun mentoring when Martin played for him with the Oakland Oaks, which won the Pacific Coast League championship in 1948.[18]

The nightclub patron accusing the players, a deli owner named Edwin Jones, claimed that he got sucker punched as he tried to enjoy some time with his bowling club at the famed establishment, colloquially known as the Copa. Martin and his group had been seated at a nearby table and appeared drunk, Jones accused: "They were feeling no pain, too. All I remember until I woke up at Roosevelt Hospital was that one of our party walked over to the Yankees' table and talked to Martin. Then I got up and went over, too, when I was suddenly hit with a sneak punch. That was the last I remember."[19]

More than sixty years later, Copa bouncer Joey Silvestri confessed: "There were no Yankees involved in the fight. Nobody threw a punch but me."[20]

Even if Silvestri had admitted his involvement after the incident, it likely wouldn't have mattered. Martin equaled trouble. Plus, he was the reason for the Yankees and their wives being at the Copa—a celebration of Martin's twenty-ninth birthday. The outburst at O'Hare, the criticism of Steinbrenner and Jackson, and the brouhaha regarding the bunt sign recalled the Copa episode and other tales that bolstered Martin's legend as a figure prone to the darker side of fervor.

Still, Martin's removal as manager in July 1978—whether of his own volition or under pressure from Steinbrenner—couldn't really tarnish his record of managerial success with the Yankees. He had notched two World Series berths in his first two full seasons at the helm, one resulting in a championship title. His earlier record indicated his bona fides as a manager.

Back in 1968 the Minnesota Twins were a seventh-place team with a 79-83 record. Martin took over a year later and piloted the Twins to the AL West title in 1969, his first season as a Major League manager and the first season that the AL and NL used the structure of West and East divisions. Baltimore beat Minnesota 3–0 in the best-of-five AL playoff, then lost to the Mets in the World Series.

Martin began a three-year stint as the Detroit Tigers' manager in 1971. Also having a 79-83 record the year before, Detroit turned around under Martin's leadership, ending the '71 season with a 91-71 record and a second-place finish behind the dominant Orioles. In 1972 the Tigers finished a pulse-raising AL East pennant race in first place, half a game ahead of the Boston Red Sox. The A's won the AL playoff and began a string of three straight World Series titles.

Like his managerial successes, controversy had also accompanied Martin before he became the Yankees' manager. After losing two out of three games to the Brewers in May 1973, he declared, "If they can win with this club, then I'm a Chinese aviator. The Brewers have a good young ballclub, a hustling ballclub. But to be honest about it, no way are they going to win."[21]

Detroit was 14-17.

At the end of August, Martin publicized a retaliatory mandate for Tigers pitchers to throw spitballs in violation of baseball rules for what he considered a lack of enforcement against Cleveland hurler Gaylord Perry. The spitter had been banned in 1920. AL president Joe Cronin suspended the Tigers' skipper, but general manager Jim Campbell fired him.

It didn't take long for the controversial but effective manager to find employment; Texas Rangers owner Bob Short let Whitey Herzog go and replaced him with Martin. The Rangers were 48-91. Under Martin, they went 9-14 for the remaining games on the 1973 schedule. But he flourished in 1974 with an 84-76-1 record and a second-place finish in the AL West, thanks in large part to a key acquisition in the off-season—Ferguson Jenkins tied with Catfish Hunter to lead the Major Leagues in 1974 with twenty-five wins. They also tied for eighth place in win-loss percentage. Jenkins placed fourth in strikeouts behind Steve Carlton, Bert Blyleven, and Nolan Ryan. He tied for second place in shutouts with Phil Niekro and Hunter.

Martin clashed with Rangers owner Brad Corbett, who had bought the team before the 1974 season. In July 1975 Martin wanted to sign Tom Egan, a catcher available through free agency. But Corbett, who had built his wealth on the sales of pipes for plumbing, put the kibosh on it. Foreshadowing his derogatory comments about Steinbrenner, Martin opined about Corbett's lack of baseball insight, declaring that the owner "knows as much about baseball as I do about pipe."[22]

Music at the ballpark contributed to the ire between Corbett and Martin. "Thank God I'm a Country Boy" replaced "Take Me Out to the Ball Game" under Martin's instruction and against Corbett's command.[23] Frank Lucchesi replaced Martin as the Rangers' skipper, and it was then that Steinbrenner tapped the fiery manager for his dream job—managing the Yankees. Martin succeeded Bill Virdon, leading the team to thirty wins and twenty-six losses to close out '75 with an 83-77 record.

A *Sports Illustrated* story highlighted the impact of the controversies causing Yankee players to consider employment elsewhere in the middle of the 1978 season. In addition to Lyle and Figueroa, there were Thurman Munson, Roy White, Cliff Johnson, and Jim Spencer. Jackson's future relied on a question: was the drama worth keeping him?[24]

July began with the Yankees in third place and owning a 43-32 record, nine games behind the first-place Red Sox. After the home stand, the Bronx Bombers were 47-42 and mired in fourth place; Boston increased its lead to fourteen games. Catching the Red Sox looked as likely as the Yankees breaking tradition and putting players' names on the back of the jerseys.

While Jackson, Martin, et al. provided drama in July, Hollywood showcased baseball as comedy in two movies featuring kids. Paramount released *The Bad News Bears Go to Japan*, the third and final installment in the *Bears* series revolving around a Little League team from the North Valley League in the San Fernando Valley.

The Bad News Bears premiered in 1976. Directed by Michael Ritchie and written by Bill Lancaster, son of Burt Lancaster, it starred Walter Matthau as former Minor League pitcher Morris Buttermaker, with a cast that was 180 degrees from the cute, saccharine kids usually depicted in films and TV shows. One player cursed. Another smoked and rode a motorcycle. The catcher had a weight problem. Plus, there wasn't the typical Hollywood ending where the underdogs beat a better team. The Bears lost a close game with the Yankees.[25]

The Bad News Bears in Breaking Training followed in 1977. It mentioned that the Bears were the California champions scheduled to play their counterparts, the Houston Toros, in the Astrodome; William Devane played the role of a coach who happened to be the estranged father of Bears star Kelly Leak. Unlike the first film, *Breaking Training* had a climactic moment of victory for the Bears plus reconciliation between the Leaks.

It's mentioned in *Breaking Training* that the winner of the Toros-Bears match-up will go to Japan. Tony Curtis played Marvin Lazar, a promoter who sees dollar signs in the Bears' upcoming trip. Lazar's selfishness was old hat for Curtis, who had played characters of varying similarity in *Operation Petticoat*, *Sweet Smell of Success*, and *Boeing Boeing*.

Lancaster scripted *The Bad News Bears Go to Japan*; Ritchie returned as well but as a producer. *Chicago Tribune* film critic Gene Siskel offered the premise that the movie got produced because the story would appeal to Japanese movie audiences who embraced the first incarnation.[26]

Curtis got kudos from Vincent Canby in the *New York Times*, though the filmmakers didn't get the same praise. "When given a chance by the material, Mr. Curtis projects a picture of second-rate hucksterism that is all the more funny for being so blatantly rude and transparent," wrote Canby. He also said that *Japan* "has the appearance of a movie made by people who didn't know how, or who didn't care, or who possibly turned over their responsibilities to Japanese Airlines and the Japanese Tourist Bureau, whose principal interests are prominent among the screen images."[27]

In something of a parallel, Curtis's scheming to leverage the U.S.-Japan game for lucre in the form of a TV broadcast dominates the film's plot. Two prominent characters are missing from the third installment: Ogilvie the genius and Tanner the loudmouth. There's also a lack of closure. The game takes place but gets cut short after a brawl between the players. They get together outside the hotel and play an informal game; Lazar suggests to his Japanese counterpart that they bring both teams to Cuba—a tease for a fourth *Bears* movie, which never happened. Richard Freedman of Newhouse News Service used a baseball analogy in his analysis, saying that "the Bad News Bears are definitely headed for the showers."[28]

His forecast was partly correct. The *Bears* film series ended, but Paramount fashioned the franchise for TV with Jack Warden in the role of Buttermaker. CBS aired twenty-three episodes intermittently: March–June 1979, September–October 1979, June–July 1980. Three episodes went unaired. There was a reboot of the original film in 2005, starring Billy Bob Thornton.

Here Come the Tigers was a cross between the *Bears* movies, a 1950s sitcom episode, and an ABC Afterschool Special. The *Los Angeles Times* lacerated the story, direction, and production but acknowledged an aura that the *Bears* trilogy lacked: "The movie has a good-natured spirit that successfully downplays the more brutal aspects of children's championship competition."[29]

Before Sean S. Cunningham went on to fame and fortune as the creator of the *Friday the 13th* film series, he directed this entry in the baseball movie genre. The Tigers' coach is a cop who has a mental break, so Eddie Burke, a younger cop, not only takes over the coaching duties but also agrees to host a juvenile delinquent with a penchant for destroying cars when he's not stealing them. Francis "Buster" Rivera comes from an abusive home but finds comfort with Eddie and his wife, as well as a sense of belonging with the Tigers. His parents have given up their parental rights in juvenile court, so he's without a home until the Burkes take him in.

Eddie has some limited credentials regarding baseball besides his optimism, having played in high school and earned All City honors at third base in his junior year in college. The Tigers, however, are basically misfits. Their pitcher has two kinds of pitches in his repertoire: hard and wild or slow and easy. The catcher has a flatulence problem. There are two girls—a tomboy and a beauty queen. But the latter's transformation into a cheerleader has no background information, just one of several points left unexplained or undepicted. A running gag is the announcer taking swigs of booze as he calls the game.

Eddie lucks into finding a Japanese kid who's a karate expert with tremendous power and a deaf kid who's an ace pitcher; they lead the Tigers to the championship against the Panthers, clearly a superior team. In a nod to horror genius Wes Craven, Cunningham's friend and collaborator on 1972's *The Last House on the Left*, a banner on the right-field wall advertises Craven Septic & Sewer Service owned by "Cesspool Wes."

Here Come the Tigers was filmed in 1977. Several of its characters, after seeing *Star Wars*, that year's blockbuster, debate about the "force" that Obi-

Wan Kenobi teaches Luke Skywalker to use. Rivera, clearly the worst hitter on the team, remembers the words of one of his teammates during a crucial at bat: "All you gotta do is believe in the force of good; that way you can hit your target with your eyes closed."

And so he does. The Tigers win.

The Bears and the Tigers appealed to kids, but their parents enjoyed terrific filmmaking in 1978. Hollywood escalated its portrayal of women in the late 1970s as vulnerable but ultimately self-sufficient, self-confident, and powerful, with Jill Clayburgh as the face of that revolution in *An Unmarried Woman*.

Paul Mazursky wrote, directed, and produced this film about the tumult created when Clayburgh's character—middle-aged Erica Benton, living an upper-middle-class life on the Upper East Side of Manhattan—gets betrayed by her husband, Martin, a stockbroker who leaves her for a twenty-six-year-old woman. When Martin discloses the affair after a lunch date with Erica, her face registers shock, anger, and disgust. She walks away; her emotional volatility affects her physically as she stops to vomit on the street.

On the surface, Erica had a solid, prosperous, and fulfilling life in an upscale Manhattan neighborhood. The couple jogged together adjacent to the East River, and their morning banter reflects a familiarity that's been honed through seventeen years of marriage. Sex seems to be emotionally and physically satisfying. They have a smart, personable fifteen-year-old daughter. Erica does not confine herself to the neighborhood, though. She has a part-time job at an art gallery downtown in Soho, the neighborhood that got its moniker from its geography—south of Houston Street, pronounced HOW-stun instead of the pronunciation used for the city in Texas.

Navigating the journey of dating, love, and sex during her separation on top of being the mother of a teenaged girl unveils insecurities, rage, and resilience.

Clayburgh had experienced success with *Silver Streak, Semi-Tough,* and *Gable and Lombard*. But *An Unmarried Woman* had a gut-wrenching impact because its reality reflected the era. Erica Benton's journey signified America's rising divorce rate. "The role of Erica is a genuine study of a woman with practically all the emotional range an actress could ask," said Clayburgh. "The audience gets to know and love her and identify with her."[30]

Heartbreak linked the actress and her character. After a five-year relationship with Al Pacino ended in the early 1970s, Clayburgh experienced the same volatility she portrayed: "I went through it all, self-loathing, loathing him, pain, anger, fear."[31]

Johnny Holmes of the *Corpus Christi Times* credited Mazursky for capturing Clayburgh's spectrum of emotions, most evident in a "masterful sequence" when Martin Benton, played by Michael Murphy, reveals that he wants a divorce. Mazursky isolates Clayburgh's face. "That shot, showing Clayburgh's transition from numbness to surprise, shock, fear, anger, frustration and determination, pretty well sums up the movie's course," wrote Holmes.[32]

Clayburgh revealed that the breakup scene differed from Mazursky's original script. "My character said a lot more than she does now," said the actress in a joint interview with Dallas TV journalist Bobbie Wygant. "I felt that in that position, I would be much more unable to speak than he had had the character written in that scene." In that interview, Mazursky agreed and said he had changed the scene accordingly. "The look on her face when he tells her is worth twenty-five pages of dialogue," opined the director, who received Golden Globe and Oscar nominations for Best Director and Best Screenplay.[33]

Her anger manifests further after she meets her girlfriends for drinks and support, a gathering that happens often so they can share stories, vent frustrations, and encourage each other. Erica's not the only one struggling. One of her friends is dating a nineteen-year-old and another is a self-admitted manic depressive who battles low self-esteem with sex and a veneer of contentment. It's not explicit, but the characters are presumed to be Jewish. Still raw from the implosion of her marriage, Erica expresses her anger when a well-dressed, handsome man enters and says, "Hello." Her response: "Fuck you."

A psychiatrist helps her through the aftermath of Martin's announcement. When Erica says that she hasn't had sex in the seven weeks since Martin left her, the prescription is to go out and do so. Her first encounter with a sexual partner other than Martin finds her with a man who's lecherous but familiar to Erica—her coworker, Charlie. They run into each other at a bar; she asks him to take her to his loft, but it's only a one-time thing.

A more substantive encounter occurs spontaneously with an artist, Saul Kaplan, played by Alan Bates. Erica and Saul begin to sow the seeds of a relationship, which he wants to solidify by having her spend nearly half the year at his home in Vermont with his children. But that would mean leaving behind her friends, daughter, and Manhattan lifestyle. It's a price too high for Erica, who has found resilience, independence, and confidence within herself.

Meanwhile, Martin's lover, whom he had hoped to marry, has left him. He asks Erica for another chance. She declines. Simply, Martin doesn't deserve one.

Moreover, the fullness of Erica's voyage to self-realization not only gives heft to the character but also provides a universality with which audiences can relate. "The complexities of the role of Erica, as she begins to discover her own identity, are enough to carry the film successfully from beginning to end," wrote Lorna Sutton in Spokane's *Spokesman-Review*.[34]

While the Bears and Tigers tried to master baseball's choreography and Erica Benton traipsed over Manhattan to build a new life, a different type of footwork took place at America's nightclubs, bars, and catering halls in the summer of 1978. Disco balls hung from their ceilings while "Boogie Oogie Oogie," "Heaven Must Be Missing an Angel," and other songs in the disco genre provided lyrics of love, desire, and promise backed by a syncopated bass line, violins, and horn instruments. John Travolta's portrayal of Brooklyn clubgoer Tony Manero in 1977's *Saturday Night Fever* had turbocharged disco's popularity, enhanced by the film's soundtrack blaring through stereo speakers, headphones, and transistor radios as listeners imagined themselves dancing like Travolta.

Feminism played a strong role in disco's emergence as a force in 1978. Gloria Gaynor inspired heartbroken women with her anthem of independence from a former lover who took her for granted; "I Will Survive" pulsated with the strength that comes from declaring the breaking of unhealthy ties. But another woman, crowned with the title "Queen of Disco," dominated the radio airwaves and stereo systems along with the soundtrack to *Saturday Night Fever*.

Donna Summer had been a rising force in the music industry. "Love to Love You Baby" combined whisper-like singing with orgasmic moans to describe intense, ecstatic, and fulfilling sex. It reached the No. 2 slot in 1976. When Casablanca Records released "Last Dance" two years later in July, it catapulted Summer to icon status as the song dominated radio airwaves and record sales. Plus, "Last Dance" marked the end of weddings, bar mitzvahs, proms, reunions, and other gatherings where a DJ or band provided the musical entertainment. It was—and remains—a sonic caveat for one final whirl on the dance floor before doing the social equivalent of circling the wagons by uttering words of appreciation, congratulations, and goodwill to the hosts before departing.

Disco was powerful. It fostered an aura of positivity created by the music, something sorely needed after suffering, enduring, and recovering from events that had tested America's collective resolve. From Bainbridge Island to Boynton Bay, Americans were exhausted. Gaynor, Summer, and their peers revived listeners with their songs, though disco's supremacy in popular culture would end by the early 1980s.

Americans wanted to learn disco dances because it gave them a sense of belonging. Disco music was everywhere, especially in the home of the Schunick family in Pikesville, Maryland. Shelley Schunick, an entrepreneur with the blond, feathered hairstyle popularized in the late 1970s by Farrah Fawcett, linked her energy to this latest fad by hiring a dance instructor to teach the necessary steps to her and her husband, Howard, a premier dentist in the Baltimore-Washington region who once performed emergency dental surgery on one of America's most famous singers so she could keep a concert tour date later that night.

When dance teacher Reynold English came to the Schunick house on Winterset Avenue, he saw the couple's AMC Pacer and Oldsmobile in the driveway as the Schunicks waited inside with their friends and children—oldest daughter Sarla and fraternal twins Lacey and Jory, who were a couple of years away from their bat mitzvah and bar mitzvah.

The Schunick matriarch suggested that English create drawings of footsteps that people could look at on the floor as they practice their moves. She conceived, financed, and produced the album *Disco Steppin'*, complete with stock music, directions, drawings, and free admission for two to Baltimore's top discotheque—Girard's. English narrated the instructions on the album. Thanks to Shelley Schunick's hustle for the Hustle, which included selling the album to local record stores, *Disco Steppin'* became a minor success in the Baltimore area and a regional reflection of disco's power in 1978. "I think my mom found Reynold English in the Yellow Pages because she wanted to learn about the disco dance craze," recalls Jory. "There would be six couples—friends of our parents—who came over for the classes. Lacey and I also learned the steps."[35]

Lacey expands, "We converted our family room (where we normally all watched TV) into a Pikesville disco nightclub. Yes, we moved furniture, area rugs, etc. doing the best we could to create our own private dance club with as large a dance floor as possible in order to lay down all the instructional dance sheets that they were developing and tweaking!

"We kids did not take lessons, per se. Jory, Sarla, and I were mom's props to work out the kinks in the dance diagrams/instructions that would go in the album. Remember the game Twister? The objective was to produce Twister-like plastic sheets that would go on the floor, which would have dance steps for both male and female, teaching the 'students' the various disco dances that were popular. Jory and I were like chess pieces on a chess board, testing out the steps while our mom and the dance instructor made changes as they watched us walk/dance as we moved from number to number. From those sessions, the diagrams and instructions were honed.

"I loved it because I loved to dance, having had ballet, jazz, and any other dance lessons my mom would introduce me to. Mom taught me the jitterbug; my grandmother taught me the Charleston. So therefore, I was thrilled to learn disco, especially since it was an opportunity to learn from the most prestigious dancer in Baltimore.

"I saw it as an honor to do our part in the process. When our names were called from the other room, indicating they were ready for us to test out the new dance diagrams, I was ecstatic. As a teenager, I felt like it was such an honor. Occasionally, my mom would pull my father out of his comfortable chair, somewhat reluctantly after his hard day's work. Although dancing was not at the top of my dad's list of things to do, he was secretly taught how to dance by my mom's mom in her basement. She explained that in order to win her daughter's heart, he needed to learn the jitterbug. So, he did just that, and turned out to be pretty good.

"However, my conservative endodontist dad quickly was immersed in this 'disco nightclub scene' happening right in his family room, getting into the swing of things and testing out all the dance steps. He got a real hoot out of the fact that my mom landed this premier dance instructor for her latest entrepreneurial endeavor who was now right in the middle of our family room."[36]

The lessons paid off. When Jory and Lacey had their joint bar/bat mitzvah a couple of years later at Chizuk Amuno Congregation, a reception followed at the Pikesville Hilton, where the twins far outpaced their friends on the dance floor. At another bar mitzvah party, Jory won Best Dancer honors. His prize—Billy Joel's latest album, *Glass Houses*.

When the Schunicks weren't listening to *Disco Steppin'*, Donna Summer's voice resounded on Top 40 radio in their household along with millions of others. As the "Queen of Disco" reigned over popular culture in the summer of 1978, baseball was about to get a new king.

8

A ROSE BY ANY OTHER GAME

AUGUST

It had to happen sometime.

Pete Rose's hitting streak ended at forty-four games on August 1, tying Wee Willie Keeler's National League record set in 1897. Going 0 for 4 with two line outs, a groundout, and a strikeout plus a walk against the Atlanta Braves sent the Cincinnati Red noted for his hard-nosed style of ballplaying to the Atlanta–Fulton County Stadium visitors' clubhouse completely lacking in hits but full of anger after the 16–4 drubbing by the home team. His target: Braves relief pitcher Gene Garber.

"The guy pitched me like it was the last out in the seventh game of a World Series," said the twelve-time All-Star and six-time Major League hit leader.[1] Garber, a right-hander who threw sidearm, struck out the side in the top of the ninth to secure a 16–4 rout for the home team. Rose's final at bat ended the game.

Cincinnati began with firepower, building a 3–0 lead in the top of the first. Rose led off with a walk, sprinted to third base on Ken Griffey's double, and scored when Dave Concepción grounded to Braves shortstop Jerry Royster. George Foster struck out—one of 138 times he did so in 1978, which put him just behind Gary Alexander and Dale Murphy for the third-highest number of strikeouts in the Major Leagues that season—and Johnny Bench followed with a two-run clout.

The Braves rebounded with a pair of tallies on four straight hits. Royster pounded a lead-off double and scored when Barry Bonnell followed suit with a two-bagger. Gary Matthews's single put Bonnell on third base; Jeff Burroughs scored him with another single.

Rose lined out to Braves left-hander Larry McWilliams during his second at bat to end the top of the second inning. Atlanta tied the score 3–3 in the bottom of the fourth when Bob Horner cracked a lead-off double and scored on Rod Gilbreath's single. The Reds went up by a run in the top of the fifth. Rose led off with his third out—a grounder to Royster—and Griffey flied out to Braves left fielder Burroughs, but Concepción hit a solo homer, a rarity considering he only compiled six throughout 153 games in the '78 season.

The Braves scored five times to go up 8–4 an inning later, courtesy of a Bonnell RBI single, Horner's three-run blast, and Murphy's solo home run. In the bottom of the seventh, the Braves extended their lead to 11–4. Bonnell went yard to lead off the barrage. Burroughs then drew a walk with one out, the Braves' manager sent Rowland Office to pinch-run, and Horner banged a base hit. After Murphy's flyout to right fielder Ken Griffey, Gilbreath hit an RBI single that scored Office, followed by an RBI single to score Horner.

Crossing the plate another five times in the bottom of the eighth gave plenty of cushioning for Garber, who struck out the side in the top of the ninth—Junior Kennedy, Vic Correll, and Rose. The streak was finished.

Andy Abel, a lifelong Reds fan, recalls Rose's accomplishment with pride.

"My grandfather was an avid baseball fan. I believe my family to be the oldest Reds season ticket holder. My grandfather got his first season tickets in 1930 and we still have them today. He attended, on average, 80 games per season from 1930 to 1995. The point is my grandfather and I were very close, so baseball meant a lot to me growing up. I vividly remember Pete Rose's hitting streak as it was the talk of the town and front-page news in the *Cincinnati Enquirer* from 40 games on.

"As I stated, I watched and listened to a great deal of baseball as a kid and Pete Rose was, without any doubt, the greatest baseball player of his era. He was not as physically gifted as many of the greats, just an absolute winner! He willed himself and his teams to greatness and, in doing so, set several records that will NEVER be broken."[2]

Boston owned a comfortable if not dominant lead in the American League East over its competitors at the beginning of August: five and a half games ahead of Milwaukee, seven and a half games ahead of Baltimore, who tied with New York for third place. After the Yankees went 6-1 on a late July road trip, they opened a seventeen-game home stand in which they compiled a

6-3 record before hosting their archrivals from New England for a two-game series on August 2–3.

Despite standing atop the AL East, the Red Sox had not been faring well. Or even mediocrely. After a five-game winning streak in mid-July, they were 3-11 leading up to the pair of games in the South Bronx. The August 2 game spanned two nights because of the American League's curfew restriction, which had ended play at 1:16 a.m. in the pitch-black hours of August 3.[3] New York struck early and often, building a 4–0 lead in the bottom of the second inning. Every Yankee had an at bat. Andy Hassler got nicked for three singles, a double, a walk, and a batter getting on base because of a rare error by left fielder Jim Rice, who made three errors in 114 games that season. Cliff Johnson and Mickey Rivers struck out during this sequence, but the Yankees had pounded Hassler enough for Red Sox manager Don Zimmer to call in Tom Burgmeier, who struck out Thurman Munson to end the barrage.

New York made the run count a quintet in the bottom of the third. Piniella led off the bottom of the third with a double; Reggie Jackson struck out but Piniella crossed home plate when Chris Chambliss got a base hit. Boston responded with two runs in the top of the fourth and another two in the top of the sixth, when Dick Tidrow loaded the bases and relief pitcher Goose Gossage walked in both runs.

Rice crushed a lead-off double in the top of the eighth, then a thirty-five-minute rain delay occurred. The Red Sox tied the game when Rice went to third base on a wild pitch by Gossage and scored on Carl Yastrzemski's sacrifice fly.

The rivals remained tied at 5–5, sending the game to extra innings. Another rain delay happened in the bottom of the twelfth. It lasted seventeen minutes. For curfew restrictions, the umpires suspended the game at 1:16 a.m. It resumed the following night with the visitors going ahead by two runs in the seventeenth inning; the Bronx Bombers didn't score in their half. Boston's 7–5 victory happened after Dwight Evans and Butch Hobson hit back-to-back singles. Evans scored from third base on Rick Burleson's single; Hobson advanced to second base, and Rice knocked him in with another single.

Boston won the second game 8–1. New Englanders welcomed the news, particularly Rice's performance—two RBIs in the first game and three RBIs complemented by three runs scored in the second game. Rice had been less than effective at the plate with a 2-for-20 record against the Royals and White

Sox during the five-game home stand at Fenway Park preceding the two games at Yankee Stadium.

Faltering as well, the Red Sox gave pause to New Englanders who believed 1978 would be a year of destiny given the enormous fourteen-game lead in July. Zimmer agreed that the offense needed a boost but underscored that his team doubled down on the work during difficult times. "Our problem's been hitting," said Zimmer, who had taken over the skipper job from Darrell Johnson in the middle of the 1976 season. "But these guys don't figure to be stopped forever, they're too good. When Jimmy Rice slumps for five or six days, he goes out to the batting cage and works with Johnny Pesky and the other coaches. He's done the same thing during this slump, too, but nothing happened for awhile."[4]

Rick Burleson, who reached fourth place in the 1974 American League Rookie of the Year voting and made his second of four All-Star teams in 1978, pointed out the importance of the victories beyond adding two entries to the "W" column. "We're definitely turned around," stated Burleson, who had two hits in seven at bats with an RBI and two runs scored in the seventeen-inning game and 1 for 4 with a run scored in the next game. "It wasn't that we were doubting our abilities, but we were really wondering how long this thing was going to go on. Then we came out here today."[5]

New York lost the following night against Baltimore at Yankee Stadium, then won six in a row to complete the home stand with an 11-6 record. The fifth game in this streak emphasized the offense as the Yankees mounted a 9–0 score balanced by Ron Guidry tossing a three-hitter against the Brewers and registering nine strikeouts. His record to that date stood at 16-2.

Both Guidry and the offense pounded the opposition early. In the first three innings, New York's standout hurler had seven strikeouts and a 5–0 lead, which expanded to 8–0 in the fourth inning. He proved that pitching is a thinking man's occupation, full of strategy and estimation as well as power and finesse. "The last time I faced them they hit every fastball I threw up there," said Guidry. "Tonight I used the fastball as a kind of set-up pitch, and came in with the slider. I made them aware of the slider early."[6]

Vengeance belonged to the lanky southpaw; Milwaukee had been responsible for Guidry's first loss, a 6–0 contest at Milwaukee County Stadium on July 7. "Sure there was added incentive," said Guidry. "It was a little bit of a payback. No-hitter? Naw, I don't think about them, I got to save something for later."[7] Even if Guidry didn't think about a no-hitter, conversation probably began to percolate among the more than thirty-five thousand people in attendance after realizing that he kept the Brewers hitless through five innings. Robin Yount punctured the idea with a lead-off double in the top of the sixth. Dick Davis banged a one-out single in the top of the eighth for the second hit followed by Yount's single.

Guidry seemed to come out of nowhere in 1978. But the Yankees had at least one staff member who had appreciated his potential before this terrific season. "I knew he was a great prospect," said Yankees manager Bob Lemon, who had been the team's pitching coach in 1976 before helming the White Sox. "When you saw that arm, you had to fall in love with it. I don't know where you could find a better one."

Lemon also disclosed a factoid that would have changed the Yankees' fortunes in 1978. During his Chicago tenure, he attempted to include Guidry in the trade that sent Bucky Dent to New York.[8]

In the National League West, three teams battled for first place when August began. The Giants topped the division with a half-game lead over the Reds and one and a half games over the Dodgers. At the tail end of July, the Dodgers lost two in a row followed by four more losses from August 1 to August 4. Fortunes changed. Starting on August 5, they won eight of the next ten games. But there was more drama inside the Dodgers' clubhouse than on the field.

It began on August 16, when *Washington Post* sportswriter Thomas Boswell highlighted the unsung contributions of Reggie Smith in a feature article quoting Don Sutton: "This nation gets infatuated with a few names. All you hear about on our team is Steve Garvey, the All-American boy. Well, the best player on this team for the last two years—and we all know it—is Reggie Smith. As Reggie goes, so goes us." Dodgers skipper Tommy Lasorda chimed in that Smith should have won the MVP in 1977. Sutton continued, "Reggie doesn't go out and publicize himself. He doesn't smile at the right people or say the right things. He tells the truth, even if it sometimes alienates people. Reggie's not a facade or a Madison Avenue image."[9]

Sutton embraced publicity, leveraging his fame to make several appearances on the game show *Match Game* beginning in 1976. Two days after the *Post* article's publication, the *Los Angeles Times* quoted Boswell's piece. Garvey approached Sutton in the clubhouse before the August 20 game against the Mets; their conversation escalated to a clash that might have had some people looking around for boxing announcers from *Wide World of Sports*.

The battle was real. As UPI reporter Milton Richman described it, "I've seen plenty of baseball fights before, but I've never seen one where the participants showed more cold, concentrated fury amounting to an almost homicidal desire to take one another [a]part than in the struggle between Garvey and Sutton." It took "an extraordinary effort" from their teammates—plus coach Preston Gomez and general manager Al Campanis—to separate the ballplayers turned battlers.[10]

Garvey believed what is considered a bedrock rule in any community, whether it be a baseball team, a family, or a Fortune 500 company's board of directors: opinions are for other members of the group, not anyone else. "We're a team and we should act as a team," declared the first baseman. "If we've got differences, they should be kept inside the clubhouse."[11]

Versions differed, of course. Sutton denied being the instigator, claiming that Garvey "poked his finger in my chest making a point." Garvey said that Sutton mentioned Garvey's wife, a turning point in the encounter and an accusation that Sutton neither confirmed nor denied. Justifying his own actions, Garvey said, "I apologize to my teammates. It was a bad time for something like this to take place, but my approach (to Sutton) did have to come; it was a necessity." *Times* columnist Jim Murray advocated for Garvey in a piece laced with more sarcasm than a Don Rickles performance in Las Vegas. Among his theories for Sutton's ire: Garvey was the Hillside Strangler, a jewel thief, or a communist.[12]

Described as having "eyes red and voice wavering" before a home game against the Phillies, Sutton noted his religious faith as a Christian, shortcomings as a human being, and gratitude to a higher power in a statement on August 24 that read, in part, "I thank God for Steve Garvey and for the role He has let him play in my life and I can now thank Him for the Washington Post article and the disagreement in New York. Because together they have helped to point out to me very vividly that as long as my life isn't right, then I can't be a good example for anyone." Garvey accepted the apology, which he watched on a monitor in a TV truck.[13]

For Dodgers fans, *mirabile dictu*, the drama did not seem to have any significant consequence regarding the team's effectiveness. From August 16 until the end of the month, the Dodgers had a 10-4 record.

AUGUST 16

Bob Welch limited the Phillies to six hits as he threw a complete game for a 5–2 victory in which Smith bashed a grand slam at Veterans Stadium. Gomez offered his acclaim as he appraised the slugger with a substantial comparison: "Mickey Mantle and Reggie Smith are really the only switch hitters I've seen who could beat you with power from both sides of the plate."[14]

AUGUST 17

Another 5–2 victory against the Phillies gave Burt Hooton his thirteenth victory of the season and Terry Forster his fifteenth save. Garvey contributed the quintet of runs with an RBI single, a bases loaded triple, and a run scored.

AUGUST 18

Continuing their road trip to New York, the Dodgers won, 7–3, for Tommy John's fourteenth victory in 1978. Again Garvey gave a standout performance at the plate with a 2-for-3 night, three runs scored, and four RBIs from a single and a three-run homer.

AUGUST 19

The Mets scored four unearned runs in their 8–4 defeat of the Dodgers, but the score only told half the story. Rage ruled the day on both sides.

Believing that he checked his swing, Mets fan favorite Lee Mazzilli argued with the third base umpire about a third strike. Smith and Lasorda confronted the home plate umpire about Smith being called out. There was another altercation involving Smith when he jawed with Mets backstop John Stearns about an umpire calling a ball instead of a strike. Dodgers third baseman Lee Lacy escalated an argument with Tim Foli from words to fists when he "charged Foli, only to be tackled by Sutton." The right-hander lasted five and a third innings against the Mets, who tagged him for five hits, seven runs, and five walks. On the plus side, Sutton had seven strikeouts. After the game, he shared his insight into the team's psyche: "Our club is just an emotional, intense club and it doesn't take a whole lot to get us on edge (to) react emotionally."[15]

AUGUST 20

After the clubhouse scrap with Sutton, Garvey factored into the ninth-inning comeback that began with the Dodgers at a 4–2 deficit. Smith began the rally with a lead-off walk, followed by Garvey's single. Mets manager Joe Torre selected Skip Lockwood from the Shea Stadium bullpen to replace Craig Swan; Smith scored from second base on Ron Cey's single, and Garvey arrived at third base thanks to an error by Steve Henderson in left field.

After Dusty Baker pinch-hit for Charlie Hough and struck out, Lacy's sacrifice fly scored Garvey to tie the game at 4–4. Joe Ferguson had the game-winning hit—a line drive double to left that allowed Cey to score; Henderson took responsibility for misjudging that hit. "The ball just sailed over my head," explained Henderson, who had come to the Mets in 1977 via the trade for Tom Seaver and attained second place in that year's Rookie of the Year voting. "I thought I had it but it sailed."[16]

AUGUST 21

Garvey had another exemplary performance, going 3 for 4 and scoring a run in the Dodgers' 4–2 loss against the Expos. But the five-time All-Star and four-time Gold Glove Award winner made a couple of rare defensive mishaps—an error in the first inning and a miscommunication leading to a balk in the fifth inning. Bob Welch did not follow through on his attempt to pick off Del Unser at first base because Garvey wasn't in position. Lasorda disclosed, "He thought Garvey was holding the runner on. Someone's supposed to tell the pitcher. Garvey's supposed to tell him if he's playing behind (the runner)." Andre Dawson's single likely would have put Unser on second base, but he scored on a throwing error by Dodgers shortstop Bill Russell.[17]

AUGUST 23

Montreal pecked away at Burt Hooton for nine hits, but the righty limited the opposition to one run through eight innings. After Hooton gave up a single to Warren Cromartie and a double to Gary Carter in the top of the ninth, Lasorda replaced him with Charlie Hough to protect LA's 4–1 lead. Larry Parrish's grounder to third baseman Ron Cey scored Cromartie, but Charlie Hough struck out Chris Speier and pinch hitter Tom Hutton to end the game and secure Hooton's fourteenth victory of the season against eight losses.

Garvey praised the hurler, who had thrown a no-hitter as a twenty-two-year-old rookie with the Cubs in 1972 and got second place in the Cy Young Award voting for 1978. "I think Happy (Hooton) has a tendency to be overlooked," said the Dodgers' first baseman. "He's so steady, so consistent. It's guys who play in streaks that tend to be chronicled and written about. Happy does it every time out; he sneaks up on you."[18]

AUGUST 24

Los Angeles began a thirteen-game home stand with another comeback win, beating the Phillies 5–4. Lopes and Cey each had three hits and scored a run against the Phillies; a Cey hit began the decisive rally in the bottom of the eighth with the Dodgers trailing 4–2. Baker doubled his teammate to third base; they both scored on Russell's single to tie the game.

Then a couple of switches happened. Lasorda wanted Rick Monday to pinch-hit for starting pitcher Tommy John; Phillies manager Danny Ozark sent Tug McGraw to replace Warren Brusstar, who had replaced Steve Carlton in the bottom of the fifth. Instead of using Monday, Lasorda sent in veteran Manny Mota, whose Major League career began in 1962, to face McGraw. Mota hit a single "off third baseman Mike Schmidt's glove" that scored Russell to put Los Angeles up 5–4, but he tried to extend it into a double and got thrown out at second base.[19]

AUGUST 25

Garvey and Sutton had outstanding performances in a 6–5 victory against the Phillies. Sutton struck out ten in eight innings; Garvey had a 2-for-4 night with three RBIS and a run scored. Philadelphia led 5–4 when the Dodgers went to bat in the bottom of the ninth. Ozark used Ron Reed in the bottom of the ninth; Smith tagged him for a base hit. After Garvey's flyout to right fielder Bake McBride, Reed plunked Cey, who left the game for pinch runner Ted Martínez.

Baker's single scored Smith to tie the game. Martínez scampered to second base, stayed there when Monday fouled out, and sprinted home when Jerry Grote singled for the game-winning RBI.

AUGUST 26

The Phillies delivered a 3–1 loss to the Dodgers. Their trio of tallies happened in the top of the fourth. It was quite a barrage. Greg "Bull" Luzinski led off with a single then went to third on José Cardenal's double. Bob Boone sent both runners across the plate on a double, followed by Garry Maddox getting on first base because of Russell's error. Bud Harrelson's groundout to Russell sent Boone and Maddox to second and third. Randy Lerch aided with a single to center field that scored Boone, but Monday threw out Maddox at home.

AUGUST 27

Philadelphia dominated in a 9–3 victory led by the top of the order: Bake McBride, Larry Bowa, Mike Schmidt, and Greg Luzinski. McBride went 4 for 6, including a home run, yielding four runs scored and a couple of RBIs. Bowa contributed two runs scored and a 3-for-6 performance; Schmidt had two RBIs, a run scored, and three hits in five at bats. Luzinski doubled home a run in the top of the fifth and singled home two more in the top of the eighth. The fifth-inning smash could have been a home run because the ball "actually cleared the fence [but] was knocked back into the field of play by a leaping Reggie Smith."[20]

AUGUST 28

Hooton got his fifteenth win—a complete-game, four-hit shutout of Montreal: 4–0. The Expos and Dodgers both fought in a scoreless tie through the top of the seventh; Lopes hit a two-run homer with two outs in the bottom half of the inning. Lacy followed with a two-run clout an inning later.

Lopes noted the passion of Dodgers fans, who marked the twenty-first season of professional baseball in Los Angeles since team owner Walter O'Malley moved the team from Brooklyn in 1958. "The fans are becoming more involved than at any time in the past," observed the second baseman. "The last two home stands have been like Philadelphia was last year (in the playoffs). I got goosebumps all over and I think all of the guys have. I think these fans have caught the fever."[21]

AUGUST 29

The Expos went up 1–0 in the top of the second. Hal Dues walked Smith to begin the bottom of the fourth, but Garvey's grounder to Dues resulted in a force out of Smith at second base. Cey singled; both he and Garvey scored when Joe Ferguson, a part-time catcher playing the outfield for this game, bashed a three-run homer. Garvey's sacrifice fly in the bottom of the fifth scored Lopes, who had singled, stolen second base, and advanced to third base on Bill Russell's groundout to Expos shortstop Chris Speier.

Tommy John threw a complete game in the 4–1 victory and improved his record to 16-9.

AUGUST 30

The Expos had a 3–0 lead until the Dodgers tied the game in the bottom of the eighth on Reggie Smith's homer with Bill North on base and Cey's solo shot. With two outs in the bottom of the ninth, it seemed like the Expos and Dodgers might be headed to extra innings. North singled for his third base hit of the night, moved to second on a wild throw by Wayne Twitchell trying a pick-off, and scored on Garvey's single.[22]

At the end of August, the champions of Chavez Ravine led the NL West by two games over the Giants and distanced themselves from the Reds by seven games. Leadership of the NL West wasn't the only thing in Southern California getting shaken up during August. Hollywood had an unexpected summer blockbuster.

"Double secret probation." "A really futile and stupid gesture." "Fat, drunk, and stupid is no way to go through life, son." Mention any one of those pieces of dialogue to an *Animal House* fan, and you'll likely get one of the remaining two in response or perhaps another from the script written by Harold Ramis, Douglas Kenney, and Chris Miller.

Filmed at the University of Oregon and set during fall of 1962 at the fictional Faber College, *Animal House* starred Tim Matheson—whose career dated back to the early 1960s, when he was a child actor with guest roles on *Leave It to Beaver*, *My Three Sons*, and *The Farmer's Daughter* along with voicing the title role in the Saturday morning cartoon show *Jonny Quest*—and John Belushi, who had gained stardom with *Saturday Night Live*, which finished its third season in the spring before *Animal House* hit theaters.

Matheson's character, Eric "Otter" Stratton, is Delta Tau Chi fraternity's rush chairman and inspirational leader. He reflects confidence, charisma, and pride as he seduces Dean Wormer's wife, gives a passionate defense of the fraternity's antics before Faber's Pan-Hellenic Council, and revives the spirit of his expelled fraternity brothers with a speech that convinces them to commit "a really futile and stupid gesture" to get revenge on the dean.

His plan: create havoc, destruction, and panic at Faber's homecoming parade. It's climaxed by fraternity brother D-Day driving a pledge's car that's been converted into the "Deathmobile"—decorated with the head from Emil Faber's statue as a hood ornament—into the parade viewing stand.

Belushi plays John "Bluto" Blutarsky, a Delta brother still in college after seven years. His voracious appetite allows him to chug a quart of whiskey when the dean shuts down the Delta house and stuff his face with just about every food in the Faber cafeteria as he moves his tray down the line.

Film critics were often lukewarm, not completely bashing *Animal House* nor raving about it. *Newsday*'s Alexander Keneas wrote that Belushi's "characterization is a stereotype; it's also funnier than anything that actually occurs in the film." Delawareans read Harry F. Themal's appraisal in the *Sunday News Journal*, underlined by the declaration, "This film offers little but sophomoric humor that even a high school freshman would scorn." Janet Maslin of the *New York Times* concluded that the film "is by no means one long howl, but it's often very funny, with gags that are effective in a dependable, all-purpose way."[23]

Syndicated columnist Bob Greene validated the casting as "so on the mark as to be eerie" and revealed, "It was the only time in memory that an audience was screaming so hard with laughter that a significant portion of the dialog [*sic*] was lost."[24]

Film critics may have been uneven in their assessments. Audiences weren't. On a $3 million budget, *Animal House* grossed $120 million.[25] Technically, the title is *National Lampoon's Animal House*. Two of the film's three writers—Doug Kenney and Chris Miller—came from *National Lampoon*, a humor magazine that Kenney had started with Henry Beard and Robert Hoffman. It derived from *Harvard Lampoon*, an iconic magazine from that Ivy League institution associated with the color crimson. Kenney was an alumnus of Harvard; Miller used his fraternity experiences from Dartmouth as comedy fodder. Ramis had college experience as well, and he brought his stories from the Jewish fraternity Zeta Beta Tau at Washington University in St. Louis.

Matty Simmons ran *National Lampoon*. Experience, instinct, and vision in the business world gave him a solid foundation to lead this media empire that shaped comedy in the 1970s and 1980s. Simmons headed publicity during the formative years of Diners Club, a pioneering credit card company that began operations in 1950. One of his creations: the *Diners Club Magazine*. Simmons departed the company in 1967 and began his publishing business—21st Century Communications. With fellow Diners Club executive refugee Len Mogel, Simmons published *Weight Watchers Magazine* and *Cheetah*, a short-lived rival to *Rolling Stone*, then brought the Kenney-Beard-Hoffman trio into the company's fold in 1969 to create *National Lampoon*. It debuted the following year.[26]

Extension of the magazine's brand into other media followed with *National Lampoon's Radio Hour* and the off-Broadway play *Lemmings*, a parody of Woodstock. Records became part of the portfolio as well. Part of *Animal House*'s DNA can be found in the magazine's *1964 High School Yearbook Parody*, which included the characters Mandy Pepperidge and Larry Kroger, later portrayed in the film scripted by Ramis, Kenney, and Miller. *Animal House* became a summer blockbuster.

The journey in making *Animal House* has become Hollywood lore. Jack Webb was the first choice to play Dean Wormer, but the *Dragnet* star declined. The writers created the character of Otter for Chevy Chase, but director John Landis didn't want the *Saturday Night Live* star for the suave Delta brother. Donald Sutherland's decision to play a professor over two days of shooting for a flat fee of $35,000 rather than a percentage of the gross ticket sales cost him millions of dollars. The filming on location in Eugene, Oregon, took thirty-two days.[27]

Matheson credits Landis for setting the tone of camaraderie that gave the characters dimension, believability, and empathy. In a 2021 interview for the Library of Congress marking the twentieth anniversary of the film joining the National Film Registry for being "culturally, historically or aesthetically significant," Matheson lauded Landis for doing "something really brilliant.

'Animal House' was a five-week shoot, but he had the Deltas come in a week early to just hang out. For a week, we ate together, toured the set, watched the Deathmobile being built, and just hung out. We had a bond before everyone else showed up."[28]

Before they started filming, the actors portraying the Deltas had been invited to a party at the Sigma Alpha Epsilon fraternity house hosted by brothers who would have felt at home with the film's antagonists from Omega Theta Pi. Only SAE brothers were allowed in the house. They didn't like the actors flirting with the young women who had invited them, and the friction led to a melee in which Matheson et al. got thrown out of the house and pummeled. "I mean, it was like a wave hit us," recalled Peter Riegert, who played Boon. "And we were out the door. 'They've got Tim! They've got Tim!' And then I saw Bruce [McGill] charging back in to get Tim. Tim was down like this [covering up his face]. And everybody was getting the shit kicked out of them."[29]

The incident mirrors a scene in the movie where Otter gets baited by Barbara Sue "Babs" Jansen to meet her at a hotel only to find five Omega brothers, who beat him to a pulp.

Elmer Bernstein's score accompanied the film's comedy with austere arrangements. It was part of the twenty-four-year-old Landis's strategy for Bernstein, a legendary composer responsible for a roster of scores that helped define excellence in twentieth-century filmmaking. Without Bernstein's music, would *To Kill a Mockingbird* have the same emotional impact regarding racism? Would *The Great Escape* be as compelling? Would *The Man with the Golden Arm* be as provocative?

Landis had a connection to Bernstein that other filmmakers didn't—he was a childhood friend of Bernstein's son, Peter. But when Bernstein screened *Animal House*, which he believed was funny, he didn't see a path for his musical contributions. In a 2002 interview, Bernstein described how Landis had convinced him to participate in the endeavor. "I would like you to score this film as if it were a drama," the composer recalled the director saying. "Score these scenes as if they were drama without any reference to funny sounds and funny music, anything like that.

"Of course, the effect is hysterical," said Bernstein, who had won an Academy Award for *Thoroughly Modern Millie* and Golden Globe Awards for *To*

Kill a Mockingbird and *Hawaii*. "If you score funny scenes seriously they are much funnier, so long as they are funny to begin with. It set a trend on how to score comedies."[30]

Indeed. Bernstein also scored *Meatballs*, *Airplane!*, and *Ghostbusters*. The soundtrack to *Animal House* complemented Bernstein's score, created a celebratory aura, and amplified the early 1960s setting, as did the cars, fashion, and women's hairstyles. That soundtrack boasted such hits as "Twistin' the Night Away," "Shout," "Wonderful World," "Louie Louie," "Hey Paula," "Tossin' and Turnin'," and "Let's Dance."

Simmons borrowed a line from the movie for the title of a book he wrote about the behind-the-scenes tales of the film's genesis, production, and success. In *Fat, Drunk, and Stupid: The Inside Story behind the Making of "Animal House*," he underscores the vibrancy of friendships that he saw even in their embryonic phase during the filming on location. "When a movie shoot is over, everybody tells one another how much they loved working with them and they go on their way," explains Simmons. "Frequently there's a tear or two. But I've never since seen the sadness that I saw in those leaving the set of *Animal House*."[31]

At the end of August, summer's relief began to wane. Bolstered by the exuberance created in *Animal House*, college kids prepared to return to school for the upcoming semester. Vacationers enjoyed the last sliver of sunshine before heading back to work. TV network executives implemented their marketing campaigns for the fall schedule. Baseball fans looked forward to the home stretch of the season.

September would be full of surprises.

9

THE BOSTON MASSACRE

SEPTEMBER

Labor Day weekend in 1978 began on Friday, September 1, with two divisions in tight pennant races.

A two-game gap separated the Dodgers and Giants in the NL West, and the same held for the Royals and Angels in the AL West. Their counterparts in the NL East and AL East had comfortable though not impenetrable leads. Aiming to get a third consecutive pennant in the Senior Circuit, the Phillies led the Pirates by five games; a barrier of six and a half games distanced the Red Sox from the Yankees. Having enjoyed a fourteen-game lead in mid-July, the fellas from Fenway then suffered a reduction in their lead by more than half. The Yankees winning their last seven games in August gave them momentum, which the Red Sox paced by winning six of their last seven.

September began with a less than prosperous sequence for the Red Sox, who completed a ten-game home stand at Fenway Park by losing two of three to the A's, then traveling to Baltimore for a three-game set and losing two to the Orioles.

Yankee Stadium opened the month by hosting a seven-game home stand—three games against the Mariners, four games against the Tigers. The home team added five victories and two losses to its '78 tally, winning two in the first series and three in the second series. In their last fourteen games, the Yankees were 12-2, clipping Boston's lead in the AL East to four games.

Jim Spencer, who played in seventy-seven games in 1978 as a part-time first baseman for the Yankees, lauded the serenity fostered by their new helmsman Bob Lemon, whose steadiness had replaced Billy Martin's volatility. "There is a more relaxed atmosphere in the clubhouse," admitted Spencer. "Lemon is a low key guy. You don't have to worry about all that other stuff [and] what's going on up there [in the press box]."[1]

The next series for both teams consisted of four games at Fenway Park, where the Red Sox had a 52-14 record for the season, including winning six of eight games against the Yankees. Boston took two of three at Fenway in June, followed by splitting two games at Yankee Stadium later in the month.[2]

Nasty weather in Boston truncated another two-game series in early July—the Red Sox won on July 3, but the July 4 game got postponed to September 7. At Yankee Stadium in August, the visitors swept a two-game series for wins No. 5 and 6 against the Bronx Bombers to that date. Despite the Yankees' recent encroachment in the standings, the Red Sox were on solid ground when they opened the four-game series at Fenway Park with the September 7 make-up game. Or so New Englanders believed.

Boston then amassed a quartet of losses that became known as the "Boston Massacre."

SEPTEMBER 7

It began with a 15–3 thumping involving twenty-one hits by the invading squad. Yankees second baseman Willie Randolph led the offense with three hits, five RBIs, a run scored, and a walk.

The Yankees scored twelve runs in the first four innings. Randolph had the honor of being the first to cross the plate, though it was an unearned run. After Mike Torrez caught Mickey Rivers looking, Randolph got to first base because of an error by Red Sox third baseman Butch Hobson, who "bounced the ball into the dirt and through [first baseman George] Scott's legs and set the tone for Boston's longest night of the year," described Joe Gergen in *Newsday*.[3]

Thurman Munson's single put Randolph on second, and Reggie Jackson's single scored him as Munson went to third, then scored on a sacrifice fly by Chris Chambliss for a 2–0 lead.

Three more runs went on the Fenway Park scoreboard for the New Yorkers in the second inning. Lou Piniella, Roy White, Bucky Dent, and Rivers pecked away at Torrez for four singles and two runs, which sent Don Zimmer to the dugout phone for reinforcements. Andy Hassler gave up another run, which gave the Yankees a 5–0 lead.

A couple of scores an inning later put them up 7–0. In the top of the fourth, they batted around the order. Chambliss and Graig Nettles hit back-to-back singles; Dick Drago relieved Hassler and gave up five runs. The Red Sox scored two runs in the bottom of the fourth when Carl Yastrzemski tripled off Catfish Hunter, who left the game with a strained groin muscle, and Carlton Fisk homered off relief pitcher Ken Clay to make the score 12–2.

Yankees shortstop Bucky Dent led off the top of the sixth with a triple. After Rivers grounded out, Randolph sent his double-play partner home with a single for the Yankees' thirteenth run. The Red Sox got their final run in the bottom of the seventh, though unearned. Hobson banged a single, but Piniella's error allowed him to scamper to second base. The next two batters grounded out to Randolph. Hobson ran to third base on Rick Burleson's grounder and scored when Fred Lynn did the same.

The Yankees scored their final two runs in the bottom of the eighth off Bill Campbell. It was a standout night for the visiting team with several contributors in addition to Randolph.

Piniella: 2 for 5, 3 runs scored.

White: 3 for 4, 2 RBIS, 3 runs scored.

Dent: 2 for 6, 2 RBIS, 2 runs scored.

Munson: 3 for 3, 1 RBI, 1 run scored.

"The only good thing is that this is only one game," offered Zimmer. "Maybe we tired them out."[4]

He couldn't have been more wrong.

SEPTEMBER 8

Repeating their paradigm from the previous night, the Yankees had a 2–0 lead after the first inning. Both runs were unearned. They began another offensive barrage, resulting in seventeen hits as the Red Sox saw the score amplified to 8–0 in the second inning, 10–0 in the fifth inning, 11–0 in the sixth inning, and 13–0 in the eighth inning. The home team scored twice in the bottom of the ninth, a noble effort with negligible impact. Losing 13–2 turned the Fenway faithful into the Fenway frustrated.

Like the impact of an icy wind off the Charles River in February, New England's baseball community felt these devastating losses in their bones. Growing up in New Hampshire, Fisk knew the importance of baseball to the region and expressed the confusion that Red Sox fans felt. "I can't believe we could have hitting, pitching and defense all go like this at once," said the six-time All-Star and 1972 American League Rookie of the Year.[5]

Another New England native had the spotlight. Yankees starting pitcher Jim Beattie had stayed close to his roots: graduating from South Portland High School, going to Dartmouth, and playing in the Cape Cod Baseball League. But any notions of joining the Red Sox got quashed when the Yankees drafted him in 1975; Beattie journeyed through the farm system to Syracuse, Oneonta, West Haven, Fort Lauderdale, and Tacoma before joining the Yankees in 1978.

His performance against the Red Sox on June 21 prompted the Tacoma assignment: Beattie gave up a run in the bottom of the second and three more runs in the next inning before Martin pulled him with no outs. The Red Sox tallied three more against Dick Tidrow. Final score: 9–2.

Beattie had been transformed. He struck out eight, walked one, and lasted eight and two-thirds innings; Fred Lynn's double in the first inning was the sole hit for Boston until Jim Rice's single in the seventh. During their ninth-inning rally, the Red Sox banged four hits and scored the pair of runs before Ron Davis spelled Beattie with two outs and retired Garry Hancock on a grounder to second baseman Willie Randolph.

Adding to the home team's woes: seven errors. It was a combination of victory and vengeance for the six-foot-five-inch right-hander. "Coming from New England, no matter how many years I'm in the big leagues, it will always be a thrill for me to pitch at Fenway Park," stated Beattie. "And I really wanted to change things around from the last time. You try to forget about those things, but you can't."[6]

Beattie got offensive support throughout the Yankees' lineup, just as Catfish Hunter and Clay had the previous night.

Mickey Rivers had a 3-for-3 night and scored twice. Also, Randolph went 2 for 4 with a run scored and an RBI. Reggie Jackson clocked a three-run homer, his twenty-first of the season. Chris Chambliss hit two singles in five at bats; he scored three times and batted in a run. Roy White's four at bats yielded two hits, two runs scored, and an RBI. Lou Piniella bashed the ball for three hits and two RBIs, complemented by scoring a run.

Dejection hovered around Boston. To lose two games to the Yankees at Fenway Park was one thing. To be stifled was another. The Yankees were an inferno. The Red Sox, a candle. But Boston's baseball brethren faced a disquieting problem more compelling than being pummeled for twenty-eight runs in two games. Dwight Evans left the game with dizziness in the sixth inning after he dropped a ball that allowed Chambliss to advance to second base; Chambliss scored on a Graig Nettles single. During the game against the Mariners on August 28, Evans had been beaned by Mike Parrott, a rookie hurler, who said the ball "slipped" from his control. It broke the helmet and leveled Evans; X-rays didn't show a fracture.[7]

The incident had a lasting effect confirmed by the team doctor, William Southmayd, who said, "The swelling is still there. Dwight doesn't know about it himself. He's all right when he's looking straight ahead and at the plate. But looking up and down, he has a problem." Only Evans, who won his second of eight Gold Glove Awards in 1978, was not the type to let a setback exclude him from the lineup, particularly with the Yankees creeping forward in the standings. "He probably shouldn't have been out there," opined Fisk. "But Dwight is such a tough kid. He wants to play so badly. He might be back right away. I just hope he doesn't hurt himself. He's too valuable to this team and too nice a guy to go out there and hurt himself."[8]

The Yankees had closed the gap in the AL East to two games, though the Brewers remained a threat to the Red Sox's leadership as well. In the past twenty-seven games, they were 19-8 and trailed by five and a half games. Anything could happen.

SEPTEMBER 9

Ron Guidry had twenty wins and two losses in 1978 when he dressed in his road uniform for the third game of the series, which took place in the afternoon after night games on two consecutive nights. His performance in '78 would join other examples of dominance in baseball history. Sandy Koufax went 27-9 in 1966, his last season in the Major Leagues. Denny McLain's 31-6 record and Bob Gibson's 1.12 ERA in 1968 reflected a season of power for pitchers and caused Major League Baseball to lower the mound. Nolan Ryan steamrolled through opposing lineups in 1973, compiling 383 strikeouts.

Even though they had their ace on the mound, this was no time for the Yankees to take anything for granted. Dennis Eckersley sported a 16-6 record—including a 9–0 output at Fenway Park so far that season—when he kept the opponents from the South Bronx scoreless for the first three innings. Two Yankees reached first base; Munson got hit by a pitch in the top of first, and Nettles banged a single in the top of the second. Their curbing ended in the fourth inning, when the Yankees scored all their runs in the 7–0 victory.

Munson began with a single but became the second half of a double play. Carl Yastrzemski caught Jackson's fly ball to left field and fired to second baseman Frank Duffy, who threw to George Scott and got Munson out at first base. Chambliss revived the Yankees with a double. Eckersley gave an intentional pass to Nettles; Piniella's double allowed Chambliss to score the first run and Nettles to move from first to third. Roy White drew another intentional walk.

The Yankees made the score 3–0 when Dent's single brought Nettles and Piniella home as White sprinted to third base; Yastrzemski's error gave Dent the opportunity to go to second. White and Dent scored on Rivers's single. Rivers took second on Yastrzemski's throw to Fisk and third on a wild pitch during Randolph's at bat, which ended in a walk. Munson's single knocked in Rivers, amplifying the score to 6–0.

Zimmer selected Tom Burgmeier to take over. A passed ball sent Randolph home for the seventh run; Munson went to second base. Jackson drew a walk, but Chambliss's flyout to center fielder Fred Lynn capped an extraordinary display for the Yankees.

Piniella had another fantastic game, going 3 for 5 with an RBI and a run scored; Munson went 2 for 4 and contributed an RBI; and Dent's single sent home two runs. Guidry gave a stellar performance—a two-hitter raising the record for "Louisiana Lightning" to 21-2. Both hits came in the first inning; Rick Burleson and Jim Rice singled. Guidry walked four and whiffed five in his complete-game effort. Three strikeouts came in the bottom of the fifth, when he struck out the side.

Was there something supernatural going on? Was there really a curse inflicted upon the Red Sox because they had sold Babe Ruth to the Yankees after the 1919 season? At the very least, the weather factored into New York's latest emphatic victory. Piniella's two-out blooper to "short center" with Nettles on first and Chambliss on second looked like an easy out to end, but a strong wind prevented the defense from capturing the sphere. It scored Chambliss and set off the series of seven runs scored.

If anyone could have gotten it, second baseman Frank Duffy looked like the logical choice. Eckersley commented, "When the ball went up, I thought it was just a fly ball. But when I looked around, I knew it was trouble. I mean it drifted over 100 feet away from him. The wind was just that bad." Duffy took the blame. "I should have stopped and let it drift back to me. But I lost it momentarily in the sun, and when I picked it up again it was too late." Eckersley refused to make either Duffy or the wind culpable for causing the barrage by the Bronx Bombers, stating instead that he "lost the game" when he had two strikes on Dent and gave up a two-RBI single.[9]

Yastrzemski also didn't acknowledge the wind as a component in the loss, calling it "an alibi." A thirty-nine-year-old veteran who made "a pair of sensational catches" and had been with the team since 1961, Yaz exemplified a workman-like approach to the game. Quiet. Determined. Focused. He had been through the Cinderella season of 1967, winning the Triple Crown and leading the team to the World Series against the mighty Cardinals led by Bob Gibson. That series went seven games, as did the 1975 World Series against the Reds. Both ended in losses. A perennial All-Star, with 1978 being his fifteenth year getting that recognition, Yastrzemski reminded the team that they needed to look forward: "This one is history and will be forgotten in a few hours. Tomorrow's game is the one that counts."[10]

In the past three games, the Yankees had scored thirty-five runs. The Red Sox, five. Winning a trio of games at Fenway Park gave the visitors sixteen wins in their last nineteen games. *Boston Globe* sports columnist Ray Fitzgerald tried to deflect ill will, lest anyone believe the Red Sox were going through the motions. He pointed out defensive attempts: Yaz dove for a ball with the score 7–0, and Hobson followed suit in the sixth inning. With two outs in the bottom of the eighth, there was Burleson hitting a grounder to Guidry and "sliding into first base in a futile attempt to beat out a slow bouncer."[11]

The Red Sox occupied first place with a one-game lead as they headed into the fourth and final game of the series.

SEPTEMBER 10

When fans of Boston's AL ball club went to Fenway Park on the afternoon of September 10 or anticipated catching the game on radio or television, the weight of recent losses needed to be put aside in typical New England fashion.

Acknowledge pain and ignore it to focus on the job at hand—maintain hope, confidence, and enthusiasm in their beloved squad that gave them joy in a year that needed it. Desperately. The February blizzard had been deadly, bringing the metropolitan area to a halt and costing millions of dollars in damage. Boston's heavily Catholic population mourned the passing of Pope Paul VI in early August, succeeded by Pope John Paul I.

By comparison, baseball games are trivial. But that calculus does not account for the very essence of sports—optimism. It balances the accuracy of Henry David Thoreau's observation about the mass of men leading lives of quiet desperation. We need sports as an outlet for our frustrations. The team's success is our success; we live vicariously through strikeouts, home runs, no-hitters, and batting records.

Red Sox fans don't need this analysis because they feel it as part of their everyday existence along with their loyalty to the Bruins, Celtics, and Patriots. But their optimism had been tested in these first three games. The Yankees won the final game 7–4, completing a sweep and vaulting them into a tie for leadership of the American League East.

Ed Figueroa got credit for the victory—which improved his record to 16-9—and Goose Gossage attained his twenty-third save of the year. "We've been playing well since the All-Star break, but we weren't sure the Red Sox would ever have a slump," observed Gossage, who would lead the AL in 1978 with twenty-seven saves. "When we gained six games on them to go from 14 down to 8 down in a week, we felt good, but I can't say I ever thought we'd be in a position like this."[12]

George Scott had been with the Red Sox since 1966, when he placed third in Rookie of the Year voting. He went 0 for 11 in the series and scored a run in the last game after drawing a walk, then going home on Jack Brohamer's double and an error by Chambliss; his blunt appraisal reflected pain and professionalism. "These were the worst four days in my career," said the slugger. "But no one here will quit. I like to think about it this way—that the Yankees were great just for four days, unbelievably great. But I don't want to think in terms that they're hot. Because if I think that way, they can stay hot for the next 20 games."[13]

Twenty-two-year-old rookie Bobby Sprowl started for the Red Sox. One of five pitchers employed by Zimmer throughout the game, Sprowl had joined the team in late August. He began his professional baseball journey in the team's farm system with other teams named Red Sox, going 9-4 for Winter Haven in the Class A Florida League, then playing for two teams in 1978 before joining the parent club. With Bristol in the Double-A Eastern League, Sprowl registered a 9-3 record; Pawtucket benefited from his seven wins against four losses in the Triple-A International League.

Mickey Rivers led off the first inning with a walk, then stole second base, followed by Willie Randolph drawing another walk. Munson grounded into a Burleson–Jerry Remy–Scott double play; Rivers got to third base and scored on Reggie Jackson's single. Sprowl loaded the bases with walks to Piniella and Chambliss, motivating Zimmer to cut the rookie's tenure short and replace him with Bob Stanley. Dismay reigned when Nettles tagged him for a two-RBI single and a 3–0 lead. Scott fielded Roy White's grounder and threw to Burleson for a force out.

The New Yorkers padded the score to 5–0 in the second and added their sixth run in the fourth. Boston responded with two runs in the bottom of the fourth, beginning with Lynn's lead-off walk. Rivers snared Rice's fly ball in center field for the first out, but Figueroa gave up another walk to Yastrzemski. Fisk doubled home Lynn. Yaz reached third base and scored on Garry Hancock's sacrifice fly to right fielder Piniella; Scott ended the inning with a groundout to Nettles.

Lynn's lead-off homer in the bottom of the sixth narrowed the scoring gap to 6–3; the Yankees scored their seventh run in the top of the seventh. In addition to Sprowl and Stanley, Zimmer sent Andy Hassler, Dick Drago, and Bill Lee to the Fenway Park mound. The Yankees had keen eyes against the hurlers, sustaining three strikeouts, smashing eighteen hits, and drawing eight walks. It provided a victory of finesse, not power. There were no home runs. In Figueroa's six innings, he notched three strikeouts while limiting Boston's batsmen to three hits and three walks; Gossage allowed two hits and struck out two.

Winning four games against a first-place team would normally be cause for celebration, but the aura of optimism intensified given the circumstances of New York whittling down Boston's mid-July lead of fourteen games to four by the time the series began. Now the teams found themselves tied in a battle for the AL East flag at 86-56 with twenty games left in the season. Despondency would have to be temporary for the Red Sox, and the same went for the Yankees regarding rejoicing. "Boston hasn't folded," counseled Reggie Jackson, who scored a run and went 2 for 5 with a pair of RBIs. "They've got the best record in baseball. And so do we."[14]

Willie Randolph concurred: "We have to keep a level head and not get too carried away."[15]

Red Sox ace Luis Tiant did not pitch in the series because of Boston's rotation. He had gone the full nine in a 2–0 shutout against the Orioles on September 6, which gave him a 10-7 record so far. Though eager, the right-hander with a corkscrew windup would have to wait until September 11 for his next opportunity. "Luis actually wanted to pitch, but Zim didn't want to use him with three days' rest," confirmed Yastrzemski in his autobiography.[16]

The Red Sox do not merely provide a diversion for New Englanders. They are part of the region's lifeblood. Middle-aged fans in 1978 could share stories about not only the excitement, passion, and ultimate disappointments of 1967 and 1975 but also their childhoods marked by 1946, when the Red Sox led by Ted Williams, Johnny Pesky, and Bobby Doerr faced the Cardinals in the World Series and lost it in seven games.

Another series against the Yankees awaited the boys from Boston.

SEPTEMBER 15

The Yankees went to Detroit following the Boston series and won two of three games against the Tigers. The Red Sox continued their slide with a 1-3 record in the next four games; they split a two-game series against the Orioles and lost two games to the Indians. The losses put them one and a half games behind the Yankees when the teams began a trio of contests at Yankee Stadium. The Brewers had inched up as well. Though still in third place, they were four games out of first place.

But the Yankees maintained their solemnity. Piniella warned, "Sure, they can come back. They're very capable of coming back." Gossage also issued a caveat. "They don't have guys who quit," said the star reliever. "Look at Yastrzemski. They're down seven runs and he's still making those plays in the outfield."[17]

THE BOSTON MASSACRE • 119

But it was Yastrzemski's error when he made a rare appearance playing first base on September 15 that opened the door for a four-run Yankees rally and their 4–0 victory. Rivers and Randolph began the bottom of the fourth with back-to-back singles. Hobson fielded Piniella's grounder and began a double play by throwing to the second baseman, Remy, who completed the two-fer by firing the ball to Yaz, who saw an opportunity for a triple play by nailing Rivers at third base.

Rivers had turned and tried to get back to the base because a sprint for home plate was futile if Hobson caught the first baseman's throw and threw to Fisk. "I had seen Rivers a few seconds before and finally I just threw it," explained Yastrzemski. "But I was off balance. I should have set my feet. After I threw I could see the ball sail."[18]

Hobson dove and missed; Rivers scored. Tiant walked Jackson, and Chambliss homered to raise the score to 3–0. Nettles followed with a solo clout for the fourth run.

SEPTEMBER 16

Boston lost the next game in dramatic fashion. With the score tied 2–2, Rivers led off the bottom of the ninth with a triple; stayed put when Randolph grounded out to Burleson; and scored on Munson's lineout to Jim Rice, who "made the running, falling catch" in right field. Rice had switched from left field before the Yankees came to bat; his first-inning homer—and forty-first of the season—with Remy on base accounted for Boston's pair of runs.[19]

New York's other two tallies came off Reggie Jackson's bat—an RBI single in the bottom of the first and a solo homer in the bottom of the fifth. His game-tying bash happened with a thumb injury thanks to performing a good deed. Jackson waited in the on-deck circle while Munson fouled off a ball that could have hurt some fans. "I rarely ever touch a ball like that because of what could happen," said Jackson. "But the ball was headed for the stands and I saw three or four kids sitting back there, so I just tried to bat it down." His effort resulted in a damaged, though not dislocated right thumb. "The nail was bent back, but the trainer taped it down," revealed the slugger, who proceeded to hit his twenty-third homer of the season.[20]

The 3–2 victory on September 16 pushed the Yankees ahead in the standings with a lead of three and a half games. Ray Fitzgerald communicated an unthinkable finality to the readers of his *Globe* column: "A look around the locker room transmitted only one message: The season is over."[21]

He would change that view within twenty-four hours. Sort of.

SEPTEMBER 17

After the Red Sox won 7–3 on September 17, giving Dennis Eckersley a 17-8 record for the season to date, Fitzgerald explained to his readers how the Red Sox went into the game more lighthearted than in recent days. Their fusillade of hits reminded the Yankees, the press, and themselves of how potent they could be on offense, although the fact remained that they were two and a half games behind the Yankees with two weeks left in the season. "I buried this ball team Saturday," wrote Fitzgerald. "I'm not going to grab a shovel and exhume them simply because they hung on for a win Sunday. But I'll hold off for another day working on a proper epitaph for the tombstone."[22]

Eckersley had an exemplary tenure of six and two-thirds innings. The six-foot-two-inch right-hander allowed three hits, two walks, and a run while striking out four batters; Bob Stanley finished the game. George Scott's RBI double broke a 0-for-36 fever; Boston's first baseman hadn't added a hit to his stats since September 2.

New York's first run occurred in the bottom of the seventh when Chambliss singled, moved to second base on Roy White's walk, and scored on Gary Thomasson's single. In the bottom of the eighth, the home team scored two unearned runs.

As the Yankees battled the Red Sox for AL East supremacy, there was another Boston-area icon getting notice from millions of Americans that September. *The Paper Chase* premiered on CBS on September 9. John Jay Osborn Jr. had penned the same-named 1971 novel based on his experiences as a student at Harvard Law School. A 1973 movie version had starred John Houseman in an Oscar-winning performance as the feared but respected contracts professor Charles Kingsfield; Houseman reprised his role for the TV show.

Kingsfield's aura creates anxiety familiar to anyone who has been to law school, where contracts traditionally is the most difficult course during the first year. Dissecting the nuances of bailments, conditions, offers, acceptances, intent, consideration, and breaches can cause law students to wake up in a cold sweat with hearts racing on the days they have contracts class. Houseman brought the character to life, resplendent with intimidation, authority, and knowledge.

But there's an underlying purpose to the Socratic method in law schools, requiring students to recite the facts of cases in the assignments and analyze the legal principles used in the judges' decisions. Kingsfield orates, "You teach yourselves the law. But I train your minds. You come in here with a skullful of mush and if you survive, you'll leave thinking like a lawyer."[23]

The venerable actor—who had collaborated with Orson Welles during the 1930s in the Federal Theatre Project of the Works Progress Administration and Welles's radio program *The Mercury Theatre on the Air*—further explained the character's demeanor of pressure in the classroom. "He acts imperiously and cruelly," stated Houseman. "He's a great teacher. One of the ways he teaches is by being tough on his students. He's aware of the effect he has. He does it purposely. Like many teachers of his generation, he enjoys the myth he's created."[24]

The Paper Chase was a quality show requiring attention, discipline, and patience, especially from those who didn't understand the legal terminology. CBS used it to counterprogram ABC, which had the dominance of *Happy Days* and *Laverne & Shirley* on Tuesday nights. Those two shows, set in the same fictional universe of late 1950s Milwaukee, attracted an enormous audience of Americans looking to escape from present-day chaos in the headlines to what they considered a simpler, slower era.

Happy Days and *Laverne & Shirley* were powerhouses in the Nielsen ratings for ABC. To use a baseball analogy, they were the prime-time equivalents of Babe Ruth and Lou Gehrig. Or Willie Mays and Willie McCovey. Or Hank Aaron and Eddie Mathews. Or Sandy Koufax and Don Drysdale. CBS's other network competition in the 8:00 to 9:00 p.m. time slot (7:00 to 8:00 p.m. Central) was NBC's comedy-drama *Grandpa Goes to Washington*, starring Jack Albertson as a new U.S. senator in his midsixties.

The buzz around *The Paper Chase* praised its quality, due in part to the multidimensional characters, but a theory about TV stipulates that a diamond may shine too brightly for a prime-time audience. Houseman disclosed, "I'm laughing because everyone has been saying our show is 'too good' to last on television. I don't know what that means. If it's true, that's sad. I don't think those who watch 'Laverne and Shirley' will switch, but I think there are viewers who avoid 'Laverne and Shirley' like the plague."[25]

The Paper Chase lasted twenty-two episodes on CBS. It later aired thirty-seven episodes across three seasons on the cable network Showtime from 1983 to 1986.

Other rookie shows in prime time included the sitcoms *WKRP in Cincinnati*, *Taxi*, and *Mork & Mindy*, starring Robin Williams as the alien he played in a February episode of *Happy Days*. WKRP focused on an AM rock-and-roll station with an eccentric group of characters, among them a fast-talking sales manager named Herb Tarlek, whose loud sport coats are his signature; beautiful blonde receptionist Jennifer Marlowe, whose intellect and people skills match her beauty; and morning drive-time disc jockey Dr. Johnny Fever, whose on-air moniker is just the latest in a series for this once great DJ.

Created by former advertising executive Hugh Wilson, WKRP had touches of authenticity in its portrayal of a radio station. Dayton TV columnist P. J. Bednarski talked to people in local radio and noted, "Those disc jockeys who wander from station to station, like WKRP's Johnny Fever, reflect a real way of life for a radio personality, for whom cities become bus stops."[26]

Readers of the *Cincinnati Enquirer* curious about this cultural depiction of their city found some insight about Johnny Fever from his portrayer, Howard Hesseman. "It wasn't so much specific things I'm lifting but more a spirit or a pummeled version, a general style," said the actor, whose previous TV credits had included guest spots on *Sanford and Son*, *Rhoda*, *Mannix*, *Harry O*, *The Rockford Files*, and *The Bob Newhart Show*. "I think of Johnny as pretty laid back, like he's been burned and is hiding out, like he's withdrawn and inside walls."[27]

WKRP used Cincinnati references in dialogue plus items in the set dressing to reinforce the setting, for example, a pennant for Xavier University in the station's "bullpen" where the staff work. "They go very lightly on those references because they don't want it to be too localized," explained Hesseman.[28]

Produced by Mary Tyler Moore's production company—MTM Enterprises—WKRP had solid reviews. In the *Dayton Daily News*, Tom Hopkins wrote, "If you have the courage to watch the pilot episode tonight, you may wind up in the hospital with a severely tickled funny bone."[29]

The *Miami Herald* TV and radio editor Jack E. Anderson concurred: "It has mustered an ensemble of relatively new but cracking good players and the writing is laugh-loaded."[30]

Putting WKRP in the same category as lofty TV comedies of the 1970s, *Chicago Tribune* scribe Gary Deeb posited, "Under the loving care of producer Wilson, 'WKRP' seems pointed toward the same literate, occasionally elegant comedy that characterizes 'M*A*S*H,' 'Barney Miller,' and the old 'MTM' show. Rather than glorify stupidity and antisocial conduct, 'WKRP' gently spoofs the human condition."[31]

Baltimore TV critic Bill Carter was pointed in his appraisal: "This show is the bright shining star of the new TV season; if the American TV public doesn't take a shine to it, they deserve all the kiddie-porn, jiggle-junk and dumb-numbers that the networks dish up for them."[32]

Some actors reprised their roles and others made guest appearances when a sequel series aired for two years in first-run syndication in the early 1990s—*The New WKRP in Cincinnati*.

Mork & Mindy gave more ballast to the success of Garry Marshall, the producer and showrunner responsible for *Happy Days* and *Laverne & Shirley*. Aaron Spelling, ABC's other powerful producer, added *Vega$* to his portfolio of hits, which included *The Love Boat*, *Fantasy Island*, and *Charlie's Angels*. Robert Urich starred in *Vega$* as Dan Tanna, a private investigator who drove a red 1957 Thunderbird and also worked as a security consultant for the Desert Inn.

Taxi, created by the foursome of James L. Brooks, Stan Daniels, David Davis, and Ed. Weinberger, revolved around the staff of the fictional Sunshine Cab Company in Manhattan. These television veterans had fantastic pedigrees in comedy—all were alumni of *The Mary Tyler Moore Show*, which Brooks had co-created with Allan Burns. *Taxi* also benefited from its lineup placement, the fourth sitcom in a two-hour block led by *Happy Days*, *Laverne & Shirley*, and *Three's Company*.

WKRP, *Mork & Mindy*, and *Vega$* aired for four seasons. *Taxi* had five seasons—four on ABC and a fifth when NBC made a rare move in network TV by buying a show that another network had canceled. Tony Danza played cab driver Tony Banta, often wearing a Yankees jacket with the intertwined "NY" logo on the chest. Yankees fans were undoubtedly pleased. Whether they'd see that logo in the playoffs remained a question—the Red Sox were a game behind with one game left in the season for both teams as they went to bed on September 30.

The Yankees were 99-62. The Red Sox were 98-63.

If the Yankees won their game against the Indians, the pennant belonged to them no matter what happened with Boston's game against the Toronto Blue Jays.

If both teams lost, the Yankees would get the pennant.

If the Red Sox won and the Yankees lost, then the teams would be tied for first place, forcing a one-game playoff to determine the 1978 American League East champions.

On the Senior Circuit, Phillies manager Danny Ozark led his team to the NL East pennant for the third time in a row. The Dodgers repeated as NL West champs with their second flag under Tommy Lasorda. Davey Lopes, noting the team's lack of success at the beginning of the season, pointed out the value of resilience for the ball club. "They said the Dodgers weren't capable of repeating after we didn't get off to the kind of start we had last year," recounted the team captain. "They said we were not a good second half ballclub, that we'd fold under the pressure. Well, I think we proved a lot of people wrong."[33]

Besides these iconic rivalries, September held uplifting triumphs and demoralizing tragedies in baseball. Angels outfielder Lyman Bostock was shot and killed in Gary, Indiana, while riding in a car with a woman whose estranged husband thought they were having an affair. The shooter pulled up alongside and attempted to shoot the woman but hit Bostock in the head; she had pellet wounds.

In federal court, sportswriter Melissa Ludtke won her lawsuit against MLB commissioner Bowie Kuhn, AL president Leland MacPhail, and the New York Yankees for having denied her the same access to locker rooms as her male counterparts.

Jim Bouton concluded his comeback with the Atlanta Braves at the age of thirty-nine with a 1-3 record after last playing in the Major Leagues in 1970, Ron Guidry ended the season at 25-3, and the Kansas City Royals won the AL West for the third consecutive season.

Americans interested in world affairs noted the passing of Pope John Paul I, who died after only thirty-three days as Catholicism's leader, plus the Camp

David Accords bringing Egypt, Israel, and the United States together for a step forward in the Middle East peace process. There was a better chance of lasting peace in the Middle East than Red Sox fans smiling at the prospect of seeing their team play the Yankees again.

10

THE WORLD SERIES

OCTOBER

On October 1 the Indians thrashed the Yankees at Yankee Stadium, 9–2. Cleveland southpaw Rick Waits allowed five hits, complemented by a thirteen-hit barrage for the Tribe. With the score tied 2–2 after one inning, the visitors scored four times in the top of the second, starting with Gary Alexander's lead-off homer off Catfish Hunter. Dan Briggs—whose playing time in '78 amounted to fourteen other games—walked but got forced out by Duane Kuiper's ground ball to first baseman Chris Chambliss, who fired to shortstop Bucky Dent, covering second base. Kuiper took second when Hunter threw a wild pitch. After Tom Veryzer grounded out to Graig Nettles at third, Rick Manning's single scored Kuiper and padded Cleveland's lead to 4–2.

Yankees manager Bob Lemon replaced Hunter with Dick Tidrow. It didn't help. Jim Norris's double put Manning on third base and Buddy Bell's single scored them. In the top of the fourth inning, the Indians got their seventh run when Manning doubled home Veryzer, who had singled.

Dave Rajsich became the third of five hurlers in the game for the Yankees when Tidrow had two outs with two Indians on base from a double and a walk in the top of the seventh. Designated hitter Wayne Cage walked to load the bases, but Rajsich thwarted a rally by striking out Alexander.

The Indians got their last two runs in the top of the ninth. Larry McCall took over pitching duties for the home team and got nicked by Norris's single and Bell's walk. Andre Thornton's grounder to Dent resulted in a double play, but Norris got to third and scored when Cage doubled. Alexander's double scored Cage. Paul Lindblad came into the game and retired Briggs on a fly ball to Mickey Rivers in center field for the third out.

Cleveland's offense gave a bravura performance. Manning went 3 for 5, scored twice, and knocked in two runs. Norris also had three hits and scored twice. Cage had an RBI while Bell, Thornton, and Alexander each sent two Indians across home plate.

The Red Sox won their last game of the '78 regular season thanks to Luis Tiant pitching a two-hitter in a 5–0 victory over Toronto. At least one Boston player had confidence overflowing like a pond after a thunderstorm. "There was no question we'd win," said George Scott. "I say that for one reason. In a big game, no matter what anyone wants to tell you, Luis Tiant is the greatest pitcher I've ever seen. He'll be doing this when he's 90."[1]

Both teams tied for the season, forcing a one-game playoff at Fenway Park for the AL East title. Mike Torrez started for the Red Sox; he sported a 16-12 record and insider knowledge regarding the opposition, as he had spent most of the 1977 season with the Yankees. Lemon put Guidry on the hill. In the West, Gaylord Perry reached his 3,000th strikeout in a 4–3 win for the Padres over the Dodgers, but the drama taking place at Fenway Park dominated the attention of baseball fans.

It seemed like a Hollywood ending would be scripted for Boston. Carl Yastrzemski, a beloved veteran with eighteen years in a Red Sox uniform, bashed a lead-off homer in the bottom of the second. Torrez protected his 1–0 lead through the top of the sixth inning. Boston scored again in the bottom of the sixth when Rick Burleson hit a lead-off double, went to third base on Jerry Remy's sacrifice bunt, and crossed home plate on Jim Rice's single.

New York scored four runs in the top of the seventh; a home run by Bucky Dent accounted for three. After Torrez retired Nettles on a fly ball to Jim Rice in right field, Chris Chambliss and Roy White banged consecutive singles. Jim Spencer pinch-hit for Brian Doyle and flied out to left fielder Yastrzemski. Then Bucky Dent became the focal point of baseball when he smashed a ball over the Green Monster to put the Yankees up 3–2.

Torrez walked Mickey Rivers, prompting Zimmer to send Bob Stanley to the mound. Rivers stole second base, then scored when Thurman Munson doubled. Lou Piniella flied to Rice for the third out. Reggie Jackson hit a solo homer off Andy Hassler to begin the top of the eighth and give the visitors a 5–2 lead.

The Red Sox weren't done yet. They battled back in the bottom of the eighth. Remy led off with a double. Right fielder Piniella caught Rice's fly ball, but Yastrzemski got a base hit to score Remy, went to second base on Carlton Fisk's single, and scored on Fred Lynn's single to make the score 5–4. Hobson's fly ball to Piniella in right field and Scott's strikeout prevented the home team from going further. The Yankees failed to score in the top of the ninth.

Boston showed signs of a comeback in the bottom of the ninth. Burleson walked with one out and advanced to second when Remy singled. Rice flied out to Piniella for the second out; Red Sox fans all over New England and especially those in the ballpark heightened their hopes when Carl Yastrzemski took his place in the batter's box. Unfortunately, he connected for a foul pop-up that Nettles snared to give New York the division title. Final score: 5–4.

Yankees owner George Steinbrenner belied his boastful, arrogant persona when he visited the Red Sox locker room and highlighted the honorable battle between the rivals. "It's a shame that this is not the World Series, that our series is not seven games and when we're finished with each other that the season then isn't over," said Steinbrenner. "We are the two best teams in baseball. We said that on the field today. We won, but you didn't lose."[2]

The Yankees beat the Royals in the best-of-five AL championship series for the third straight year. It took four games. Los Angeles also needed four games against Cincinnati in the NLCS to secure the NL flag, but it was a bittersweet time for their fans. Dodgers coach Jim "Junior" Gilliam died of cardiac arrest at the age of forty-nine on October 8. He had been in a coma since mid-September after surgery for a brain hemorrhage.[3]

The Dodgers had employed Gilliam since 1953, when he replaced Jackie Robinson as the team's second baseman. In 1965 Gilliam became a player-coach and stayed with his coaching duties when he retired from ballplaying a year later. His imprint on the ball club went beyond teaching mechanics, giving his death a terrible weight as the Dodgers marched toward the World Series to avenge their '77 loss. "I had an almost spiritual feeling for Gilliam," said Dusty Baker. "I had problems on and off the field this year, and Gilliam was right there, helping." Dodgers manager Tommy Lasorda explained the team's view on losing a cornerstone of the franchise dating back to its final years playing in Ebbets Field: "We dedicated the playoffs to a great man, a great human being and we're dedicating the Fall Classic to him."[4]

GAME ONE, OCTOBER 10

It was déjà vu all over again.

Yogi Berra's statement rang true as the Yankees and Dodgers took the field at Dodger Stadium for Game One, which ended in an 11–5 victory for the home team. They had squared off in the 1977 World Series, which culminated in storybook fashion when Reggie Jackson bashed three home runs in Game Six to give New York its first championship since 1962.

The teams' tremendous World Series rivalry spanned more than twenty years, with Series face-offs in 1941, 1947, 1949, 1952, 1953, 1955, 1956, 1963, and 1977. In the Fall Classic encounters of 1977 and 1978, one couldn't help but think of a competition reborn. Tales abounded regarding Jackie Robinson, Pee Wee Reese, Mickey Mantle, Yogi Berra, Don Drysdale, Sandy Koufax, and Whitey Ford. Don Larsen's perfect game, Robinson stealing home, and the Dodgers' 1955 World Series title—the only one in Brooklyn—were talking points that proved baseball is a game handed down from generation to generation.

Octogenarians who had seen the Dodgers in the 1916 and 1920 World Series could further mine the well of nostalgia by talking about the leadership of Wilbert Robinson, the batting of Zack Wheat, and the pitching of Burleigh Grimes. A discussion of Indians shortstop Bill Wambsganss's unassisted triple play in the 1920 showdown would undoubtedly arise.

Tommy John took the mound at Dodger Stadium to begin Game One, a welcome sight for fans of the home team. The Dodgers' offense gave John—who had a 17-10 record during the season—a 3–0 lead in the bottom of the second sparked by Dusty Baker's lead-off homer. Rick Monday doubled off Yankees starter Ed Figueroa, who was 20-9 in the season. Lee Lacy followed with a walk, but Steve Yeager's ground ball to Dent resulted in a double play. Monday advanced to third base; Davey Lopes smacked a home run. Ken Clay relieved Figueroa and retired Bill Russell on a pop fly to Dent.

Los Angeles put up three more runs in the fourth inning when Lopes hit another homer, this time with two runners on base. "Sinker ball and slider pitcher," said Lopes, who hit seventeen round-trippers in the '78 season. "I moved up half a step in the batter's box. He threw me a sinker, and I timed it just as it was starting to go down. Nine times out of 10, I'd pop it up, but the way I'm going now . . . it's like I said. I'll hit anything."[5]

The score became 7–0 an inning later. Ron Cey hit a lead-off single off Clay, went to third on Baker's single, and scored when Clay threw a wild pitch.

New York responded with three runs in the top of the seventh. Reggie Jackson's lead-off clout provided the first score, and Dent's RBI single accounted for Piniella and Chambliss crossing the plate.

The Dodgers added another trio of runs for a 10–3 lead in the bottom of the seventh. Pinch-hitting for Monday, Bill North hit a two-RBI double and scored when Lacy singled. The Yankees reduced LA's lead to 10–5 in their half of the eighth. Terry Forster relieved John with two outs and remained for the rest of the game; LA tallied another run in the bottom of the eighth when Russell led off with a double and Reggie Smith singled him home.

Figueroa disputed the home plate umpire's decisions after the game: "The umpire was calling an awfully small strike zone on me. He was calling my low fastballs too low. In the American League they would be strikes."[6]

Lopes acknowledged a higher power, pointing to "Jim Gilliam's spirit" affecting the Dodgers. "He's with each ballplayer out there. If they look out there, they'll see Jim Gilliam."[7] Regarding his two-homer night, Lopes brimmed with optimism about LA's chance to avenge the 1977 World Series loss and give Southern California its first World Series title since 1965. "I've never been more relaxed in my life than I was tonight," said the LA second baseman. "Why? Because I have extreme confidence that we are the best team until the Yankees prove different. No doubt in my mind we're going to win."[8]

GAME TWO, OCTOBER 11

A classic scenario.

Bottom of the ninth. Trailing 4–3. Two out. Two runners on base. One of the greatest sluggers in baseball at the plate.

"I just went in and figured the best pitch I had was the fastball so I let it go," said twenty-one-year-old rookie right-hander Bob Welch of striking out Reggie Jackson.[9] The Dodgers notched their second win in the 1978 World Series.

Jackson's fury erupted. "As he neared the Yankee dugout, he flung the bat and stormed down the steps," wrote Henry Hecht in the *New York Post*. "That was when Bob Lemon tried to calm him down. Reggie, according to witnesses, shoved Lemon. Lemon backs down from no one. He shoved Jackson."[10]

Although Jackson had led the AL in strikeouts four times and the Major Leagues twice, he also owned four World Series rings, two American League home run titles, an AL RBI title, and three AL slugging percentage titles. The slugger had been responsible for the first two Yankees runs when he doubled home Roy White and Thurman Munson in the top of the third. White had hit a one-out single and stolen second base; Munson walked. Los Angeles got a run in the bottom of the fourth thanks to an RBI single by Ron Cey, who also homered in the bottom of the sixth with two men on base to make the score 4–2.

In the top of the seventh, White scored again for the visitors. He had gotten on base with a lead-off single and went to third on Paul Blair's double. After Munson struck out, White crossed the plate on Jackson's grounder to second baseman Lopes. "We've got the spirit of Gilliam with us," said Cey, LA's stalwart third baseman. "We want to win it all. We played our best baseball down the stretch. We've got a lot going for us, including momentum."[11]

Catfish Hunter pitched six innings for the Yankees; Goose Gossage threw two innings in relief. Burt Hooton started for the Dodgers. He lasted six innings, gave up eight hits, and struck out five. Terry Forster tossed two and a third innings, followed by Welch's exploits. Hunter, Gossage, and Hooton had World Series experience, but Welch's lack of it, combined with his young age, did not matter. Lopes used the moniker "Iceman" for Welch. "There's something about the guy that's hard to explain," said Lopes. "When he was out there I know he didn't hear the hollering. He's cold out there on the mound. I can't really explain it. He does things at his age a lot of guys never do."[12]

Junior Gilliam's death and winning the first two games at home created a sense of inevitability for the National League champs. Since moving to Los Angeles in 1958, the Dodgers represented the NL in the World Series six times: victorious in 1959, 1963, and 1965, but defeated by the Orioles in 1966, the A's in 1974, and the Yankees in 1977.

The Dodgers had a strong offense against the 1978 Yankees. Davey Lopes was third in the National League for stolen bases, with forty-five. Steve Garvey ranked third in total bases, second in batting average, and ninth in slugging percentage for the Senior Circuit. Reggie Smith's prowess at the plate earned him second place in slugging percentage. Regarding RBIS, Los Angeles had three players in the top ten: Garvey, Smith, and Cey.

Being down 2–0 was not a cause for Yankees fans to panic. Going back to their home field would be a boon against the powerful swaths of LA's batsmen. "The Dodgers have more right-handed power than most teams," said Lou Piniella. "Balls they are hitting out to left center are pop shots in Yankee Stadium." Plus, the Yankees infield would be better suited for defense. Graig Nettles observed, "The two dives on that cement infield took everything out of me. I felt like I had been hit by a truck. That's what they should do with that infield, run a truck over it. That freeway doesn't even have a number on it."[13]

GAME THREE, OCTOBER 13

Rituals define mornings.

The suburbs of New York City are awash with homes inspired by William J. Levitt, who after World War II pioneered the building of neighborhoods with houses that all have the same floor plan. A typical dawn might have the patriarch in one of these abodes rising an hour before his clan to enjoy the quiet and anticipate the energy of the day. He makes himself his usual breakfast—scrambled eggs, lightly buttered pumpernickel toast, and a cup of Sanka—while he listens to WINS-AM for news updates. His wife soon awakes to make breakfast for the kids.

The youngest, a junior high school student, might have set his GE clock radio alarm so he wakes up to the comedic antics of disc jockey Jay Thomas and the latest hit records on 98.7 FM, WXLO, otherwise known as 99X. Disco music is in heavy rotation. His sister, a high school senior with good but not great grades and an SAT score barely above 1100 has begun to consider college applications; SUNY-Albany, Maryland, Delaware, and Rutgers are the most probable, with her "reach" schools being GW, Emory, and Northwestern. Her morning routine includes reading the early edition newspaper for her AP history class, where they try to put current events in a historical context. She then learns the story that shocks the music world. Punk rock star Sid Vicious of the Sex Pistols has been arrested for the murder of his girlfriend, Nancy Laura Spungen. It happened in a stabbing at the Chelsea Hotel, where the couple resided. He was released on $50,000 bail.

This fictional construct is a composite of thousands of families across the tri-state area of New York, Connecticut, and New Jersey. But if they rooted for the Yankees, then a discussion of the World Series would be added to the morning ritual, along with a mention that everyone should avoid black cats, broken mirrors, and walking under ladders because of the date—Friday the Thirteenth.

With Ron Guidry on the mound at Yankee Stadium, New York had an excellent chance to absolve themselves of the two-game deficit. Don Sutton started for LA and claimed that Lasorda referred to him as a "sacrificial lamb" against the lanky lefty who had won twenty-five games and lost three during the season. Although the Dodgers skipper presumably said it as a joke, Guidry's dominance in '78 was as evident as the Empire State Building in the Manhattan skyline on a cloudless night.

Still, Sutton brought considerable skill to the mound. A Dodger since his rookie season of 1966, he had compiled a record of more than two hundred wins. In 1978 he went 15-11 and tied with Gaylord Perry for ninth place in strikeouts in the National League. His self-appraisal offered evidence of humility: "I may not be the best pitcher in baseball but I think I give a creditable performance every time out."[14]

Roy White slammed a solo homer in the bottom of the first to put the Yankees up 1–0 in Game Three. Graig Nettles scored in the bottom of the second after hitting a lead-off single, advancing to second base after Chris Chambliss drew a walk, and he went to third after Brian Doyle's grounder to shortstop Bill Russell forced out Chambliss at second base. Bucky Dent's ground ball to Ron Cey forced out Doyle, allowing Nettles to score.

Los Angeles drove in one run in the top of the third, and the score stayed 2–1 through the top of the seventh. The Yankees added three runs in their half of the inning. Dent singled and Rivers got on base with a bunt; Lemon sent Blair to be a pinch runner for Rivers. White grounded to Russell, which forced out Blair, but Dent went to third base and scored on Munson's single. White got to second base, then scored when Jackson singled off relief pitcher Lance Rautzhan. Munson went to third base; Piniella's ground ball to Russell resulted in the second out and scored the Yankees catcher. Rautzhan retired Nettles on a fly ball to Bill North in center field.

The Yankees won 5–1. But the defensive play of Yankees third baseman Graig Nettles proved to be a key factor in the victory as much as—if not more than—the offense. "It was one of the greatest exhibitions by a third baseman that I've ever seen," admitted Lasorda. "It's difficult to determine how many runs he cost us but he was definitely the difference."[15] Los Angeles sportswriter Melvin Durslag testified that Nettles's prowess cost the Dodgers and "created a debate among viewers over whether he saved five runs for New York, or six."[16]

Sports Illustrated's Ron Fimrite calculated, "Nettles robbed Los Angeles of at least five hits and perhaps as many as seven extra bases and seven runs."[17] It was a depressing night for those who donned Dodger blue, whether on the field, in the stands, or at home. Comparisons to Brooks Robinson's outstanding performance in the 1970 World Series abounded, per the tendency of sports observers to compare and contrast players.

Rick Monday offered a bit of exaggeration in his assessment of Nettles during the evening's activities at Yankee Stadium, but the 56,447 in attendance might have felt the same way about the Yankees third baseman being an unstoppable force on defense. "There's no way to beat him," said Monday. "We could handcuff his right arm to his left leg and his left arm to his right leg, put a ball and chain around his neck and a blindfold around his eyes, and he would still make the play."[18]

Nettles was a godsend for Guidry, who threw a complete game with 137 pitches. The Dodgers walked seven times against the lefty, who allowed seven hits and struck out four batters. According to the man nicknamed "Louisiana Lightning," he didn't have his best stuff from the first pitch onward. Munson told him so.[19]

Sutton lasted six and a third innings. Rautzhan and Charlie Hough pitched in relief.

GAME FOUR, OCTOBER 14

The Yankees won Game Four. It took ten innings marked by a forty-minute rain delay, a rebound from being down 3–0, and high drama involving Reggie Jackson's base running.

Tommy John took his turn in the Dodgers' rotation and got tagged for six hits across seven innings. Neither team scored a run for the first four innings;

Los Angeles scored three runs on Reggie Smith going yard in the top of the fifth, with Yeager and Lopes having gotten on base through a double and a walk.

New York scored a pair of runs in the bottom of the sixth. John struck out Paul Blair to start the inning, then gave up a single to White, a walk to Munson, and a single to Jackson, thereby scoring White. The next play set off the temper of Tommy Lasorda. Piniella hit a liner that Russell dropped, then recovered to step on second base for a force out and throw to Garvey for a double play. But the ball hit Jackson's hip and veered to right field, allowing Munson to score. Or did Jackson purposely extend his hip to interfere with the ball? Henry Hecht reported, "He did move his hip about six inches as the throw approached him, if you watched the TV replay."[20]

Lasorda became the human equivalent of Mount Vesuvius, exploding with rage about Jackson staying—freezing, actually—in the middle of the base path and interfering with the ball's flight. The umpires tried to calm him down; he didn't. Jackson offered an explanation that underscored his lack of intent. "When Lou hit the ball, it looked like a hit," said the man who wore No. 44 for the Yankees. "My instinct was to break for second. Then when I saw Russell had a chance for it, my instinct was to go back to first. Then I saw Russell drop the ball. I had nowhere to go, so I just froze."[21]

Garvey had a terrific vantage point at first base. He did not buy Jackson's argument that the action—or lack thereof—just happened. "There is no doubt in my mind it was intentional," said the Dodgers first baseman. "The throw was headed right at him. Instinct tells you to get out of the way of a ball coming right at you. He moved his leg just enough to deflect the ball. He knew what he was doing. It was quick thinking, but dirty pool."[22]

According to *Sports Illustrated*, Jackson confessed "that his freezing near first was more a matter of convenience than confusion."[23]

Adding to the controversy was the question of whether Russell intentionally dropped the ball. Lasorda denied that to be the case. "It happened too fast for him to think about dropping it," said the Dodgers' manager. Second base umpire Joe Brinkman concurred. Lasorda theorized that the umpire's call meant any runner could do the same thing: "stop and stand directly in the way of the first baseman." He also argued that the Dodgers would have won the game because Munson wouldn't have scored if the umpires had called Jackson out. Baker and Monday disagreed. "After that play, we were still ahead," said Baker. "We just messed it up, we did a lot of stuff wrong."[24]

The Yankees tied the score at 3–3 in the bottom of the eighth. John left the game after Paul Blair led off with a single; Forster replaced him, but the reliever lasted about as long as a first-time comedian doing a stand-up routine on *The Tonight Show*. White sacrificed the runner to second with a bunt, and Blair scored when Munson bashed a double. Goodbye, Forster. Hello, Welch.

In the bottom of the tenth, White scored the winning run. He had drawn a one-out walk off Welch, advanced to second base on Jackson's single, and sprinted home when Piniella singled.

Ed Figueroa started for the Yankees, giving up four hits and Smith's homer in his five-inning tenure. Dick Tidrow took over for three innings; Gossage began the top of the ninth and got credit for the victory.

GAME FIVE, OCTOBER 15

The Yankees offense was potent in Game Five. The Dodgers offense, not so much.

Known historically for power because of Babe Ruth, Lou Gehrig, Mickey Mantle, and, more recently, Reggie Jackson, the Yankees pecked at LA's pitching with eighteen hits. Sixteen were singles. Munson and Dent both doubled; they were the only Yankees to get extra base hits.

LA's lads jumped to a 1–0 lead in the top of the first for this game that started at 4:30 p.m. Davey Lopes got a base hit off Jim Beattie to start the game and stole second base. Russell flied out, but Smith singled home Lopes, who scored again in the third to put the Dodgers up 2–0 after hitting a one-out single and going home on Russell's double. No Dodger crossed the plate for the rest of the game.

The Yankees pounded Burt Hooton in the bottom half of the inning for four runs. Hooton started by walking Dent, followed by Rivers singling his teammate to second base; Roy White knocked him in with another single, which sent Rivers to second base.

Rivers and White committed a double steal, and both scored when Munson hit the third single of the half inning. He went to third base because of an error by right fielder Smith and scored the fourth Yankee run after Jackson's strikeout and Piniella's single. Lasorda called the bullpen for Rautzhan, who prevented further hemorrhaging by getting Nettles to ground into a double play.

New York added three runs an inning later to amplify the lead to 7–2. Jim Spencer grounded to Garvey for the first out, but Doyle and Dent hit back-to-back singles. Dent's was "a hard ground ball, one hard hop right at Russell." But it "bounced off" the Dodgers shortstop.[25]

Dodgers left fielder Baker threw to third base, but not in time to get Doyle, while Dent got to second base.

Rivers sent Doyle home with a single, which allowed Dent to advance to third base. White's grounder—like Spencer, he hit it to Garvey—resulted in a put-out, but there was a bonus. Usually a stellar fielder, Garvey "bobbled the ball for a split second, stepped on first for the out and then threw wildly home, the third Dodger error."[26] What could have been a double play gave Dent an opportunity to score the Yankees' sixth run of the game. Rivers went to third base because of Garvey's error.

Hough relieved Rautzhan. Rivers scored on Munson's single off the reliever. Jackson drew a walk, but Piniella's flyout to North in center field ended the inning.

In the bottom of the seventh, the Yankees scored four more times; they did so once again in the bottom of the eighth for a final score of 12–2. A dozen to a deuce. Beattie had stifled the Dodgers' offense. Although the right-hander allowed nine hits, he also notched eight strikeouts and limited the opposition to four walks in his complete-game performance. Steve Garvey opined, "The kid can pitch. He wasn't as overpowering as we'd heard but he kept making good pitches. We had him on the ropes, but we never could put him away. He made great pitches on me both times I struck out."[27]

New York Post sportswriter Paul Zimmerman partly blamed Russell's fielding for the loss that gave the Yankees a 3–2 lead in games and sent the teams back to Los Angeles. There was "no play on a single that went through him and could have gotten the Dodgers out of the three-run fourth," stated Zimmerman.[28] Russell said, "I'm not gonna make excuses, I missed the first one but the others were tough plays," he said. "I'm only human. I'm not a golden glove by any means."[29]

Dodgers catcher Steve Yeager addressed the weather before offering his blunt conclusion: "It's tough to play in this kind of weather. Your hands are cold and it's hard to hold on to the ball. It's slippery; it just pops out of your hand sometimes. Happened to me a couple of times today. But the weather's not what beat us. We just got our butt kicked."[30]

Everything came together for the Bronx Bombers. Munson had three hits in five at bats, knocked in five runs, and scored once. White contributed two hits, three RBIS, and two runs scored. Doyle and Dent each tallied three hits and scored twice. After three losses to the Yankees, Russell summarized the despondency: "We had all the confidence in the world when we came here. They just tore everything down."[31]

The teams went to Los Angeles for the conclusion of the Series.

GAME SIX, OCTOBER 17

New York may be a terrific sports venue for natives, but it's not for everyone, particularly those who hail from a region defined by sunshine, celebrities, and glamour. When the Dodgers boarded the team plane to make their egress from the Big Apple and head to Southern California, nobody seemed happier than Dodgers shortstop Bill Russell: "The press, the people, the fans, everything about New York makes me sick. We haven't played well defensively in this Series, that's no secret, but I don't see any reason for being crucified."[32]

Two teams from the two biggest markets, with rich, glorious histories stretching back several decades, including legendary World Series moments, created a high-intensity spotlight for Game Six. Los Angeles needed to win and force a seventh game, igniting the prevalence of the word "pressure" to describe the mission. Veteran hurler Don Sutton put the moment in perspective, lest anyone think that whatever team wins the World Series has any real impact on the fans' day-to-day lives. "Pressure is trying to feed nine kids on one small paycheck," said Sutton. "That's pressure. I don't have any pressure on me. No one is going to shoot me at sunrise if I don't get anybody out."[33]

The Yankees repeated as World Series champions without the benefit of two stalwarts who were injured—second baseman Willie Randolph and relief pitcher Sparky Lyle. Doyle substituted for Randolph, flourishing with stellar fielding and a 7-for-16 output at the plate. In Game Six he went 3 for 4, scored twice, and knocked in two runs. "I don't think anyone expects little guys like me in the bottom of the batting order (he hit eighth) to hit much so the RBI's are a bonus," said Doyle.[34] Bucky Dent had a great game as well: 3 for 4 with three RBIS.

Lopes banged a lead-off homer off Catfish Hunter in the bottom of the first to put the Dodgers up 1–0. The Yankees scored three runs in the top of the second. Nettles singled with one out and Spencer walked, followed by Brian Doyle doubling home Nettles and Dent's single scoring Spencer and Doyle.

LA reduced the Yankees' lead to 3–2 in the bottom of the third. Joe Ferguson led off with a double and advanced to third on Vic Davalillo's sacrifice bunt fielded by first baseman Spencer, who then flipped to Hunter. Lopes's single scored Ferguson. The Yankees made the score 5–2 with a pair of runs in the bottom of the sixth and enhanced the lead with Jackson's two-run homer in the bottom of the seventh.

The final score of 7–2 cemented the Yankees as champions for the second year in a row. Bucky Dent was voted MVP of the World Series. He played in all six games, notched seven RBIS, and batted .417 (10 for 24). Brian Doyle scored four times and batted .438 (7 for 16). Thurman Munson had seven RBIs and five runs scored. Lou Piniella knocked in four runs. Reggie Jackson, eight.

Dent underscored an intangible asset as the reason for the Yankees chugging along like the Little Engine That Could. "We've got some big hearts on this team," said the Yankees shortstop. "People say we're the best team money can buy but you don't buy their hearts, you don't buy what's inside of them."[35]

The Dodgers showed true sportsmanship by acknowledging their opposition's excellence.

Rick Monday: "They deserved to win."

Ron Cey: "They are a super team, one of the best I've ever seen."

Davey Lopes: "There's nothing wrong if you do your best and get beat by a better team and that's what happened."[36]

Lemon credited the team that he had begun managing in the middle of the season. "They're the world champions, and I rose [on] their coattails," he said. "They won it last year, and they took me along with them this year."[37] Figueroa believed otherwise. "We are here today only because of that man," said the pitcher, who went 20-9 in 1978.[38]

Seeing the Yankees and Dodgers compete again in the World Series offered nostalgia for those who recalled the epic battles in the Fall Classic between 1947 and 1963. That emotion got compounded when TV viewers watched prime time and saw a familiar actor starring as Dr. David Banner in CBS's *The Incredible Hulk*, based on the Marvel Comics character. Bill Bixby had starred in the comedies *My Favorite Martian* and *The Courtship of Eddie's Father*; both shows lasted three seasons. *The Magician*, a one-hour detective show about a magician who uses his skills to solve crimes, aired for one season.

Bixby had played Banner in a 1977 TV movie about the Hulk; CBS commissioned a series that premiered in March 1978 and returned for the fall schedule. It went off the air in 1982, but NBC aired three TV movies with the character between 1988 and 1990.

The Incredible Hulk benefited from Bixby's celebrity plus the popularity of the title character in comic books; Lou Ferrigno played the Hulk after Banner transforms. But there were critics of the show, including Bixby himself. "I didn't blame people too much at first," said Bixby. "I'll admit I also had a snobbish attitude about the project when it was first suggested to me. But after I read the script and realized the Hulk could become a classic character, well, I've always wanted to be different. I'd rather fail trying to do something different than never try to be anything more than pedestrian."[39]

But pedestrian fare can be alluring. *Rescue from Gilligan's Island* reunited the characters that had been on *Gilligan's Island*, a sitcom created by Sherwood Schwartz about seven castaways stuck on an island three hundred miles from Hawaii after encountering a vicious storm during a three-hour cruise. It aired on CBS from 1964 to 1967 and became a huge success in TV syndication. But *Gilligan's Island* didn't have a proper finale. Schwartz conceived a reunion TV movie depicting their escape. They constructed rafts and strung their huts together to leave the island during a storm and finally landed safely in Hawaii.

NBC aired *Rescue from Gilligan's Island* after Game Four of the World Series and *CHiPs*, a drama about California Highway Patrol officers, on Saturday night, October 14. Nostalgia begat Nielsen ratings that made network programmers and advertisers swoon: a 52 share. This meant that 52 percent of televisions that were on that Saturday night were tuned to the escapades of SS *Minnow* captain Jonas Grumby aka Skipper, first mate Gilligan, movie star Ginger Grant, farm girl Mary Ann Summers, professor Roy Hinkley, and millionaire Thurston Howell III and his wife, Lovey Howell.[40]

The story ended with a reunion cruise commemorating their return to civilization only to endure another storm and wind up on the same island. NBC aired two sequels: *The Castaways on Gilligan's Island* and *The Harlem Globetrotters on Gilligan's Island*.

11

A TALE OF TWO SPARKYS

NOVEMBER

"This is the best thing for me."[1]

Sparky Lyle's declaration regarding a ten-player trade on November 10 sending him to the Texas Rangers underlined his displeasure with the team that had yielded three consecutive World Series berths and two titles from 1976 to 1978. Chaos reigned; Lyle revealed. A week after the trade, Crown Publishers held a press conference at 21, the famed Manhattan bar and restaurant, touting the pitcher's account of the 1978 Yankees. Co-written with Peter Golenbock and debuting the following March, *The Bronx Zoo* chronicled the genesis, impact, and consequences of the drama that permeated the team, from an insider's perspective. It became a best seller.

Jim Bouton had caused a stir with *Ball Four*, which hit the bookstores in 1970. In 1978 Lyle's recent status as a star reliever and the drama of the Yankees amplified the impact of the tell-all tome. In his coverage of the Crown press conference, *Daily News* columnist Dick Young previewed Lyle's prose, including the pitcher's observation about the Yankees' star slugger: "We're a better team when Reggie [Jackson] is not playing the outfield, and we're a better team when he's not hitting in the No. 4 spot because he strikes out too much."[2]

It seemed like every time something good happened for the Yankees, something bad happened to cancel it out. Signing Jackson added power to the lineup, but a disastrous interview with a *Sport* magazine reporter set off a tsunami of controversy in the spring of 1977. The Yankees won the 1977 World Series; Billy Martin departed the managing job halfway through the 1978 season. Lyle won the Cy Young Award, then got traded a year later. Winning the 1978 World Series capped a tremendous season of comebacks for the Yankees, but *The Bronx Zoo* pierced the privacy of the clubhouse. One example is Lyle quoting his fellow pitcher Catfish Hunter on the team's star slugger: "When you unwrap a Reggie Bar, it tells you how good it is."[3]

Lyle broke into the Major Leagues with the Boston Red Sox during their Cinderella season of 1967, appearing in twenty-seven games and finishing eleven. Boston traded him to the Yankees in 1972. He flourished. Lyle led the Major Leagues in games finished and the American League in saves, capturing third place in the MVP voting. He led the AL again in saves in 1976, then won the Cy Young Award in 1977 after topping the Junior Circuit in games played and games finished.

Getting the prestigious award elevated respect for Lyle and his bullpen brethren. "It gives them more recognition and it means people are beginning to realize the importance of relief pitchers," said Lyle. "That's what this award means to me."[4]

During his first year with the Yankees, Lyle emphasized the role that baseball's firemen have on the team: "A relief pitcher is a specialist. Probably more of one than anyone else in baseball. You can't feel pressure. I know I'm going to either be the hero or the goat. There's no second chance."[5]

His prowess would be missed. In addition to Lyle, the World Series champions bargained fellow hurlers Larry McCall and Dave Rajsich in addition to backup catcher Mike Heath and infielder Domingo Ramos, plus $400,000, for the November 10 trade. In exchange, Texas parted ways with pitchers Paul Mirabella, Dave Righetti, and Mike Griffin along with Greg Jemison, an outfielder, and Juan Beníquez, a center fielder.[6]

Another Sparky received news of getting removed from his employer's payroll in November when the Cincinnati Reds fired Sparky Anderson, who had guided the squad to five NL West titles, four World Series appearances, and two titles since taking the manager job in 1970. It came on the heels of Pete Rose becoming a free agent earlier in the month. On November 28, *Cincinnati Enquirer* sportswriter Bob Hertzel addressed the void created by Rose's departure, a possible transformation of the Reds' lineup, and Anderson's challenges in this new paradigm. Hertzel's description of Anderson as "a devoutly loyal employee" mirrored the thoughts of Reds fans and personnel. The silver-haired skipper had become a fixture in Cincinnati.[7]

Anderson had known about the firing but promised to keep quiet. By that evening, his pink slip had become public. The evening edition of the *Cincin-*

nati Post reported that the Reds fired him with a year left on his contract. Reds fans learned that team president Dick Wagner went to Anderson's home in the Los Angeles suburb of Thousand Oaks to break the news and his reasoning. Wagner talked with the press about dissatisfaction with two second-place finishes in the NL West after World Series titles in 1975 and 1976, but details remained elusive. "I do not want to get into specifics with regard to the move we have made," stated Wagner.[8]

Getting rid of Anderson was questionable at best and scandalous at worst. Reds fans adored their team's leader, making Wagner's decision a provocative topic. *Enquirer* columnist Mark Purdy posited, "He says his goal is to make the average fan happy, but Wagner appears intent on becoming as absolutely unpopular as is humanly possible."[9]

There was talk about the problem being discipline. Or lack of it. In August Bench critiqued his manager as being "too low key" in his role.[10] Former Reds pitcher Jack Billingham suggested that Anderson's familiarity with star players became an obstacle for the forty-four-year-old manager. "When you have nine superstars, they almost handle you instead of you handling them," observed Billingham.[11]

His appraisal had merit. Cincinnati was a powerhouse club with stellar talent. Johnny Bench had been a Rookie of the Year, two-time MVP, eleven-time All-Star, and ten-time Gold Glove Award winner. Pete Rose also won Rookie of the Year, later earning membership on twelve All-Star teams before Anderson's dismissal. In addition, he won an MVP Award. George Foster's recent statistics evidenced his supremacy: leading the National League in RBIs for the third straight season in 1978 and topping the Major Leagues in 1976 and 1977. Plus, Foster topped the Major Leagues with fifty-two homers in 1977 followed by forty to lead the NL in 1978.

Further, Wagner purged the quartet of coaches who had advised Anderson since his 1970 debut as the Reds manager. Ted Kluszewski, Larry Shepard, and George Scherger reportedly got other positions with the ball club. Not so for Alex Grammas. "If Alex were around, it would be like having another Sparky Anderson on the premises," wrote Pat Harmon in the *Cincinnati Post*.[12]

Kluszewski was a fan favorite as a Reds player from 1947 to 1957, later finishing his career with the Pirates, White Sox, and Angels before retiring in 1961. He had a career .298 batting average, marked by outstanding years in the mid-1950s. "Big Klu" led the Major Leagues in home runs and RBIs in 1954 while placing third in slugging percentage, fourth in extra base hits, and seventh in batting average.

The following season, he had the second-highest number of home runs in the Majors behind Willie Mays. His 1955 output resulted in the sixth-highest slugging percentage, third-highest number of hits, seventh-highest number of extra base hits, and eighth-highest batting average.

Anderson's departure did not sit well with Rose, who sought a new team with better compensation. "I can understand why they can't get together with me, because it's a matter of economics," stated the hard-nosed player nicknamed Charlie Hustle. "But it wasn't Sparky's fault that we finished second. Without him we would have probably finished third. Sparky has never been a guy who took credit when we enjoyed success so why should he have to take the blame for our failure?"[13]

Before he took the helming job in Cincinnati, Anderson managed in the Minor Leagues for the Toronto Maple Leafs, Rock Hill Cardinals, St. Petersburg Cardinals, Modesto Reds, and Asheville Tourists. St. Petersburg won the Florida State League championship under Anderson, whom the Reds tapped to replace Dave Bristol. Anderson had coached for the Padres during 1969 and had already agreed to coach for the Angels in 1970 when the Reds offered him the skipper position.

Before his inaugural season with Cincinnati, Anderson ingratiated himself by joking about his age and sole season as a Major League second baseman with the 1959 Phillies. He batted .218 and struck out fifty-three times over 152 games. "People laugh when I tell them I'm 35 because I look like I'm 50," said Anderson. "But if you took as many zeroes for four at the plate as I did, you'd look old, too."[14] Cincinnati's press emphasized Anderson's unknown quality, but that status changed rapidly. He became a cornerstone of Cincinnati culture, as identifiable with the southern Ohio metropolis as the Tyler Davidson Fountain, Kings Island, and Scotti's Italian Eatery. Anderson guided the Reds to a World Series appearance in his first season; they lost to the Orioles in five games.[15]

Throughout his nine seasons with the Reds, Anderson—who got the nickname "Sparky" as a Minor League ballplayer in the 1950s when a broadcaster observed his enthusiasm and dubbed him accordingly—shared his philosophy regarding the nuances of managing.[16]

ON STRATEGY

"You can't read a book and learn about baseball. You have to see it with your eyes" (advice offered during his first spring training with the Reds).[17]

ON MANAGERS

"I never won anything. The players are going to win it. Also, they're going to lose it. The manager's big job is to keep a good relationship with the team. Call guys in and straighten 'em out" (during the off-season after losing the 1972 World Series in seven games to the A's).[18]

ON THE CINCINNATI REDS

"I came from nothing and I was given a helluva club. I owe everything to the people who hired me. I wouldn't leave Cincinnati unless I was fired. I owe them that" (during the off-season after losing the 1973 NL championship series to the Mets).[19]

ON POSITIVE THINKING AND GOD

"The real source of strength and power, of course, is not in any attitude or idea, but in the Creator Himself who made us and loves us and wants us fulfilled" (at the beginning of the 1974 season).[20]

ON HIS APPEARANCE

"My mother was snow white," said the skipper. "So was my father" (during the 1974 season, when he was forty years old).[21]

ON UMPIRES

"If I pit them against each other and hear three or four different stories, then I know they are lying. I want to hear the stories, catch them individually, then tell them together what each one told me. Sure, I put words in their mouths. I work them one against another. They will always try to cross themselves up and I try to confuse them" (during the off-season between 1975 and 1976).[22]

ON PLAYERS

"Players win or lose games, not managers" (during the 1975 NL championship series).[23]

"This club has more pride and class than any other club in sports" (comparing the Reds to the Brooklyn Dodgers of the 1950s after sweeping the Yankees in the 1976 World Series).[24]

"With the kinds of players I have, it's easy to look smart" (during the off-season after the 1976 World Series).[25]

ON GETTING FIRED FROM THE CINCINNATI REDS

"I have no animosity toward anyone. I was nobody and Bob Howsam gave me a chance to manage a big-league club, which I thought I'd never get. Everything in this house I owe to Bob Howsam."[26]

"There's already too much dirt and too much mud-slinging. I'm going to be straightforward. I got fired. It's no disgrace. The only disgrace is if you make it one."[27]

"That was no coincidence. They didn't want Rose to have an excuse to leave. If Rose had said he was leaving two weeks later, I would have been fired two weeks later."[28]

"When [Dick Wagner] fired me, he flew me back to Cincinnati, gave me all the time I needed, gave me a credit card, and let me take care of my business. There never was any personal (bad) feeling between Dick and I."[29]

Lifelong Cincinnatian Andy Abel was eleven years old in the summer of 1978. He recalls that, "unfortunately, we were not shocked, rather dismayed, when the Reds fired Sparky Anderson and Pete Rose left the team. Bob Howsam had been the GM of the Reds from 1967 to 1977 and the absolute key to building the Big Red Machine. His successor, Dick Wagner, was hellbent on proving that he could duplicate Howsam's success by rebuilding the team in his image. He was absolutely wrong!

"Of course, I am biased, but I believe Sparky Anderson to be one of the great managers in MLB history. Keep in mind the talent, and with that talent the egos, that one had to bring together for the eight-year run that the Reds had. Then to duplicate this success with the Tigers in the American League was unprecedented. Keep in mind, there are only 23 managers in the Hall of Fame and Sparky is one of them. I will leave the debate about the best up to the experts."[30]

John McNamara replaced Anderson, but the beloved silver-haired skipper found work during the middle of the 1979 season when the Tigers hired him as the third of three managers that year.

In his autobiography, Anderson recalled the 1978 firing from the Reds and advising Joe Morgan, who was "really upset" that the Reds would lose their leader. "You've got a new manager," Anderson remembered telling his star second baseman. "Whether you like it or not, that man don't deserve to be greeted by what you have to say about me. We're friends. I have to ask you this favor. I don't want no defense on my behalf."[31]

Anderson returned to Cincinnati during the off-season, in a manner of speaking. He made a guest appearance as himself on WKRP in Cincinnati. The premise seemed a bit incongruous with the station's rock-and-roll format—hosting a sports radio show for two hours a day, five days a week. Despite his celebrity, the fictional radio show *Sparky's Bullpen* is a disaster.[32]

Anderson made another guest appearance in prime time the following year on *The White Shadow*. A funny bit of dialogue happens when one of the Carver High School basketball players says that he voted for him, confusing the baseball manager with John Anderson, a 1980 third-party presidential candidate running against Ronald Reagan and Jimmy Carter. WKRP and *The White Shadow* aired on CBS; MTM Enterprises produced both shows.

The White Shadow premiered during the week that Anderson got booted from the Reds. Revolving around a classic fish-out-of-water storyline, it starred Ken Howard as Ken Reeves, a former NBA player and college All-American who had suffered a career-ending knee injury and been hired by his former Boston College teammate, now a principal at Carver High School in "South Central," an area of Los Angeles. Reeves is white. Most of his team members are Black, though the team does have a non-WASP trio consisting of one Hispanic player, one Italian, and one Jew. CBS unveiled this one-hour drama on November 27, 1978.

The beginning of the pilot episode sets up Reeves's dilemma. While playing for the Chicago Bulls, he gets fouled during a lay-up attempt, falls hard, and tries to rehabilitate in a montage of Windy City locations, all accompanied by a jazzy instrumental piece. As Reeves leaves the locker room for the last time, he heads toward the basketball court that held so many memories for him. A basketball catches his attention. After he makes a shot, a voice echoes through the arena: "You stink!"

It's Jim Willis, his Boston College teammate. In a line that might seem insensitive in subsequent decades, Reeves references Willis's color. "Where are you, Willis? You know I can't see you in the dark." Willis's claim that he's in Chicago for sightseeing doesn't figure for Reeves, who explains that it's winter. Then, a brief but effective dialogue indicates the deep respect that only two longtime friends could have as they josh one another.

Reeves: "You still like being a high school principal?"
Willis: "It beats digging gold. You still like being a pro ball player?"
Reeves: "Beats being a high school principal."

After Willis points to the reality that Reeves will not play basketball again, he offers the injured ballplayer a job—basketball coach at George Washington Carver High School in South Central Los Angeles. When the issue of salary arises, Willis explains that it pays "less." Reeves inquires, "Less than what?" Willis says, "Less than you can live on." Reeves accepts by saying, "That makes it irresistible."

Carver's new coach and his squires clash. To earn their respect, Reeves, who's in his midthirties, selects two players for a two-on-one game. Ten baskets win. Reeves puts them through their paces, though he works up quite a sweat doing so. But the players aren't the only obstacle for Carver's basketball leader. Vice Principal Sybil Buchanan sees him as a glorification of athletics distracting Carver's players from their studies. Plus, he doesn't have any real experience in teaching.

Although Carver loses its first game under the new Reeves regime, it wins the next game in the last second. By this time, the coach and his team are functioning as a unit. In the locker room, the show's title is explained in dialogue between Morris Thorpe—one of the players in the two-on-one game—and Reeves. Carver's coach says, "Yeah, but vacation's over. Now we really go to work. I'm gonna be leanin' on you guys. And I'll be behind you. Every step of the way."

Thorpe acknowledges, "Yeah. Like a white shadow."[33]

Reviews of *The White Shadow* ranged from promising to predictable for its premiere.

> Associated Press: "Howard's talent is wasted."[34]
>
> *Evening Sun* (Baltimore): "'The White Shadow' had better decide if it wants to be funny or touching. Right now, it isn't anything."[35]
>
> *Journal Herald* (Dayton OH): "*White Shadow* isn't, by anyone's standards, a classic television series. But it has some merit."[36]
>
> *Orlando Sentinel Star*: "With most of the scenes shot on location, the production looks good. The acting ranges from good to excellent. With these basics under control, it shouldn't take too much work to whip this well-intentioned dramatic series into top shape."[37]
>
> *Palo Alto Times*: "I just choked in disgust.... May it pass quickly and quietly."[38]
>
> *Philadelphia Inquirer*: "MTM series have been characterized by intelligence and maturity, and 'White Shadow' is no exception."[39]
>
> *Tampa Tribune*: "But surprise, surprise. 'The White Shadow' is good. Very good, in fact."[40]
>
> *Los Angeles Times*: "Despite that silly title which sounds like something rising from the black lagoon, this is a first-rate show and worthy of your attention."[41]
>
> *New York Times*: "If CBS decides to get a touch more confident, about itself and its public, television could discover it has a nice new series."[42]

Created by Bruce Paltrow, *The White Shadow* explored hot-button topics in a thoughtful manner; writers kept moralizing to a minimum in favor of expressing how these issues affected the characters. The show often centered an episode on the arc of a player's dilemma, suffering, and resolution. Examples: Ricky Gomez rejoins his old gang; Curtis Jackson is discovered to be an alcoholic; Abner Goldstein tires of being the team's outsider and stands up for inclusion in off-the-court activities; Thorpe genuinely likes a girl who has a salty reputation; Mario "Salami" Pettrino has an affair with his teacher; Warren Coolidge suffers from body image because he towers over his friends; and Milton Reese's girlfriend is pregnant.[43]

Episodes that made a guest character the center of the story included stories on homosexuality, illiteracy, autism, and teacher burnout. *The White Shadow* highlighted racism in an episode in which a friend of Carver High's Black basketball players—Albert Hodges—is released from prison because he was wrongfully convicted. He convinces them that Coach Reeves and his policies are racist, culminating in them refusing to suit up for a game. Unbeknown to Albert, Reeves arranged for his alma mater to offer him a minority scholarship. The team discovers this and heads to the gym just in time to prevent a forfeit.[44]

Another episode touching on racism showed the players getting refused entry by a country club even though Reeves was a guest and operating under the assumption that he could bring them for a visit. They later go to a public golf course and get a tutorial on Charlie Sifford, the "Jackie Robinson of golf."[45]

Real events also impacted *The White Shadow*. Salami becomes an amateur boxer in an episode undoubtedly influenced by the popularity of *Rocky*, the 1976 Oscar-winning movie written by and starring Sylvester Stallone as Rocky Balboa, aka the Italian Stallion. NBA player Kermit Washington's devastating punch to Rudy Tomjanovich's head during a melee that broke out in a 1977 Lakers-Rockets game gave fodder for another episode, one that put Salami in the role of the assaulter. In the Washington-Tomjanovich incident, Tomjanovich entered the fray to break it up; Washington's reaction decked him. An NBA statement read, "Tomjanovich is hospitalized with injuries reported to be a fractured cheek bone, a broken nose, a fractured skull and a concussion." *The White Shadow* also had the other player in the hospital, but he admitted that he joined the fight specifically to hit Salami.[46]

The Cold War inspired an episode where a Russian team visits Carver. One of the Russian players asks for asylum but gets strong-armed by his overseers and returns to the Soviet Union with the rest of his team.[47]

Ego was a resonant theme with Coolidge, Carver's star center. He nearly quits school in two episodes, first to sign with an unscrupulous manager and the second time because he thinks he has a chance to play for the Harlem Globetrotters. Coolidge's self-importance later balloons when he gets a role on a TV show set in a high school but then confronts the director and loses his job when he refuses to portray an insulting Black stereotype. Ed Asner makes a cameo as himself; he starred in the title role of the MTM-produced *Lou Grant*, a spin-off of *The Mary Tyler Moore Show*.[48]

The White Shadow launched the directing careers of cast members who became prominent in television, thanks to Paltrow. The first was Thomas Carter, who played James Hayward. His journey began by using filming breaks to trail the crew and learn about production. "I really used *The White Shadow* as my own film school," said Carter. Paltrow took notice and gave him an opportunity to direct an episode. Three more followed.[49]

Carter's dedication paid enormous dividends. He became the helmsman for the pilots of *St. Elsewhere* and *Miami Vice*, both highly significant factors in NBC's success during the 1980s, as well as the three-part miniseries *A Year in the Life* in 1986, which later spawned a TV show of the same name that lasted one season. His directing credits over several decades include *Hill Street Blues*, *Midnight Caller*, *Bosch*, *Shades of Blue*, SEAL *Team*, *Elementary*, and *The Morning Show*.

Kevin Hooks and Timothy Van Patten—who played Thorpe and Salami—followed Carter in learning about production from the crew of *The White Shadow*. Although neither had an opportunity to direct episodes of the show, they became blue-chip directors in television. Hooks's résumé includes *St. Elsewhere*, *Fame*, *Hotel*, *China Beach*, *I'll Fly Away*, ER, NYPD *Blue*, *Castle*, *911*, *The Orville*, and *This Is Us*.

Van Patten has directed episodes of *New York Undercover*, *Homicide: Life on the Street*, *The Wire*, *The Sopranos*, *The Pacific*, *Boardwalk Empire*, and *Perry Mason*. His work has yielded fourteen Emmy nominations and two Emmy Awards—one for *Boardwalk Empire* and the other for *The Pacific*. In addition to directing an episode of *The Pacific*, Van Patten was supervising producer for the show; his production efforts garnered him the Emmy Award for Outstanding Miniseries.

The White Shadow aired for three seasons on CBS. "We had this incredibly loyal fan base that even today people recognize me from the show and I haven't acted in years," said Carter in a 2013 interview. "But I would go to New York and I couldn't walk two blocks down the street without people just recognizing me and saying hello and saying how much they like the show. It just had a real intensity to it in terms of the people's loyalty to it."[50]

Carter also expounded on the show's realism. "In being authentic, it seemed universal. Even though these characters lived in a specific place and they were from a specific background, I think a lot of young people, certainly, and other people who had lived lives in various communities, just related to what they were going through in growing up.... We did it honestly. I think it was fresh because these characters hadn't been seen on television before on a weekly basis.... People just embraced that.

"That's just a big lesson ... that you don't have to do a white show with white characters to get a white audience.... Anybody can like anything if they feel those characters are true and that their stories are common, human stories. I think that's mostly what we did, whatever the subject matter might have been. I think there was that kind of authenticity that made the show appealing."[51]

The actors' basketball skills provided another component of authenticity. "They knew basketball so well that if we asked [a cast member], 'What are you going to do when so-and-so throws the ball to so-and-so?' he knew exactly how he'd wind up and where he'd be," said Jackie Cooper, who directed five episodes of *The White Shadow*, in an interview for a segment on the show's DVD.[52]

"For it to be legitimate, to hold an audience, they have to believe that we're the real deal," said Ken Howard. Further, the six-foot-six-inch actor revealed a benefit from his portrayal of Coach Reeves: "Coaches, I mean the big coaches, Mike Krzyzewski and Jim Calhoun, they treat me like I'm another coach," said Howard, who passed away in 2016. "They just kind of include me. Somehow, I'm the make-believe coach who did it well enough that they just kind of include me. 'Come on, meet so-and-so.' They're always very good to me. So, it's a whole world that opened up to me in a way. I am still part of that world of basketball that I love."[53]

The White Shadow's last episode aired on March 16, 1981, but it resurfaced for two stalwarts of popular culture. Byron Stewart reprised the role of Coolidge in more than twenty episodes of *St. Elsewhere*, which aired on NBC from 1982 to 1988; Paltrow was an executive producer of the show set in the fictional Boston hospital St. Eligius. In the medical drama, Coolidge, after graduating from Carver High, played for Boston College on Reeves's recommendation; an injury ended his aspirations. He works as an orderly and often wears his Carver jersey under a white hospital coat.

Van Patten appears in one episode as a different character. Coolidge sees him and shouts, "Salami!" To his shock and chagrin, he learns that it's not his old teammate.[54]

ESPN utilized Stewart and Howard in their *White Shadow* roles for two installments of its "This Is *SportsCenter*" advertising campaign. Participating with ESPN personnel in "Fans against Traveling"—a parody of the "We Are the World" music video—they admonish NBA players for traveling violations. Coach Reeves points out that they're pros. Coolidge has two lines: "It started with Kareem Abdul-Jabbar!" and "What would Naismith say today?"[55]

Their other commercial is set in the ESPN office, where they attempt to convince anchor Gary Miller about the caliber of basketball playing on *The White Shadow*. Reeves underscores Carver's weak side offense, Coolidge's potential to be All-World if a three-point shot existed in the late 1970s, and the team's ability to beat the Globetrotters in a second-season episode but holding back for the sake of the show.[56]

On the same night that *The White Shadow* premiered in 1978, San Franciscans and the gay community at large endured what Dianne Feinstein, president of the city's Board of Supervisors, described as "a double tragedy of immense proportions." Supervisor Dan White murdered fellow supervisor Harvey Milk and Mayor George Moscone in city hall. Feinstein informed the press about White shooting and killing her friends, who were also her allies in the city's progressive political bloc. Press accounts noted that she was "shaking so badly that [Police] Chief Gain had to support her." Under the city's law, Feinstein became the acting mayor because of her presidential status with the Board of Supervisors.[57]

White had resigned from his position on November 10 after the latest in a series of disputes with Milk, over a drug rehabilitation facility proposed for the Mission District. Milk advocated for it; White disagreed. But a few days later, White wanted reinstatement. At first Moscone acceded, but then he reversed his decision. There were four targets for White: Milk, Moscone, Supervisor Carol Ruth Silver, and Speaker Willie Brown of the California Assembly. White got a meeting with Moscone in the mayor's office to plead his case again for reinstatement but killed him when the mayor refused. At the request of White, Milk went to his colleague's office, where he too was then shot and killed with White's .38 Smith & Wesson revolver.

White went to a police station and confessed. Nearly six months after the murders, a jury convicted him of voluntary manslaughter; White's attorneys had argued diminished capacity based on depression. His lighter sentence of seven years ignited San Francisco's White Night riots on May 21, 1979. White served five years; he received parole on January 7, 1984, and committed suicide via carbon monoxide poisoning in his garage on October 21, 1985. Feinstein and other progressive politicians carried the burden of losing two icons as they continued their agenda. She later won a special election to the U.S. Senate and subsequently won five senatorial elections. Feinstein passed away in 2023.

November 1978 had been a month of heroes. Cincinnati said goodbye to one. Basketball welcomed one. The gay community mourned two—one of their own and a mayoral ally. As 1978 headed toward the finish line, America found renewed hope with a familiar hero who stood for truth, justice, and the American way.

12

IT'S A BIRD... IT'S A PLANE... IT'S A BLOCKBUSTER

DECEMBER

Superman premiered on December 10, 1978, encompassing the hallmarks that had defined the title character's universe through comic books and other media since his first appearance in *Action Comics* No. 1 forty years earlier.

There was the origin story of Jor-El and Lara sending their baby Kal-El in a rocket to Earth to escape the impending explosion of the planet Krypton.

There was the discovery of the rocket by Jonathan and Martha Kent on their farm in Smallville, where they dubbed the baby Clark and raised him as their son.

There was the Fortress of Solitude, somewhere in the Arctic region.

There was Clark Kent growing up in Smallville, then becoming a reporter at the *Daily Planet* in Metropolis and working with eager photographer Jimmy Olsen, gruff editor Perry White, and ambitious reporter Lois Lane.

There was Superman's archenemy Lex Luthor.

The film ignores a storyline in the comic books featuring a teenage Clark Kent as Superboy, who made his first appearance in 1944. Instead, *Superman* shows Clark enduring the typical existential crisis for teenagers, but his is more pronounced. While it's common for high school students, even popular ones, to question where and how they fit into their communities, Clark's teenage isolation is compounded because he hides his abilities of speed, strength, and flight granted to him by living on a planet with a yellow sun. Krypton's red sun was stronger, thereby preventing Kryptonians from having these powers. Jonathan believes that Clark is on Earth for a reason that hasn't been determined. Scoring touchdowns and impressing his peers do not merit consideration.

When his adoptive father dies, Clark takes a crystal from the rocket ship that's hidden in a barn on the Kent farm and goes on a journey of self-discovery that brings him to the Arctic region, where he throws the crystal. After landing, it forms the Fortress of Solitude, which features video images of his Kryptonian father Jor-El—played by Marlon Brando—giving instructions about life to his offspring once known as Kal-El. After twelve years, the last son of Krypton emerges with wisdom informing his purpose—helping humankind with his powers. Christopher Reeve played Clark/Superman.

Perry White hires Clark as a reporter at the *Daily Planet* and gives him the city beat, which is Lois Lane's domain. When she protests, White reasons, "Lois, Clark Kent may seem like just a mild-mannered reporter. But listen. Not only does he know how to treat his editor in chief with the proper respect. Not only does he have a snappy, punchy prose style. But he is in my forty years in this business the fastest typist I've ever seen."

When the press discovers Superman, White shows the front pages of the *Daily Planet* and its competitors—*Metropolis Post*, *Metropolis Times*, *Daily News*—displaying this new, mysterious creature. He emphasizes that he wants the *Daily Planet* and the hero to be synonymous. The *Daily News* is a real New York newspaper, likely shown as a shout-out because the producers filmed part of *Superman* at the newspaper's building in Manhattan. Legendary *Daily News* film critic Rex Reed has a cameo appearance. Other Manhattan locations seen in *Superman* include the World Trade Center Twin Towers, Statue of Liberty, Empire State Building, and Pan Am Building. Lex Luthor, played by Gene Hackman, lives two hundred feet below Grand Central Terminal.

A montage of images features Superman protecting the public: stopping a cat burglar, rescuing a cat in a tree, ensuring that Air Force One lands safely in a storm. His bond with Lois begins when she is hanging from a disabled helicopter teetering on the roofline of the *Daily Planet* building and he rescues her just as she and the chopper are about to fall to the ground. This scene triggered a debate regarding Superman's powers in a first-season episode of the long-running sitcom *The Big Bang Theory*, which revolves around the personal and professional lives of three physicists and an engineer from Caltech. One character believes that Superman's strength and acceleration combined with the forces of gravity pulling Lois downward will result in Superman's arms slicing her into three pieces.[1]

Lex Luthor plans to hijack a test for two U.S. military missiles and adjust their trajectory for Hackensack, New Jersey, and Southern California. If the latter is successful, then the coastline will disappear, allowing Luthor to capitalize on the desert land that he owns because it would suddenly be beachfront property. Superman sends the missile bound for the Garden State into space but does not arrive in time to stop the one targeted for the West Coast. Lois dies because she's trapped in her car by an aftershock caused by the missile's impact. Superman travels back in time at super speed so he can prevent the missile from completing Luthor's California plan.

Some critics were about as kind to *Superman* as salt on Frosted Flakes. "Despite a magic moment here and there, its wings are leaden, its spirit earthbound," wrote Bernard Drew in the *Pensacola News Journal*. Devotees of the critic Charles Champlin read a similar account in the *Los Angeles Times*: "But it is, I regret to say, a very large letdown. 'Superman' has lead feet." However, Champlin was kinder to the actor in the title role. "Reeve is a fresh and welcome casting, and if he performs as well for other directors as he has for Richard Donner, who has overseen 'Superman,' he has a promising future."[2]

Vincent Canby's assessment in the *New York Times* tore apart the latest version of the Man of Steel following the portrayals in Superman movie serials of the 1940s starring Kirk Allyn, the TV show in the 1950s starring George Reeves, and cartoon depictions for Saturday morning television produced by Hanna-Barbera. "To enjoy this movie as much as one has a right to expect, one has either to be a Superman nut, the sort of trivia expert who has absorbed all there is to know about the planet Krypton, or to check one's wits at the door, which may be more than a lot of people are prepared to do for longer than two hours," wrote Canby.[3]

Holiday audiences disagreed with the disapproval, flocking to theaters from Sacramento to Sag Harbor like overweight guests heading toward the dessert tables at a wedding. *Superman* became a popular movie destination in between holiday shopping and holiday parties, continuing its success by being the highest-grossing movie in 1979 and benefiting from the nostalgia that boosted *Grease* and *Animal House*.

But Reeve took on a tremendous burden to make his characters feel approachable for a modern audience. He had stellar training to take on this challenge. When Reeve transferred from Cornell to Juilliard, he bonded with a fellow student and 1978's other breakout performer—Robin Williams. They were roommates at the lauded institution for the performing arts, where they studied under Oscar winner John Houseman, who had a resurgence of fame that year with *The Paper Chase* TV series.[4]

"I've deliberately tried to underplay Superman," said Reeve, who starred in three sequels, in 1980, 1983, and 1987. "I try to take him off the comic page, warm him up, and give him some life. The kids who go to movies in the Midwest don't know how the movie business works. When they go, they want to see Superman and you'd better have something to show them."[5]

When Reeve guest hosted on *Saturday Night Live* in 1985, he poked fun at himself in a sketch about the auditions for *Superman*. Jim Belushi has the role of Donner, the film's director, who is auditioning three prospective actors for the role. Reeve plays himself; Gary Kroeger and Rich Hall play the other two thespians—Cory Meredith and Peter Blake. They must not only act out a scene but also perform feats such as catching a bullet in their teeth, making a diamond out of coal, and melting a telephone with "heat vision." Meredith fails and gets shot. Reeve fails all three tests: he doesn't catch the bullet, he squeezes the coal only enough to liquefy it, and his heat vision ignites a window curtain next to the telephone. Blake gets the job after passing the first two tests and putting out the fire by blowing on it. But he forgoes the Superman role for a callback on a Dial soap commercial. Begrudgingly, Donner hires Reeve, whom he refers to as "this idiot here."[6]

As Gary Kroeger recalls, "Chris was a trouper from day one. Not a moment of hesitation with anything. He approached everything as an actor and so he didn't question the material, he just looked for ways to make it work. In this sketch I got the feeling that he loved doing a parody of the process and to have fun with the audition that ultimately made him a star. You can tell that he's playing the naive, eager version of himself as a young actor, desperately wanting to please the director. Chris was the consummate actor because he viewed every role as a network of support for every other actor's experience. Never an unkind word, but he made suggestions to ideas to make the whole thing come together. He played it for real.

"Chris did play himself (without parody) but at the same time it was a 'version' of himself that WAS a parody of young actors, eager to please and ambitious to the point of blindness. If Chris had camped it up and played for laughs the sketch would not have worked. He set the tone so that the rest of us could be a little bit over the top.

"Chris was one of the nicest people I have ever met in the business. He came to work, he had no 'star' attitude. In fact, he seemed to be in awe of us just a little. He made the week a pleasure and even went out to dinner with us to stay connected during the week. YES! His theatre background was key, I believe. He instinctively knew that the success of a sketch, of the show as a whole, depended on the collaboration between actors, writers and direction. He viewed SNL as live theatre.

"Chris Reeve WAS Superman to a generation. Maybe two generations. I grew up with George Reeves, but when Chris Reeve landed the role from Richard Donner and they re-booted the story, Chris became the ultimate superhero. Handsome, strong, gentle disposition as Clark, just the right comic touch, and just the right confident Superman. I've been fine with every incarnation of the character because every actor brings something different to the iconic strongman with the ethics of a Saint, but no one improved upon Chris's portrayal."[7]

Margot Kidder's interpretation of Lois Lane in *Superman* fit the late 1970s sensibility of a dedicated, independent woman competing and succeeding in a male-dominated industry. It's an identifiable burden that female moviegoers saw themselves shouldering not only in journalism but in medicine, investment banking, law, academia, advertising, and other industries.

Amy Adams portrayed the reporter in Superman and Justice League movies directed by Zack Snyder in the 2010s. Kidder disliked the filmmakers' choices for the role that she redefined. "They took one of the best American actresses around, Amy Adams, and didn't give her anything to do!" exclaimed Kidder, who used alcohol and drugs to end her own life in 2018. "I mean, how stupid is that? They made her what used to be the girlfriend, which kind of ended in the 60s with women's rights."[8]

It wasn't just the portrayal of women that changed in the 1960s. Since the latter part of the decade, movie audiences had become used to sophisticated, nuanced, and provocative stories reflective of the strife in society highlighted by the Vietnam War, Watergate, inflation, and an oil crisis. *Bonnie and Clyde*, *M*A*S*H*, *The Sting*, *The Godfather*, and *The Taking of Pelham 1-2-3* exemplified this new wave of filmmaking. *Superman* capped an extraordinary year for Hollywood.

Capricorn One displayed the distrust that Americans felt toward government in the post–Vietnam War, post-Watergate era. It revolves around a NASA cover-up regarding the first astronauts setting out on a mission to Mars—Capricorn One. The mission crew comprises a trio of astronauts played by Sam Waterston, James Brolin, and O. J. Simpson, who find themselves evacuated from the rocket before it launches because of a mechanical failure that would have been fatal during the mission. NASA sends an empty rocket into space as part of a scheme that has the astronauts faking televised footage of a Mars landing, with a duplicate for the inside of Capricorn One and a TV studio substituting for the red planet's surface.

A canceled mission would result in the money faucet being turned off for NASA, which would also lead to the termination of contracts worth potentially millions of dollars to companies supplying parts, equipment, and technology. When a flawed heat shield results in the spacecraft's destruction during its reentry into Earth's atmosphere, the astronauts face deliberate doom because in order for NASA to maintain its fraud it must kill the three men. Two are hunted down and killed. The remaining one, Charles Brubaker, Brolin's character, escapes with the help of a reporter and a biplane pilot, played by Elliott Gould and Telly Savalas, respectively.

The recently ceased war in Vietnam prompted several antiwar pictures. *The Deer Hunter* shocked audiences with its portrayal of the pressures facing Vietnam War veterans, highlighted by a flashback scene of the characters forced into playing Russian roulette with their captors. *Coming Home* won three Academy Awards—Best Actor, Best Actress, Best Screenplay Written Directly for the Screen. Its 1968 setting showed the emotional impact of the Vietnam War and a love triangle between a military wife, her Marine Corps officer husband, and a veteran who's a paraplegic.

There were other types of successful fare, too. *Halloween*, for fans of slasher movies, starred Jamie Lee Curtis as Laurie Strode battling mental patient Michael Myers in the first of her eight movies for the *Halloween* franchise. *Hooper* starred Burt Reynolds at his comedic height as an aging Hollywood stuntman taking on a record-breaking stunt in a rocket car together with a young, brash protégé played by Jan-Michael Vincent.

Warren Beatty recycled the premise of the 1941 film *Here Comes Mr. Jordan* for *Heaven Can Wait*, which he cowrote with Elaine May and co-directed with Buck Henry. But this version of the comedy made the lead character, Joe Pendleton, a football player with the Los Angeles Rams instead of a boxer whose spirit is taken from his body before death; he attempts to find a new body with athletic potential, accompanied by the angel Mr. Jordan, played by James Mason.

Baseball didn't need Hollywood for a compelling story. It faced a question—who would Pete Rose be playing for next year? At the beginning of December, he targeted four teams as potential employers: the Pirates, Braves, Cardinals, and Royals.[9] On December 4 the man who wore No. 14 for the Reds signed with an outlier—the Philadelphia Phillies. He got quite the bounty. Philadelphia's contract made Rose the highest-paid player in baseball, with an $800,000 annual salary for four years but a requirement to "play a specific number of games the fourth year" to maintain that figure.[10] Press accounts stated that he left money on the table plus some sweeteners.

The Royals offered a four-year deal at more than $1 million per year with an option to stay with the team for two additional years. Rose might have been the missing factor in an equation to beat the Yankees. For three straight seasons, Kansas City had lost to their pinstriped rivals in the American League championship series, but Rose wanted to stay with the Senior Circuit. "Switching to a new league, one in which I would have to face pitchers with whom I'm not familiar, was one reason," explained the six-time hits leader in the Major Leagues.[11] Rose reportedly also wanted to beat Stan Musial's National League record for career hits.

The Braves also offered more money, plus there was talk about a stake in Ted Turner's TV stations. Cardinals owner August Busch used his family's beer empire at Anheuser-Busch for a bonus in his offer: beer distributorships. Pirates owner John Galbreath had thoroughbreds in his investment portfolio; transferring one to Rose as a bonus could have been a terrific revenue stream for him. The offers from Kansas City et al. far outpaced Cincinnati's proposal that amounted to $850,000 over two years.[12]

Like Kansas City, Philadelphia had won the past three division titles but lost the pennant in the championship series; Cincinnati took the NL flag in

1976 and Los Angeles won the next two years. Obtaining the services of Rose not only gave heft to the Phillies' offense—which had Larry Bowa hitting .294 and Greg Luzinski bashing thirty-five home runs in 1978—but also an intangible value of leadership. Rose forecast his impact on the ball club that hadn't ever won a World Series since its inception in 1883 and last won an NL pennant in 1950. "I will make these guys grind it out," promised the three-time NL batting average leader. "They have lacked that on-the-field leader, the every-day [sic] player who has experience winning in the World Series. All I say is they should follow me on the first day of spring training. I'll make them tired if they follow me. But, I will make them winners and you never get tired of winning."[13]

Rose personified the term "everyday player." In only one season since his rookie year of 1963 had he played in fewer than 148 games, and he took the field for every game from 1974 to 1977. Knowing his limitations as a ballplayer, Rose honed his skills like an apprentice diamond cutter learning the intricacies of his trade. He didn't have the grace of Joe DiMaggio or Ted Williams. He didn't have the batting power of Reggie Jackson or Harmon Killebrew. But he knew how to swing the bat, as evidenced by his recent achievement of the forty-four-game hitting streak during the '78 season.

Another achievement reflecting dedication, discipline, and ability at the plate happened in 1977 when Rose surpassed Frankie Frisch as the leader in career hits by a switch hitter. He expounded on the achievement, revealing the weight of adding value to a team however you can. "The reason that's so important is that not many guys in baseball or any other sport become the all-time best at whatever they do," Rose explained. "I couldn't become the best home run hitter or RBI man, but I worked hours and hours on the nature of my game, which is switch-hitting. The whole secret is not trying to be something you're not."[14]

Rose would turn thirty-eight on April 14, 1979. Doubters regarding his potential need only look at his 1978 statistics of playing in 159 games, getting 198 hits, leading the Major Leagues with 51 doubles, leading the National League with 731 plate appearances, and batting .302. While some might have called him arrogant, Rose considered himself truthful when he opined on the value of experience, consistency, statistics, and records: "Where do I lack? Who does these four things better than me? There's guys who can hit better than me. There's guys who can run faster and throw better. But you put them all in a package and I have to feel that I'm the No. 1 player."[15]

Rose's style of play could be termed competitive, aggressive, or brutal depending on the person offering the opinion. In the 1970 All-Star Game, he looked more like a member of the Cincinnati Bengals than the Cincinnati Reds when he ran into catcher Ray Fosse at home plate to score the game-winning run for the National League in the twelfth inning.

Three years later, Rose and Mets shortstop Bud Harrelson got into a fistfight during the NL championship series. New York had blanked Cincinnati 5–0 in game two, prompting Harrelson to joke about the opposition's offense. With the Mets leading 9–2 in game three, Rose banged a single off Jerry Koosman in the top of the fifth inning followed by Joe Morgan grounding to first baseman John Milner; a double play occurred when Milner threw to Harrelson, who fired back to Milner. Rose took his opportunity to provoke a fight with the much smaller Harrelson. Benches cleared.

Coincidentally, Harrelson and Rose played together on the 1979 Phillies. Rose spent five seasons with the team, marking his tenure in the City of Brotherly Love with the first World Series title for the Phillies, in 1980. He played for the Expos for more than half of the 1984 season, then returned to the Reds in a midseason trade as a player-manager when the Reds fired Vern Rapp from the helmsman position. Rose retired from playing after the 1986 season as the all-time leader in the Major Leagues for games played, plate appearances, at bats, and hits.

In 1988 Rose got suspended for thirty days because he made physical contact with an umpire while arguing a call. But the following year was a flashpoint for the icon when information surfaced about him gambling on sports, including baseball; Rose admitted the other sports but denied the allegations regarding the national pastime to baseball commissioner Peter Ueberroth. A. Bartlett Giamatti succeeded Ueberroth as commissioner on April 1 and hired attorney John Dowd to investigate a few days later; his report concluded that Rose bet on the Reds while he managed them. The controversy resulted in Giamatti banning him permanently from Major League Baseball. On a parallel note, the Hall of Fame disallowed anyone on the permanently ineligible list from induction.

While the baseball world pondered the impact of Rose going to Philadelphia, the literary world celebrated another blockbuster in December: Herman Wouk's *War and Remembrance* followed his 1971 saga *The Winds of War*, which detailed the era before America's involvement in World War II, from Germany's invasion of Poland to the Japanese attack on Pearl Harbor.

Again centered on Captain Victor "Pug" Henry and his fictional naval family, *War and Remembrance* debuted in October and topped the best-seller list in November; it stayed there for much of December.

Wouk gave a sweeping account of the war, from battles in the Pacific theater to the Holocaust in Europe to President Franklin Roosevelt in the White House. Reviewers praised this sequel to *The Winds of War*. In the *St. Louis Post-Dispatch*, Harry Levins referenced another World War II novel by Wouk, *The Caine Mutiny*, which had inspired the 1954 movie of the same name starring Humphrey Bogart. "Like many in his generation, Wouk seems to have found that World War II was the central event of his life," wrote Levins. "He must have felt that the tiny bridge of the U.S.S. Caine was too small a stage for that big a story. Hence, 'Winds' and 'Remembrance.'"[16]

Wouk's chronicle of Jewish suffering at the hands of the Nazi regime in *War and Remembrance* reminded middle-aged Americans in the late 1970s of the tragedy that had astonished the world in its complexity, massiveness, and evil during their lifetime. If Wouk's words were arrows, they would hit the bulls-eye. Richard Allen Paul, an attorney in Wilmington, Delaware, contributed a review to the city's *Sunday News Journal* praising the author for devoting part of the novel to the slaughter of six million Jews: "The last third of the book contains some of the most shattering prose I've had to read, and I'm a Jew with a fairly complete knowledge of the Holocaust. I haven't wept in a long time—until now."[17]

Floyd Logan described the Jewish plight as "recounted with sickening horror" in the *Indianapolis News*.[18] But a contrasting review appeared in the *Jackson Sun*. Rima Firrone alleged that Wouk had passed over those who died during World War II except for "the hopeless Jews" and calls his religion into question: "The final Solution should not be ignored, but Mr. Wouk's heredity and the current Middle East situation make motives suspect. The book falls into the realm of rabble-rousing support for Israel and today's Jews based, not on their merits, but on the suffering of their parents.

As a work of fiction, *War and Remembrance* is a failure; as a political essay, it is inappropriate."[19]

In a lecture titled "War and Remembrance: The Paradox of Historical Fiction" presented at the Library of Congress a year later, Wouk addressed the Holocaust and other atrocities of World War II as crucial factors in his "passions" for research and in writing the sequel to *The Winds of War*: "The deepest passion was grief, grief for the terrible destruction of my Jewish people on the European continent. Grief, too, for the millions and millions of dead in this worst of man-made catastrophes, for the million people who starved in Leningrad, whose bodies fell in the snow, were covered by the snow, and emerged to stink in the spring thaw. The millions and millions of civilians killed by bombs, the brave men on both sides—over fifty million human lives in all—snuffed out; so many lost lives, very present to me as a result of all this reading I had done."[20]

Wouk wrote the script for the 1983 ABC miniseries *The Winds of War* and cowrote the script for 1988's *War and Remembrance* with Dan Curtis and Earl W. Wallace. "I ended up writing some forty hours of film in the two serials, equal perhaps to twenty feature movies," said Wouk at a 1995 Library of Congress symposium honoring him. "It was a challenge, but I developed no love for the work. I did it to preserve the accuracy and quality of the filming of my novels."[21]

His commitment to translating his novels into another medium is rooted not only in protecting the work but also in depicting a story that compels, educates, and entertains. Readers who were forty-five or older in 1978 remembered the events depicted in *War and Remembrance* and embraced Wouk's creation within the context of battles in Europe and the South Pacific as well as events at home. Perhaps a neighbor was a paratrooper on D-Day, a sailor at the Battle of Midway, or a Marine at Guadalcanal. Maybe an older cousin flew on bomber planes over Germany. Wouk had already set a new standard of excellence with *The Winds of War*, so the sequel needed to be as good. It was. *War and Remembrance* struck a chord with readers, earning its author another appearance on the best-seller list.

Wouk had credibility beyond his skills in research and writing, as he had served in the navy during World War II. Before the United States entered the war, he had attempted to get into Officers' Candidate School but got rejected because of his age—twenty-six. After the Japanese attack on Pearl Harbor, the age standards disappeared. Prior to joining, Wouk had worked as a comedy writer for radio star Fred Allen.

Serving in the South Pacific gave insight and inspiration to the man who would come to write novels that defined literary excellence in the twentieth century, including *Marjorie Morningstar*, *Youngblood Hawke*, and *The Caine Mutiny*, which was inspired by his World War II service and for which he won a Pulitzer Prize. A Broadway play and a movie starring Humphrey Bogart followed. "While in Officers' Candidate School my father died, and in no great space of time after that, I found myself whirled like a driven leaf by the winds of war to the other side of the earth, below the equator, where I landed, as mindlessly and willlessly [sic] as a driven leaf, on the deck of a destroyer-minesweeper, the USS *Zane*, where I proceeded to take part in operations I did not understand, in a war I did not grasp, performing duties that I barely was equal to," said the novelist.[22]

During his naval service aboard the *Zane* and later the USS *Southard*, he envisioned writing "a great book about the war." Though provocative, *The Caine Mutiny* did not fulfill his goal. In his diary Wouk wrote that "this is not the great war book. It is a good book, or I am the more deceived, but it is in essence an anecdote about the war."[23]

Writing *The Caine Mutiny* set Wouk on a journey of research that resulted in accumulating more than two thousand books about World War II by the time he had finished *War and Remembrance*; his first purchase was an eight-volume set titled *The Record of the Nuremberg Trial: Nazi Conspiracy and Aggression*. Wouk moved to Washington DC in 1964, which gave him access to the Library of Congress's extensive resources, which he devoured along with opuses in his collection about World War II and other wars. His reading list included *War and Peace*, *The Peloponnesian War*, and Winston Churchill's six-volume series, which gave him a detailed context from which to write a novel that encompassed the military, social, political, and emotional impacts of war.

Wouk's curiosity contradicted his outlook during his younger years. "In high school if I ever came close to flunking, it was in history," he admitted. "In college, since history was an elective, I studied no history. This was my natural bent—an iron curtain blocking my mind against history."[24]

But projects as immense as *The Winds of War* and *War and Remembrance* present epic challenges in combining facts, events, and people with the fictional characters that Wouk created, hence the reason for his lecture. His solution? Avoid playing the role of a historian. "I sensed the possibility of recreating events not as the historian presents them in the disciplined order of retrospect, but as they occurred, as they rolled over a poor lovelorn gag man in the white hole of show biz; and equally over the President in the White House, watching the slow creep of the Japanese southward towards the easy loot left by the collapse of the European empires," revealed Wouk.[25]

On the fiftieth anniversary of D-Day, in 1994, Wouk returned to Washington to give a lecture at the Library of Congress as part of its tribute to him and Dan Curtis, who directed the ABC miniseries in the 1980s based on the two World War II novels. Again, he focused on the dichotomy between history and fiction by using the analogy of oil and water but provided a caveat regarding cultural interpretations of historical events being a defining version of information as well as entertainment. "Yet consider that the French Revolution will always be, for the common reader, not so much the upheaval that Carlyle and many great historians have portrayed, but rather what the popular novelist Dickens wrote about it," opined Wouk.[26]

Indeed. It's impossible to think about Lou Gehrig without recalling Gary Cooper's portrayal in *The Pride of the Yankees*. But Wouk's World War II novels were so vast in scope and so detailed in the recounting of battles and other real-life events, it would be impossible to do them justice by making movies. Fortunately, the 1970s elevated a new type of programming—TV miniseries.

ABC enjoyed great success with *Roots* and *Rich Man, Poor Man*, and NBC aired the miniseries *Holocaust* in April 1978. Like Wouk's World War II novels, *Holocaust* centered on a family. CBS had become known as the "Tiffany Network" because of its array of stellar programming in entertainment and news. Any network would be a good fit for Wouk's novels. Although having your work displayed on TV for millions of people to watch would be enticing to the ego and potentially lucrative, especially if viewers went out and bought reprinted editions of the novels, Wouk did not jump at the chance for a miniseries. It was a matter of quality. He explained, "But Mrs. Wouk insisted with eventual success on the strictest controls: of producer, of director, of writer, and to the extent that it was possible, of cast, too; even control of unseemly products that could not be advertised, because of the seriousness of the battle sequences and Holocaust scenes."[27]

War and Remembrance gave Americans a chance to remember when the country's citizens unified with pride, patriotism, and purpose as they bought war bonds, contributed to scrap metal drives, and donated to the American Red Cross. Wouk's depiction of war's horrors was familiar to Gold Star families who received notice that a brother, son, or husband died in battle fighting the Japanese in the South Pacific or the Nazis in Europe and North Africa; their sacrifices are noted by cemeteries in Arlington, Colleville-sur-Mer, and others where soldiers, sailors, marines, and airmen are buried.

Wouk's best seller recalled the importance of national unity when confronting adversity. In 1978 Americans needed to be reminded that the country had been through hell but maintained its status as the land of opportunity, freedom, and progress. On the last day of the year, they got another reminder of a horrible event testing their resolve. Newspapers reported that the House Select Committee on Assassinations concluded that President John F. Kennedy "was probably assassinated as a result of a conspiracy." But the committee stated that evidence did not point to the involvement of the Soviet Union, Cuba, anti-Castro Cuban groups, organized crime, the FBI, or the CIA in the thirty-fifth president's murder, long attributed to Lee Harvey Oswald.[28]

It was a stark reminder that America's strength lies not only in achievements but the ability to confront, endure, and rebound from disaster.

NOTES

1. THE BEST INTERESTS OF BASEBALL

1. Franklyn Buell, "Old Friends Remember Marse Joe, Bid Farewell," *Buffalo News*, January 17, 1978, 4.
2. "Broken Kneecap He Suffered in Sandlot Game Sentences Joe McCarthy to Minors," *Mount Carmel (PA) Item*, January 22, 1937, 6.
3. McCarthy got a baseball scholarship even though he didn't complete high school.
4. "Flaherty Quits Colonels for Good of Local Team," *Courier-Journal* (Louisville), July 23, 1919, 8.
5. Edward Burns, "McCarthy Calmly Hears News of Hornsby's Appointment," *Chicago Tribune*, September 23, 1930, 17.
6. Irving Vaughan, "Hornsby Gets Job: Wrigley," *Chicago Tribune*, September 23, 1930, 1.
7. Irving Vaughan, "It's Just a Ball Game as Cubs Change Pilots," *Chicago Tribune*, September 26, 1930, 33.
8. Harold C. Burr, "Story of Joe McCarthy Just a Succession of Other Little Stories," *Brooklyn Daily Eagle*, July 5, 1931, 36.
9. Arch Murray, "Insider Reveals McCarthy Will Not Return to Yankees," *New York Post*, July 31, 1945, 34.
10. "Doctor, Wife Deny M'Carthy Has Quit Post with Yankees," *Buffalo News*, July 31, 1945, 8.
11. "Joe McCarthy Has Gall Bladder Attack," *Boston Daily Globe*, May 24, 1946, 15.
12. "McCarthy Resigns Yankee Job; Dickey Named Manager," *Buffalo Evening News*, May 25, 1946, 5.
13. "Yanks Sign Joe McCarthy," Associated Press, *Boston Daily Globe*, June 25, 1946, 10; Joe Trimble, "Yanks Leading Tribe in Arclight Contest," *Daily News* (New York), June 25, 1946, 45.
14. "Joe McCarthy Coming to Sox?" *Boston Daily Globe*, February 3, 1947, 4.
15. "Joe McCarthy Signed as Red Sox Manager," *Boston Evening Globe*, September 29, 1947, 1.
16. Harold Kaese, "Why McCarthy Accepted Job at [sic] Manager of Sox," *Boston Daily Globe*, September 30, 1947, 25.
17. Frederick G. Lieb, "'Get the Players, Keep 'Em Satisfied,' McCarthy Credo; Declares Day of Driving Athletes Like Mules Is Over," *The Sporting News*, November 24, 1938, 3.

18. Sid Keener, "How to Win? Joe M'Carthy Says: Don't Beat Yourself," *St. Louis Star-Times*, June 7, 1949, 19.
19. "McCarthy of Red Sox Arrives Home for Rest," Associated Press, *New York Times*, June 23, 1950, 39.
20. "McCarthy of Red Sox Arrives Home for Rest."
21. Gerry Moore, "M'Carthy Knew He Was Through," *Boston Post*, June 26, 1950, 21.
22. "'When Man Can't Help Club It's Time to Quit'—McCarthy," *Boston Globe*, June 24, 1950, 6.
23. In 1977 Commissioner Bowie Kuhn authorized a special committee to look into the methods of the Hall of Fame's Veterans Committee, which had twelve members. Based on the research effort's results, six slots were added to the Veterans Committee. But Bill Terry's resignation caused the total number of voting members to drop from eighteen to seventeen. Also, the Veterans Committee absorbed the responsibility for voting on Negro League players. "It's Tougher than Ever to Get Inducted into the Hall of Fame," Associated Press, *Wausau (WI) Daily Herald*, January 30, 1978, 15.
24. Joe McCarthy, "An Old Yankee Manager Recalls the Joy of His Job," *New York Times*, September 25, 1977, sec. 5, 2.
25. Frederick John, "Baseball's Greatest Manager," *Modern Maturity*, April–May 1973, 14–15.
26. "Addie Joss Is Disappointed If Batter Misses Bad One," *Democrat and Chronicle* (Rochester NY), April 2, 1911, 28.
27. Bob Saxton, "MacPhail Quits; Crosley May Take More Active Interest," *Cincinnati Enquirer*, September 19, 1936, 13.
28. Lee Scott, "Larry MacPhail's Successor Will Not Be Named until After Season Ends," *Brooklyn Citizen*, September 24, 1942, 6.
29. Larry MacPhail, statement of opinion on "The Negro in Baseball," reprinted in "McPhail [sic] Letter Shows Staunch Objection to Integrate Baseball," Negro Leagues Baseball Museum, January 19, 2015, https://nlbm.mlblogs.com/mcphail-letter-shows-staunch-objection-to-integrate-baseball-c293bab9676.
30. Max Kase, "M'Phail and Topping Brawl: McDonald Gets a Shiner at Victory Party," *New York Journal-American*, October 7, 1947, 1.
31. Kase, "M'Phail and Topping Brawl."
32. Kase, "M'Phail and Topping Brawl"; Hugh Bradley, "MacPhail Sells Yankee Stock," *New York Journal-American*, October 7, 1947, 16.
33. Ralph Berger, "Larry MacPhail," Society for American Baseball Research, Baseball Biography Project, accessed January 30, 2023, https://sabr.org/bioproj/person/larry-macphail/. According to this biographical account, "The ravages of alcohol and the onset of what is now presumed to be Alzheimer's disease were affecting his once great entrepreneurial mind."
34. "Ed Mathews Hits 2-Run Fence Blow," *Ventura County Star–Free Press*, April 6, 1949, 11.
35. Jim Munsey, "Wilson Beaten, 8–2: Mathews Star in Prep Clash," *Long Beach Press-Telegram*, May 28, 1949, A-9.

36. "Boston Braves Ink Eddie Mathews," *Santa Maria Times*, June 20, 1949, 2.
37. Howell Stevens, "Mathews Seen Sure to Stay Up," *Boston Post*, March 9, 1952, 28.
38. Lloyd Larson, "Mad about Mathews," *American Weekly*, September 13, 1953, 6.
39. Tom Meany, "The Wrists That Made Milwaukee Famous," *Collier's*, April 30, 1954, 83.
40. "Braves Said 'Ugh' to Gabe's $500,000 Pitch for Mathews," *The Sporting News*, January 5, 1963, 16.
41. Terry Bledsoe, "Career as Outfielder Apparently Is Ended," *Milwaukee Journal*, April 19, 1964, Sports News, 3; Bob Wolf, "Juggler Bragan Puts Left Fielder's Glove on Slugger Mathews," *The Sporting News*, November 9, 1963, 23.
42. Bob Wolf, "Braves, Guilty of Trade Boner, Apologize to 'Edward' Mathews," *The Sporting News*, January 28, 1967.
43. John Wilson, "Mathews Brings Touch of Class and Big Bat to Astros' Lineup," *The Sporting News*, April 29, 1967, 24.
44. Jim Hawkins, "Even as Sub, Mathews Led Tigers in '68," *The Sporting News*, August 26, 1978, 12.
45. Watson Spoelstra, "Mathews Named Scout for Tigers," *The Sporting News*, November 2, 1968, 30.
46. "Eddie Mathews to Join Brewers" (news release), Milwaukee Brewers, September 10, 1975, Edwin Lee Mathews Biography File, Giamatti Research Center, National Baseball Hall of Fame and Museum, Cooperstown, New York.
47. Vic Carucci, "Managing Not Eddie Mathews' Game," *Utica Daily Press*, August 7, 1978, 19.
48. Phil Pepe, "Eddie Mathews: They Don't Have Fun We Did," *Daily News* (New York), January 20, 1978, 23C.
49. George M. Steinbrenner III to Bowie K. Kuhn, December 23, 1977, Folder 10, Box 6, Subseries 3, Series II, BA MSS 100, Bowie Kuhn Collection, National Baseball Hall of Fame and Museum.
50. Murray Chass, "Kuhn Vetoes Finley—'Blue Is Not a Red,'" *Modesto Bee*, January 31, 1978, 5.
51. Major League Baseball Commissioner Bowie K. Kuhn, "Decision," January 30, 1978, Folder 2, Box 7, Subseries 3, Series II, BA MSS 100, Bowie Kuhn Collection.
52. Kuhn, "Decision," January 30, 1978.
53. Nancy Scannell, "Judge Rules Kuhn Had Right to Nullify Sales by Finley," *Washington Post*, March 18, 1977, D1.
54. Steve Wilson, "Rhodes Declares State of Emergency," *Cincinnati Enquirer*, January 27, 1978, A-11.
55. "Federal Help Too Little, Too Late after Blizzard Hit, Critics Charge," Associated Press, *Battle Creek Enquirer and News*, January 31, 1978, A-3.

2. "ABSOLUTELY UNBELIEVABLE"

1. Anthony F. Shannon, "Another Storm Perils Winter-Weary Jersey," *Star-Ledger* (Newark NJ), February 6, 1978, 1.

2. Paul B. Brown, "Storm Brings Middlesex to Virtual Halt," *Star-Ledger*, February 7, 1978, 3.
3. Robert Steyer, "Tools of Trade: Shovels and Snowblowers Are in Short Supply," *Star-Ledger*, February 7, 1978, 3.
4. Stuart Marques and Anthony F. Shannon, "Jersey Faces Costly Cleanup from Storm," *Star-Ledger*, February 8, 1978, 1.
5. Richard Rosen, "Flooding, Erosion at Shore," *Star-Ledger*, February 8, 1978, 1.
6. Terry Connelly and Kathleen Woodruff, "Shore Puts Damage at $20 Million," *Star-Ledger*, February 9, 1978, 1.
7. Barbara Kukla, "2-Day Freeze on Mails Marks a Jersey 'First,'" *Star-Ledger*, February 8, 1978, 5.
8. Robert Steyer, "Tire Business Benefits from Winter Woes," *Star-Ledger*, February 9, 1978, 26.
9. Jerry Krupnick, "Channel 2 Makes It to Top of the Snow Heap," *Star-Ledger*, February 9, 1978, 65.
10. Rockford ("New Jersey's Leading Furniture Chain") advertisement, *Star-Ledger*, February 9, 1978, 27.
11. Barbara Kukla, "Travel Agents Juggle Scarce Places in Sun," *Star-Ledger*, February 10, 1978, 12.
12. American Airlines advertisement, *Star-Ledger*, February 9, 1978, 56.
13. Peter Kihss, "40-Hour Snowstorm Almost Paralyzes New York City Area," *New York Times*, February 8, 1978, 1.
14. Roy R. Silver, "More Than 1,000 Cars Trapped on L.I. Roads," *New York Times*, February 7, 1978, 27.
15. Michael C. Jensen, "Snow Cripples Businesses and Forces Early Closing," *New York Times*, February 7, 1978, 29.
16. Charles Claffey and Alexander A. Hawes, "Blizzard Batters New England," *Boston Globe*, February 7, 1978, 1.
17. Charles E. Claffey, "Worst Storm of Century," *Boston Globe*, February 8, 1978, 1.
18. *The Blizzard of '78* (twenty-fifth anniversary special), WCVB, Hearst-Argyle Stations, February 7, 2003, https://www.youtube.com/watch?v=th9Ekbe_MG8.
19. *Blizzard of '78* anniversary special.
20. *The Marvelous Mrs. Maisel*, season 5, episode 8, "The Princess and the Plea," streamed May 19, 2023, on Amazon Prime.
21. *Mad Men*, season 1, episode 1, "Smoke Gets in Your Eyes," aired July 19, 2007, on AMC.
22. *61**, directed by Billy Crystal, aired April 28, 2001, on HBO.
23. Marshall, *Wake Me When It's Funny*, 35.
24. Kimberly Potts, "Anson Williams: Robin Williams Turned the Worst 'Happy Days' Episode into the Best," Yahoo! Entertainment, November 11, 2014, https://www.yahoo.com/entertainment/anson-williams-robin-williams-turned-the-worst-111306215275.html. "Nanu nanu" was Williams's creation of the Orkan greeting akin to "Hello."

25. HARDtalk, BBC, March 4, 2013, https://www.youtube.com/watch?v=xT_N9cjB8s4&list=PLYAiRXvl1Wr7PWrlbjwF-8YKDFNELzeGa.
26. Allison Samuels, "1940–2005: Richard Pryor," *Newsweek*, December 18, 2005, https://www.newsweek.com/1940-2005-richard-pryor-114071.
27. Lee Glickstein, "Three Local Comedians Return Laughing Triumphantly," *San Francisco Examiner*, March 26, 1978, Datebook, 17.
28. Dave Itzkoff, interview by Terry Gross, "He Felt He Could No Longer Be Funny, Says Robin Williams Biographer," NPR, May 14, 2018, https://www.npr.org/2018/05/14/610993828/before-his-death-robin-williams-felt-he-couldnt-be-funny-anymore.
29. *The Rachel Maddow Show*, MSNBC, August 11, 2014, https://www.youtube.com/watch?v=LdeZOJ6dn_8.
30. Marshall, *Wake Me When It's Funny*, 35.
31. *Happy Days*, season 6, episode 14, "The Magic Show," aired December 5, 1978, on ABC.
32. *Happy Days*, season 4, episode 8, "They Shoot Fonzies, Don't They?" aired November 16, 1976, on ABC.
33. *Happy Days*, season 3, episode 3, "Fearless Fonzarelli: Part 1," aired September 23, 1975, on ABC; *Happy Days*, season 3, episode 4, "Fearless Fonzarelli: Part 2," aired September 30, 1975, on ABC.
34. *Happy Days*, season 6, episode 2, "Westward Ho! Part 1," aired September 12, 1978, on ABC; *Happy Days*, season 6, episode 3, "Westward Ho! Part 2," aired September 19, 1978, on ABC.
35. *Happy Days*, season 5, episode 1, "Hollywood: Part 1," aired September 13, 1977, on ABC; *Happy Days*, season 5, episode 2, "Hollywood: Part 2," aired September 13, 1977, on ABC; *Happy Days*, season 5, episode 3, "Hollywood: Part 3," aired September 20, 1977, on ABC.
36. Andee Beck, "Donny Most Isn't Selling Himself Short," *Star-Ledger*, February 6, 1978, 21; *Happy Days*, season 5, episode 7, "The Apartment," aired November 1, 1977, on ABC. The show's other sitcom spin-offs were *Joanie Loves Chachi*, *Blansky's Beauties*, and *Out of the Blue*. The animation company Hanna-Barbera used *Happy Days* and *Laverne & Shirley* as fodder for the Saturday morning cartoons *The Fonz and the Happy Days Gang* and *Laverne & Shirley in the Army*, which aired on ABC. Combining three shows from the *Happy Days* universe, Hanna-Barbera produced the *Mork & Mindy / Laverne & Shirley / Fonz Hour*. The *Laverne & Shirley* segment was renamed *Laverne & Shirley with the Fonz* and kept the military setting; Fonzie worked in the motor pool. It incorporated Fonzie's dog Mr. Cool, who also appeared on *The Fonz and the Happy Days Gang*.
37. Phil Pepe, "Yankees Still Seeking Winfield," *Daily News* (New York), February 26, 1978, 88.
38. "Lasorda: Dodgers Stronger," *San Luis Obispo County* (CA) *Telegram-Tribune*, February 28, 1978, B-2.

39. Jack Lang, "Randle Won't Play," *Daily News* (New York), February 28, 1978, 64.
40. Larry Whiteside, "Wise: 'I Just Hope to Get Out of Here,'" *Boston Globe*, February 27, 1978, 22.
41. Whiteside, "Wise: 'I Just Hope to Get Out of Here.'"

3. GOODBYE DARK, MY OLD FRIEND

1. "Kroc Hopes Change to Dark Wakes Up Pads," *Times-Advocate* (Escondido CA), May 30, 1977, A-7.
2. "Dark Looks, Triumphs," *Times-Advocate*, May 31, 1977, A-13.
3. "Pitching Coach Replaces Alvin Dark at Padres' Helm," Associated Press, *Fresno Bee*, March 22, 1978, B1.
4. Dark and Underwood, *When in Doubt, Fire the Manager*, 230.
5. John Drebinger, "Giants Get Dark and Stanky," *New York Times*, December 15, 1949, 52.
6. Joe King, "Durocher Tags Dark as Giants' Captain," *New York World-Telegram and Sun*, February 17, 1950, 35.
7. "Dark Fired; Appling Heads A's," *St. Louis Post-Dispatch*, August 20, 1967, 5B.
8. Prescott Sullivan, "Alvin Dark and His Struggle with Satan," *San Francisco Examiner*, July 16, 1961, 35.
9. Alvin Dark with John Underwood, "Rhubarbs, Hassles, Other Hazards," *Sports Illustrated*, May 13, 1974, 42.
10. Ross Newhan, "Lasorda Names Lopes Captain," *Los Angeles Times*, March 2, 1978, E1.
11. Lasorda and Fisher, *Artful Dodger*, 161.
12. Lasorda and Fisher, *Artful Dodger*, 121–22.
13. Ray Herbat, "Ogden Successful in Baseball Deal," *Salt Lake Tribune*, August 20, 1966, 24; Lasorda quote from Cliff Hight, "The Era of Tommy Lasorda: The Ogden Dodgers, 1966–1968," *Utah Historical Quarterly* 72, no. 4 (2004), https://issuu.com/utah10/docs/uhq_volume72_2004_number4/s/10154392.
14. Phil Collier, "National League: Close Races Expected but Inter-League Trades May Upset Predictions Below," *Baseball: Street & Smith's Official 1978 Yearbook*, 41.
15. Ross Newhan, "Campanis Says Pitching Gives Dodgers Edge," *Los Angeles Times*, March 27, 1978, D1.
16. "Dodger Becomes Hero," United Press International, *The Signal* (Newhall CA), March 3, 1978, 2. In 2011 the Lindsay Unified School District eliminated the junior high school paradigm, created a K–8 program, and renamed the school Reagan Elementary. Reggie Ellis, "Garvey Day Strikes Out in Final at-Bat," *Sun-Gazette* (Tulare County CA), June 15, 2011, https://thesungazette.com/article/news/2011/06/15/garvey-day-strikes-out-in-final-at-bat/.
17. Ross Newhan, "OK, Anderson Tells the Dodgers, Let's See You Do It Again," *Los Angeles Times*, March 21, 1978, D1.
18. Newhan, "OK, Anderson Tells the Dodgers."

19. The players were Gary Thomasson, Dave Heaverlo, Alan Wirth, John Henry Johnson, and Phil Huffman. Mario Guerrero was the player to be named later.
20. Dick Young, "Randle Good Guy Who Makes Bad Mistakes," *Daily News* (New York), March 2, 1978, 75.
21. "Seaver Ponders 30 Wins," Associated Press, *Desert Sun* (Palm Springs CA), March 2, 1978, B6.
22. Joseph Durso, "Who Will Beat the Yankees?" *New York Times*, March 10, 1978, A23.
23. Bob Rubin, "Fighting Yanks Are Something Special," *Miami Herald*, March 26, 1978, 6-C.
24. Bill Brubaker, "Royals' Otis: Yankees Won't Beat Us Again," *Miami News*, March 20, 1978, C1.
25. Robert Ward, "Reggie Jackson in No-Man's Land," *Sport*, June 1977, 94.
26. "Eastwick Knows the Score," United Press International, *Ventura County Star–Free Press*, March 26, 1978, D-4.
27. Steve Jacobson, "Torrez Can't Shut Out Memory of Last Year," *Newsday*, March 11, 1978, 26.
28. Dick Young, "The Day the Yanks Could Have Kept Torrez," *Daily News* (New York), March 29, 1978, 85.

4. MOVE OVER, BABY RUTH

1. Larry Keith, "They Kept Cool during a Cold Streak," *Sports Illustrated*, May 2, 1977, 30.
2. Maury Allen, "Reggies Rain at Opener," *New York Post*, April 14, 1978, 88.
3. Red Smith, "Candy That Tastes like a Hot Dog," *New York Times*, April 14, 1978, A19.
4. Murray Chass, "Jackson Belt Brings Yanks Home with a 4-to-2 Victory," *New York Times*, April 14, 1978, A1.
5. *The Dick Van Dyke Show*, season 5, episode 10, "Go Tell the Birds and the Bees," aired November 17, 1965, on CBS.
6. Joseph Durso, "Maris Finally Hears Cheers at the Stadium," *New York Times*, April 14, 1978, A19.
7. Durso, "Maris Finally Hears Cheers at the Stadium." Baseball Reference indicates that Maris hit thirty-four home runs in 1962.
8. Durso, "Maris Finally Hears Cheers at the Stadium."
9. Murray Chass, "Maris's Feat Finally Recognized 30 Years after Hitting 61 Homers," *New York Times*, September 5, 1991, B12.
10. Allen Katz, telephone interview by author, July 24, 2023.
11. Rhoda Katz, telephone interview by author, July 24, 2023.
12. Lisa (Katz) Gruber, telephone interview by author, July 24, 2023.
13. Chris Butts, telephone interview by author, July 7, 2023.
14. Rebecca Alpert, email to author, July 9, 2023.
15. Victor Sloan, telephone interview by author, July 7, 2023.
16. James Pietras, telephone interview by author, July 13, 2023.

17. Rock Hoffman, email to author, July 21, 2023.
18. Mike Miller, email to author, July 15, 2023.
19. John J. O'Connor, "TV Weekend," *New York Times*, April 7, 1978, C26; David Foil, "'Dallas': A Big, Rotten Mess," *Town Talk* (Alexandria-Pineville LA), April 3, 1978, B-10; Noel Holston, "'Dallas' a Tacky, Trashy Potboiler," *Sentinel Star* (Orlando), April 1, 1978, 8-B; Kay Gardella, "Family Feudin'...," *Daily News* (New York), April 1, 1978, 39; Bruce Blackwell, "'Dallas' Sinks CBS to New Low Network Entertainment," Gannett News Service, *Daily Times* (St. Cloud MN), April 29, 1978, 9A.
20. Television Academy Foundation, "Larry Hagman Discusses 'Dallas' Who Shot J.R.?" Larry Hagman interviewed by Dan Pasternack, Santa Monica CA, December 7, 2004, https://www.youtube.com/watch?v=-GlWejfJhgo.
21. *Saturday Night Live*, season 6, episode 11, aired February 21, 1981, on NBC.

5. KINGMAN'S PERFORMANCE

1. "Lasorda Answers Question," YouTube, accessed April 29, 2024, https://www.youtube.com/watch?v=LIwrYH6Urbs.
2. Greg Prince, email to author, July 26, 2023.
3. Charlie Vascellaro, email to author, July 30, 2023.
4. Brian Hewitt, "Kong—Loner Didn't Like Fun City, Now Home in Homer Heaven," *Press & Sun Bulletin* (Binghamton NY), March 19, 1978, 10.
5. Richard Dozer, "Kingman Saves Day for Cubs," *Chicago Tribune*, May 15, 1978, E1.
6. Ross Newhan, "Kingman's 3rd Homer Beats Dodgers in 15," *Los Angeles Times*, May 15, 1978, E1. Kingman knocked in eight runs in the 1976 game as well.
7. Leonard Koppett, "Royals Beat Yanks, 4–3, on Inside-Park Homer," *New York Times*, May 13, 1978, 20.
8. Joe Donnelly, "A Collision Defeats the Yankees," *Newsday*, May 13, 1978, 28.
9. Donnelly, "Collision Defeats the Yankees."
10. Dick Netzley, "Rose Reaches Career Milestone, Rogers, Expos Spoil Festivities," *Troy (OH) Daily News*, May 6, 1978, 5.
11. "Pete Rose Refutes the Myths around the Infamous Ray Fosse All-Star Home Plate Collision," *The Rich Eisen Show*, July 10, 2017, https://www.youtube.com/watch?v=cxRf0eeASSs.
12. Dick Netzley, "3,000!!!!!" *Troy (OH) Daily News*, May 6, 1978, 5.
13. Kathleen Woodruff, "Byrne Cuts Casino Ribbon and a New Era Jingles In," *Star-Ledger*, May 27, 1978, 1.
14. Kathleen Woodruff and Stuart Marques, "A Smooth Opening for Jersey Casino," *Star-Ledger*, May 28, 1978, 1.
15. Luanne Axt, "Cannon Ball House to Take Historic Place," *Star-Ledger*, May 28, 1978, 50.
16. Bob Wisehart, "'Hot Wax' Takes You Back to Rock 'n' Roll Era," *Charlotte News*, March 16, 1978, 3B; Joseph Gelmis, "Rock and Roll Hero," *Newsday*, March 17, 1978, 7A.

17. Steve Dougherty, "'Hot Wax': Tribute to Alan Freed and an Infant Art Form," *Atlanta Constitution*, March 17, 1978, 26-B; Perry Stewart, "'Hot Wax' Up-Beat Film," *Fort Worth Star-Telegram*, March 31, 1978, 18A.
18. Peter Travers, "Gary Busey Is Indeed a 'Real' Buddy Holly," *Journal News* (White Plains NY), October 1, 1978, 17M.
19. Bruce A. Douglas, "'Buddy' Busey Story," *Muncie Star*, October 1, 1978, B7.
20. Rex Reed, "Busey Saves 'Buddy,'" *Daily News* (New York), July 26, 1978, 59.
21. Kenneth Stahl, "The Day the Music Died," Aircraft Owners and Pilots Association, March 1, 2020, https://pilot-protection-services.aopa.org/news/2020/march/01/the-day-the-music-died; Desiree Kocis, "Mysteries of Flight: The Day the Music Died," *Plane & Pilot*, February 4, 2020, https://www.planeandpilotmag.com/article/the-day-the-music-died/.

6. LOUISIANA LIGHTNING

1. Murray Chass, "Guidry Fans 18 Angels for Yank Mark and Wins No. 11 without Loss, 4–0," *New York Times*, June 18, 1978, S1.
2. Scott Ostler, "'From the Third Inning on, Wow!'" *Los Angeles Times*, June 18, 1978, E1.
3. Wayne Coffey, "When Lightning Struck," *Daily News* (New York), June 21, 1998, 108.
4. Guidry with Beaton, *Gator*, 103.
5. Phil Hersh, "Holtzman Goes to Yanks as Part of 10-Man Deal," *Evening Sun* (Baltimore), June 16, 1976, 1; Murray Chass, "Players Swap Memories of Yankees-Orioles 10-Player Trade," *New York Times*, June 15, 1986, S3.
6. Maxwell Kates, "The Birth of the Toronto Blue Jays," *Time for Expansion Baseball*, Society for American Baseball Research, citing interview with Elliott Wahle, January 17, 2018, https://sabr.org/journal/article/the-birth-of-the-toronto-blue-jays/#calibre_link-1106. The Toronto Blue Jays and Seattle Mariners were part of the American League's expansion. Both teams debuted in 1977.
7. Earl Lawson, "Seaver Grins, Wife Nancy Cries Tears of Joy," *Cincinnati Post*, June 17, 1978, 25.
8. *Schaap One on One*, ESPN Classic (date unknown), accessed April 14, 2024, https://www.youtube.com/watch?v=bC6-QUpIkRY.
9. Don Werner, telephone interview by author, August 18, 2023.
10. Tom Meehan, "Sutton Buttons Down San Jose in Debut as Pro," *The Sporting News*, May 1, 1965, 43.
11. John Peri, "Peri-Graphs," *Stockton Record*, June 16, 1965, 55.
12. Bob Hunter, "L.A.'s New Big D Sutton Death to Foes," *The Sporting News*, May 14, 1966, 3.
13. "300 Victories 'Out of Reach' for Don Sutton," *Boston Herald*, September 16, 1984, 58.
14. "Sutton to Play Alexander in Movie," United Press International, *Coeur d'Alene* (ID) *Press*, February 10, 1982, 11.
15. Sam McManis, "Against Claire's Wishes, Sutton Talks to Astros," *Los Angeles Times*, August 10, 1988, D1.

16. Sam McManis, "Dodgers Hand Sutton His Walking Papers and Call Up Martinez," *Los Angeles Times*, August 11, 1988, D1.
17. McManis, "Dodgers Hand Sutton His Walking Papers."
18. Nicole Pappas, "Sutton's Career Comes Full Circle with Dodgers," National Baseball Hall of Fame and Museum, accessed August 19, 2023, https://baseballhall.org/discover/inside-pitch/suttons-career-comes-full-circle-with-dodgers.
19. Eric Girard, "No. 500 . . . for Willie: But Braves Win Pair in Style," *Atlanta Journal and Constitution*, July 1, 1978, 23.
20. David Sheehan, "'Grease': Slick Production or Greasy Kid Stuff?" *Tampa Tribune*, June 9, 1978, 10.
21. Tom Burke, "A Little Hotter than the Rest," *Rolling Stone* Feature Service, *Austin American-Statesman*, June 16, 1978, E1.
22. Gene Siskel, "Travolta Cuts through Flaws in Suburbanized 'Grease,'" *Chicago Tribune*, June 16, 1978, B1; Johnny Holmes, "'Grease' Playing at The Movies," *Corpus Christi Times*, June 23, 1978, 4C.
23. Sales figures are constantly changing, but these sources provide a starting point for further discussion. SmoothRadio.com and Collider.com put the soundtrack at No. 5. Thomas Curtis-Horsfall, "What Are the Top 5 Best-Selling Movie Soundtracks of All Time?" SmoothRadio.com, January 7, 2022, https://www.smoothradio.com/news/entertainment/best-selling-movie-soundtracks-of-all-time/; Jeremy Urquhart, "The 10 Most Popular Movie Soundtracks of All Times, Ranked by Total Sales," Collider.com, July 2, 2022, https://collider.com/most-popular-movie-soundtracks-of-all-time-ranked-by-total-sales/#39-the-lion-king-original-motion-picture-soundtrack-39-1994-mdash-15-million-copies-sold. Audicus places the *Grease* soundtrack at No. 7. Elena McPhillips, "The Top-Selling Movie Soundtracks of All Time," Audicus, May 4, 2022, https://www.audicus.com/top-movie-soundtracks/.
24. Charles Champlin, "'50s as Seen Through 'Grease,'" *Los Angeles Times*, June 16, 1978, 30.
25. "Domestic Box Office for 1978," Box Office Mojo, accessed August 25, 2023, https://www.boxofficemojo.com/year/1978/.
26. "Women Wowing 'Em in the Spotlights' Glow," *Chicago Tribune*, February 5, 1971, B2; William Leonard, "Greasy Nostalgia Full of Laughs," *Chicago Tribune*, February 12, 1971, B11.
27. Jeff Lyon, "Years Ago, He Helped Light 'Grease' Fire," *Chicago Tribune*, June 19, 1978, 1.
28. Clive Barnes, "Theater: 'Grease,' 1959 as Nostalgia," *New York Times*, February 15, 1972, 27.
29. Moore, Barbeau, and Waissman, *Grease*, 216.

7. MELODRAMA IN THE BRONX

1. Larry Keith, "A Bunt That Went Boom," *Sports Illustrated*, July 31, 1978, 14.
2. Jack Wilkinson, "Reggie Suspended," *Daily News* (New York), July 18, 1978, 72.
3. "Yanks Give KC 4 in 11th, Lose 9–7," *Daily News* (New York), July 18, 1978, 72.

4. "Yanks Give KC 4 in 11th, Lose 9–7."
5. Murray Chass, "Reggie Jackson Penalized: 5 Days, $9,000," *New York Times*, July 19, 1978, 19.
6. Dave Anderson, "Reggie's World: Above It All," *New York Times*, July 20, 1978, D17.
7. "Catfish Not Worried by Diabetes," *Reporter Dispatch* (Putnam County and White Plains NY), March 2, 1978, 31; Joe Donnelly, "Hunter Working Self into a Routine of Care," *Newsday*, March 3, 1978, 109.
8. Bruno Sniders, "Catfish's Arm a Pain to Yanks," *Democrat and Chronicle* (Rochester NY), May 22, 1978, 31; Red Foley, "Rx for Catfish, Guidry—Massage & Exercise," *Daily News* (New York), May 23, 1978, 79.
9. "For Catfish, the Going Gets Tougher," Associated Press, *Journal-News* (Rockland County NY), June 22, 1978, 1D.
10. Bill Nack, "Eckersley Feels No Pain, Other than That for Catfish Hunter," *Newsday*, June 22, 1978, 175.
11. "Figueroa Stops Twins on 6-Hitter, 2–0," *New York Times*, July 20, 1978, D17.
12. "Figueroa Stops Twins on 6-Hitter, 2–0."
13. Murray Chass, "Jackson's 'Differences' Stir Turmoil," *New York Times*, July 20, 1978, D17.
14. Murray Chass, "Jackson Target of Chambliss's Criticism, Too," *New York Times*, July 21, 1978, A15.
15. "Jackson Is Back but Uneasy," *New York Times*, July 24, 1978, C6.
16. Murray Chass, "Owner Stunned by Manager's Outburst," *New York Times*, July 24, 1978, C1.
17. Murray Chass, "Martin Resigns, Bob Lemon to Manage Yankees," *New York Times*, July 25, 1978, A1.
18. Pennington, *Billy Martin*, 131–32.
19. Arthur North and David Quirk, "Bombered in Copa Brawl, Yank 'Fan' to Sue Bauer," *Daily News* (New York), May 17, 1957, 3.
20. David Margolick, "63 Years Later, a Confession in a Legendary Yankees Scandal," *New York Times*, June 19, 2020, https://www.nytimes.com/2020/06/19/nyregion/1957-yankees-brawl-copacabana-silvestri.html.
21. Matthew J. Prigge, "Billy Martin, Chinese Aviator: One of the First Great Beefs in Brewers History," *Shepherd Express* (Milwaukee), January 5, 2017, https://shepherdexpress.com/sports/brew-crew-confidential/billy-martin-chinese-aviator-one-first-great-beefs-brewers-history/.
22. Denne H. Freeman, "Rangers Fire Third Strike Past Martin," Associated Press, *Wichita Falls (TX) Times*, July 22, 1975, 9.
23. Dan Cichalski, "Did a John Denver Song Get Billy Martin Fired?" MLB, July 20, 2024, https://www.mlb.com/news/billy-martin-rangers-firing.
24. Keith, "Bunt That Went Boom."
25. *Saturday Night Live* parodied Matthau's role for its recurring "bee" characters when he guest hosted in 1978 and appeared as a coach in a sketch called "The Bad News Bees."

26. Gene Siskel, "Little Pitchers Have Big Mouths in 'Bears' No. 3," *Chicago Tribune*, July 12, 1978, sec. 3, 6.
27. Vincent Canby, "Film: More 'Bad News Bears,'" *New York Times*, July 14, 1978, C15.
28. Richard Freedman, "'Bad News Bears' Strike Out," Newhouse News Service, *Independent Record* (Helena MT), July 28, 1978, 16A.
29. Linda Gross, "'Mouse & Child,' 'Tigers'—Family Fare," *Los Angeles Times*, May 26, 1978, 23.
30. Vernon Scott, "Women Back in Movies," United Press International, *Ukiah (CA) Daily Journal*, March 1, 1978, 15.
31. Sally Quinn, "An Unmarried Movie Star's View from the Top," *Washington Post*, April 9, 1978, H1.
32. Johnny Holmes, "Film Stars Jill Clayburgh," *Corpus Christi Times*, June 1, 1978, 13D.
33. Jill Clayburgh and Paul Mazursky, "An Unmarried Woman," 1978, Bobbie Wygant Archive, accessed December 19, 2023, https://www.youtube.com/watch?v=6WJ1vci6z8g.
34. Lorna Sutton, "'Woman' a Showcase for Clayburgh's Talent," *Spokesman-Review* (Spokane WA; Idaho edition), June 30, 1978, 53.
35. Jory Schunick, telephone interview by author, April 2, 2024.
36. Lacey Schunick, email to author, October 21, 2023.

8. A ROSE BY ANY OTHER GAME

1. Earl Lawson, "Pete Boiling at Way Garber Pitched to Him," *Cincinnati Post*, August 2, 1978, 22.
2. Andy Abel, email to author, April 22, 2024.
3. Murray Chass, "Red Sox Win, Drop Yanks 8½ Back," *New York Times*, August 4, 1978, A15.
4. Joseph Durso, "A Revival in Rain for Red Sox," *New York Times*, August 4, 1978, A15.
5. Peter Gammons, "Sox Capture Rain-Shortened 8–1 Game," *Boston Globe*, August 4, 1978, 33.
6. Al Mari, "Guidry Tastes Revenge with 3-Hit Shutout," *Reporter Dispatch* (Westchester County NY), August 11, 1978, 29.
7. Mari, "Guidry Tastes Revenge with 3-Hit Shutout."
8. Hal Bock, "Guidry Gets 16th; Yanks 9–0 Winners," *Poughkeepsie Journal*, August 11, 1978, 11.
9. Thomas Boswell, "As Smith Goes, So Go Dodgers, 5–4 over Phils," *Washington Post*, August 16, 1978, C1.
10. Milton Richman, "Sutton-Garvey Fight Is Just Tip of the Iceberg," United Press International, *Santa Maria (CA) Times*, August 21, 1978, 6.
11. Scott Ostler, "Suddenly, the Hugging Turns to Punching," *Los Angeles Times*, August 21, 1978, F1.
12. Scott Ostler, "Garvey, Sutton Talk—But Not to Each Other," *Los Angeles Times*,

August 22, 1978, D1; Jim Murray, "Garvey: Case Dismissed for Lack of Evidence," *Los Angeles Times*, August 23, 1978, D1.

13. "Sutton's Prepared Statement," *Los Angeles Times*, August 25, 1978, D11; Scott Ostler, "Détente on the Dodgers: Sutton Apologizes," *Los Angeles Times*, August 25, 1978, 11.
14. Scott Ostler, "Reggie Smith and Rookie Put Dodgers Alone at Top," *Los Angeles Times*, August 17, 1978, 50.
15. Scott Ostler, "Temper, Temper . . . Mets Beat Dodgers," *Los Angeles Times*, August 20, 1978, D1.
16. Richard Rosenblatt, "Dodgers Battle on, off Field," *Poughkeepsie Journal*, August 21, 1978, 15.
17. Scott Ostler, "Dodgers Upstaged by Bit Players, 4–2," *Los Angeles Times*, August 22, 1978, D1.
18. Scott Ostler, "Expos Help Dodgers Return Home on Top," *Los Angeles Times*, August 24, 1978, J1.
19. Scott Ostler, "Mota Delivers a Hit and Dodger Victory," *Los Angeles Times*, August 25, 1978, B1.
20. Don Merry, "MVP* Bowa Does His Routine; Dodgers Fall," *Los Angeles Times*, August 28, 1978, F1. The asterisk refers to the article's subheadline: "*This Time It Means Most Valuable Phillie."
21. Scott Ostler, "Hooton Blanks Expos on 4 Hits," *Los Angeles Times*, August 29, 1978, F1.
22. Scott Ostler, "Garvey's 2-Out Hit in 9th Beats Expos," *Los Angeles Times*, August 31, 1978, F1.
23. Alexander Keneas, "Lampooning the Fraternity Bag," *Newsday*, July 28, 1978, 7A; Harry F. Themal, "All the Laughs Obscure Panther's Better Lines," *Sunday Morning Journal* (Wilmington DE), July 30, 1978, 55; Janet Maslin, "Screen: 'Animal House,'" *New York Times*, July 28, 1978, C7.
24. Bob Greene, "Life Is a Scream in the 'Animal House,'" *Commercial Appeal* (Memphis), July 3, 1978, 30.
25. *National Lampoon's Animal House*, Box Office Mojo, accessed April 16, 2024, https://www.boxofficemojo.com/release/rl994215425/weekend/.
26. Simmons, *Fat, Drunk, and Stupid*, 13–16.
27. Simmons, *Fat, Drunk, and Stupid*, 63–64; Gwen Gowen and Pavni Mittal, "'Animal House': A Look Back at the Classic Film 40 Years Later," ABC News, May 23, 2018, https://abcnews.go.com/Entertainment/animal-house-back-classic-film-40-years/story?id=55364144.
28. "On the Film Registry: 'National Lampoon's Animal House' (1978): An Interview with Tim Matheson," Library of Congress, February 2021 (date unavailable), posted online August 2, 2021, https://blogs.loc.gov/now-see-hear/2021/08/national-lampoons-animal-house-1978-an-interview-with-tim-matheson/.
29. "Animal House (1978)—The Making of Documentary," YouTube, accessed December 19, 2023, https://www.youtube.com/watch?v=ttmAGc4wH7E; Mid-Atlantic

Nostalgia Convention Panel Part 1, Hal Linden, Max Gail, and Tim Matheson, moderated by David Krell, Hunt Valley, Maryland, September 8, 2023, https://www.youtube.com/watch?v=pGr7rM5GP4U.
30. Cynthia Miller, "Guardian Interviews at the BFI: Elmer Bernstein," *The Guardian*, October 6, 2002, https://www.theguardian.com/film/2002/oct/06/guardianinterviewsatbfisouthbank1.
31. Simmons, *Fat, Drunk, and Stupid*, 104–5.

9. THE BOSTON MASSACRE

1. Bob Ryan, "Yankees Bring Their Comeback to Fenway Park Tonight," *Boston Globe*, September 7, 1978, 1.
2. Pat Calabria, "'They Got to Hear Us Breathing,'" *Newsday*, September 7, 1978, 184.
3. Joe Gergen, "Seeing Leads to a Loss of Belief," *Newsday*, September 8, 1978, 140.
4. Peter Gammons, "Yankees Come, See, Conquer and Cut Lead to 3 Games, 15–3," *Boston Globe*, September 8, 1978, 21.
5. Peter Gammons, "Sox Err 7 Times; NY Zeroes in, 13–2," *Boston Globe*, September 9, 1978, 21.
6. Joe Gergen, "Beattie Comes Full Circle as Steinbrenner Watches," *Newsday*, September 9, 1978, 24.
7. Peter Gammons, "Fastball KO's Evans; X-Rays Are Negative," *Boston Globe*, August 29, 1978, 30.
8. Larry Whiteside, "Dizzy Spell Forces Evans to Leave Game," *Boston Globe*, September 9, 1978, 22.
9. Larry Whiteside, "Ill Wind Blows Away Sox Hopes," *Boston Globe*, September 10, 1978, 50.
10. Whiteside, "Ill Wind Blows Away Sox Hopes."
11. Ray Fitzgerald, "You Gotta Have Heart," *Boston Globe*, September 10, 1978, 66.
12. Bob Ryan, "Now for a 20-Game Season," *Boston Globe*, September 11, 1978, 1.
13. Francis Ross, "Red Sox: The Power of Positive Thinking," *Boston Globe*, September 11, 1978, 1.
14. Joe Gergen, "Will the Rise or Fall Be Recalled?" *Newsday*, September 11, 1978, 88.
15. Joe Donnelly, "A March in the Key of Low," *Newsday*, September 11, 1978, 96.
16. Yastrzemski and Eskenazi, *Yaz*, 269.
17. Murray Chass, "'We've Got Them Where We Want Them,'" *Boston Globe*, September 15, 1978, 38.
18. Larry Whiteside, "Yaz 'Had Play,' But . . . ," *Boston Globe*, September 16, 1978, 20.
19. Peter Gammons, "Sox Fizzle, 3–2, Drop 3½ Back," *Boston Globe*, September 17, 1978, 49.
20. Murray Chass, "Reggie Puts Thumb in Eye of Red Sox," *Boston Globe*, September 17, 1978, 50.
21. Ray Fitzgerald, "Season Is Over," *Boston Globe*, September 17, 1978, 70.

22. Ray Fitzgerald, "Maybe, Just Maybe, Yesterday's Funeral Was Premature," *Boston Globe*, September 18, 1978, 29.
23. *The Paper Chase*, season 1, episode 1, "The Paper Chase," aired September 9, 1978, on CBS.
24. Jerry Buck, "John Houseman Brings Winning Role to TV," *Poughkeepsie Journal*, September 3, 1978, 13B.
25. Betty Utterback, "John Houseman Reprises His Oscar Role for TV," Gannett News Service, *Ithaca Journal*, September 9, 1978, 33.
26. P. J. Bednarski, "For Some Area Disc Jockeys, 'WKRP' Hits Close to Home," *Journal Herald* (Dayton OH), September 29, 1978, 64.
27. Steve Hoffman, "'WKRP' Star's Cincy Visit Was a 'Gas,'" *Cincinnati Enquirer*, September 17, 1978, F-4.
28. Hoffman, "'WKRP' Star's Cincy Visit Was a 'Gas.'"
29. Tom Hopkins, "Tune in to a Lot of Chuckles on CBS's 'WKRP in Cincinnati,'" *Dayton Daily News*, September 18, 1978, 40.
30. Jack E. Anderson, "'WKRP' Spells Lots of Laughs," *Miami Herald*, September 18, 1978, 37.
31. Gary Deeb, "'WKRP'—a Lampoon of MTM Proportions," *Chicago Tribune*, September 13, 1978, 55.
32. Bill Carter, "A Prime-Time Comedy That's Funny? Check Out WKRP in Cincinnati," *The Sun* (Baltimore), September 18, 1978, 18.
33. Lyle Spencer, "The Year That Lopes Took Charge," *Los Angeles Herald Examiner*, September 25, 1978, D-12.

10. THE WORLD SERIES

1. Peter Gammons, "Tiant's 2-Hitter Puts Sox in Playoff . . . ," *Boston Globe*, October 2, 1978, 27.
2. Peter Gammons, "Yankees Have Final Say Again," *Boston Globe*, October 3, 1978, 33.
3. "Gilliam Listed 'Critical,'" *Los Angeles Times*, September 16, 1978, B4; "Gilliam Slips into Coma; Condition 'Very Critical,'" *Los Angeles Times*, September 17, 1978, C9.
4. "Junior Gilliam Dies," Associated Press, *New York Post*, October 9, 1978, 128.
5. Paul Zimmerman, "Burst of Power Mystifies Lopes," *New York Post*, October 11, 1978, 88.
6. Earl Gustkey, "Jackson Loses Cool—But Only for a Moment," *Los Angeles Times*, October 11, 1978, E1.
7. Scott Ostler, "'Never More Relaxed'—Lopes," *Los Angeles Times*, October 11, 1978, E1.
8. Lyle Spencer, "Lopes' Obsession Is Magnificent: Homers Twice in 11–5 Dodger Win," *Los Angeles Herald Examiner*, October 11, 1978, D-3.
9. Mike Evans, "Welch's Heater Cool in Crunch," *New York Post*, October 12, 1978, 124.
10. Henry Hecht, "Reggie Strikes Out!" *New York Post*, October 12, 1978, 128.

11. Ross Newhan, "Cey Magnifique and So Is Welch," *Los Angeles Times*, October 12, 1978, F1.
12. Scott Ostler, "Dodgers Lose Their Cool over the Iceman," *Los Angeles Times*, October 12, 1978, F1.
13. Dick Miller, "Yanks Feudin', Fightin', Fussin' Again," *Los Angeles Herald Examiner*, October 12, 1978, D-2.
14. Maury Allen, "Sutton Shrugs off the Garvey Fight," *New York Post*, October 13, 1978, 126.
15. Ross Newhan, "A Third Baseman Gets a Save," *Los Angeles Times*, October 14, 1978, C1.
16. Melvin Durslag, "The Guy Doesn't Miss," *Los Angeles Herald Examiner*, October 14, 1978, A-1.
17. Ron Fimrite, "No Place Like Home," *Sports Illustrated*, October 23, 1978, 20.
18. Larry Keith, "New York's Nettlesome Man at Third," *Sports Illustrated*, October 23, 1978, 24.
19. David Israel, "Guidry Survives Ordeal, Still Champ," *Los Angeles Herald Examiner*, October 14, 1978, C-2.
20. Henry Hecht, "Yanks Refuse to Die," *New York Post*, October 15, 1978, 128.
21. Fimrite, "No Place Like Home."
22. Fimrite, "No Place Like Home."
23. Fimrite, "No Place Like Home."
24. Ross Newhan, "Yanks Get Even on Old Hip-and-Run Play," *Los Angeles Times*, October 15, 1978, C1; Scott Ostler, "Dodgers Claim 'Dirty Pool,' 'Illegal Tactics,'" *Los Angeles Times*, October 15, 1978, C1.
25. Henry Hecht, "Yankees Charge into LA to Finish Off the Dodgers," *New York Post*, October 16, 1978, 92.
26. Hecht, "Yankees Charge into LA to Finish Off the Dodgers."
27. Harvey Araton, "Beattie Beaming after Biggest Win," *New York Post*, October 16, 1978, 90.
28. Paul Zimmerman, "Russell Gloves the Goat Award," *New York Post*, October 16, 1978, 90.
29. Hecht, "Yankees Charge into LA to Finish Off the Dodgers."
30. Lyle Spencer, "Dodgers Come Home to Sanity," *Los Angeles Herald Examiner*, October 16, 1978, D-3.
31. Joseph Durso, "Now, Even Lasorda Is Frowning," New York Times News Service, *Los Angeles Herald Examiner*, October 16, 1978, D-11.
32. Mike Evans, "Lasorda Rallies Doleful Dodgers," *New York Post*, October 17, 1978, 98.
33. Paul Zimmerman, "Sutton Scoffs over Series Press," *New York Post*, October 17, 1978, 102.
34. Bob Keisser, "Doyle Simply Wanted to Do a Decent Job," *Los Angeles Herald Examiner*, October 18, 1978, D-2.
35. Henry Hecht, "How Sweet It Is!" *New York Post*, October 18, 1978, 128.

36. Mike Evans, "Dodgers Agree: Yanks Are No. 1," *New York Post*, October 18, 1978, 127.
37. David Israel, "Yankees' Bob Lemon: Far from the Madding Crowd," *Los Angeles Herald Examiner*, October 18, 1978, D-10.
38. Melvin Durslag, "Yanks' Lemon: The Great Stabilizer," *Los Angeles Herald Examiner*, October 19, 1978, D-2.
39. Marilyn Beck, "Bixby Resists Urge to Cash in on 'Hulk'-ing Success," *Star-Ledger*, October 16, 1978, 21.
40. Jerry Krupnick, "NBC Team Clouts Ratings over the Fence," *Star-Ledger*, October 18, 1978, 61.

11. A TALE OF TWO SPARKYS

1. "Yankees Deal Sparky Lyle," Associated Press, *Ithaca Journal*, November 11, 1978, 13.
2. Lyle quoted in Dick Young, "Young Ideas: Sparky Spells Relief: B-o-o-k," *Daily News* (New York), November 18, 1978, 28.
3. Lyle and Golenbock, *Bronx Zoo*, 57.
4. Phil Pepe, "Sparky Voted Best in A.L.," *Daily News* (New York), October 26, 1977, 28.
5. Barry McDermott, "Putting Out the Fires in New York: Hot Sparky Lyle Was Considered Too Special for the All-Star Game," *Sports Illustrated*, July 31, 1972, 42.
6. Murray Chass, "Yankees Send Lyle to Rangers," *New York Times*, November 11, 1978, 17.
7. Bob Hertzel, "Sparky May Have to Fiddle without Rose," *Cincinnati Enquirer*, November 28, 1978, C-1.
8. Earl Lawson, "Reds Fire Sparky Anderson," *Cincinnati Post*, November 28, 1978, 1.
9. Mark Purdy, "Even Nice Guys Who Win Can Get Fired," *Cincinnati Enquirer*, November 29, 1978, C-1.
10. Hal McCoy, "Bench Says Sparky Too Nice, Reds Need a 'Get Tough' Policy," *Dayton Daily News*, August 28, 1978, 6.
11. Bob Hertzel, "Billingham: Sparky Too Friendly," *Cincinnati Enquirer*, November 29, 1978, C-6.
12. Pat Harmon, "He Knew Somebody Would Be Leaving," *Cincinnati Post*, November 29, 1978, 21.
13. Earl Lawson, "Rose Doesn't Like Anderson Firing," *Cincinnati Post*, November 29, 1978, 24.
14. Earl Lawson, "Reds' Sparky Bats 1.000 in Laff Loop," *The Sporting News*, February 7, 1970, 42.
15. Bob Hertzel, "Sparky's Bringing Seasonin' to Season," *Cincinnati Enquirer*, October 10, 1969, 1; Pat Harmon, "'My Conscience Is Clear'—Bob Howsam," *Cincinnati Post & Times Star*, October 10, 1969, 22.
16. Cindy Thomson, "Sparky Anderson," Society for American Baseball Research, Baseball Biography Project, accessed January 8, 2024, https://sabr.org/bioproj/person/sparky-anderson/.

17. Red Smith, "Reds' Sparky No Book Manager," *Evening Press* (Binghamton NY), March 17, 1970, 12-B.
18. Charles Maher, "Sparky Anderson Takes It Easy in Thousand Oaks," *Los Angeles Times*, December 14, 1972, D1.
19. "Sparky Anderson Rejected Offer to Manage Oakland A's," Associated Press, *Wilmington (OH) News-Journal*, December 29, 1973, 8.
20. Sparky Anderson, "Lenten Guideposts: Positive Attitude a Winning Trait," *Evening Press*, April 12, 1974, 8.
21. Bob Hertzel, "Sparky Learns to Live with Gray Hair," *Cincinnati Enquirer*, July 6, 1974, 18.
22. "Umps Criticize Sparky," Associated Press, *San Pedro News-Pilot*, December 11, 1975, B9.
23. Augie Borgi, "Sparky: Managing a Ball When You Have Cannons," *Daily News* (New York), October 6, 1975. There is a photocopy of this article, without a page number, in Sparky Anderson's biographical file at the National Baseball Hall of Fame in Cooperstown, New York. The article does not appear on the microfilm copy of the *Daily News* at the New York Public Library's Stephen A. Schwarzman Building. This is not unusual because newspapers used to have different editions according to the time of day or the region; certain articles may not appear in every edition.
24. Lowell Reidenbaugh, "Reds Tinged with Greatness, Says Sparky," *The Sporting News*, November 6, 1976, 3.
25. Bud Poliquin, "Anderson Added to Banquet Dais," *Post-Standard* (Syracuse NY), January 7, 1977, 13.
26. Red Smith, "The End of Sparky's Affair," *New York Times*, November 29, 1978, B10.
27. Andy Lippman, "Sparky Won't Bad-Mouth Reds," Associated Press, *Decatur (IL) Daily Review*, December 5, 1978, 10.
28. "Sparky Anderson Raps Reds for Delaying Sacking," Associated Press, *Daily Press* (Hampton Roads VA), April 4, 1979, 19.
29. Peter King, "Old Home Still Sweet to Sparky," *Cincinnati Enquirer*, May 4, 1982, D-1.
30. Andy Abel, email to author, April 22, 2024.
31. Anderson with Ewald, *Sparky!*, 131.
32. *WKRP in Cincinnati*, season 2, episode 12, "Sparky," aired December 24, 1979, on CBS.
33. *The White Shadow*, "Pilot," aired November 27, 1978, on CBS.
34. Jay Sharbutt, "'White Shadow' Needs Fresh Look," *Des Moines Tribune*, November 27, 1978, 15.
35. Michael Hill, "'White Shadow' Isn't Anything Yet," *Evening Sun* (Baltimore), November 27, 1978, B7.
36. P. J. Bednarski, "CBS Experiments and Casts a 'White Shadow,'" *Journal Herald* (Dayton OH), November 27, 1978, 34.
37. Noel Holston, "'White Shadow' Has the Potential to Be a Winner," *Sentinel Star* (Orlando FL), November 27, 1978, 8-B.

38. Michael Munzell, "Channel Hopping: 'Shadow' of Doubt...," *Palo Alto Times*, November 27, 1978, 14.
39. Lee Winfrey, "'White Shadow' Is Intelligent, Realistic Sports Drama," *Philadelphia Inquirer*, November 27, 1978, 13-D.
40. Ben Brown, "'White Shadow' Replaces 'People,' 'WKRP,'" *Tampa Tribune*, November 27, 1978, 6-D.
41. Cecil Smith, "High Marks for School Series," *Los Angeles Times*, November 27, 1978, E14.
42. John J. O'Connor, "TV: 'White Shadow,' New Series on CBS," *New York Times*, November 27, 1978, C18.
43. *The White Shadow*, season 1, episode 7, "That Old Gang of Mine," aired January 15, 1979; season 1, episode 2, "Here's Mud in Your Eye," aired December 4, 1978; season 1, episode 14, "Little Orphan Abner," aired March 26, 1979; season 1, episode 15, "Le Grande Finale," aired April 9, 1979; season 2, episode 15, "Salami's Affair," aired January 15, 1980; season 3, episode 9, "B.M.O.C.," aired February 2, 1981; season 1, episode 5, "Pregnant Pause," aired January 1, 1979, all on CBS.
44. *The White Shadow*, season 1, episode 8, "One of the Boys," aired January 27, 1979; season 2, episode 10, "Sliding By," aired December 3, 1979; season 1, episode 13, "Mainstream," aired March 5, 1979; season 3, episode 14, "Burnout," aired March 9, 1981; season 2, episode 2, "Albert Hodges," aired September 24, 1979, all on CBS.
45. *The White Shadow*, season 2, episode 16, "Links," aired January 22, 1980, on CBS.
46. Ted Green, "O'Brien Hits Washington with $53,560 Haymaker," *Los Angeles Times*, December 13, 1977, F1; *The White Shadow*, season 1, episode 12, "The Great White Dope," aired February 24, 1979, on CBS; *The White Shadow*, season 3, episode 6, "No Blood, No Foul," aired December 30, 1980, on CBS.
47. *The White Shadow*, season 2, episode 20, "The Russians Are Coming," aired February 26, 1980, on CBS.
48. *The White Shadow*, season 1, episode 4, "Bonus Baby," aired December 25, 1978; season 3, episode 3, "Georgia on My Mind," aired October 30, 1980; season 2, episode 23, "Coolidge Goes Hollywood," aired March 18, 1980, all on CBS.
49. Television Academy Foundation, The Interviews, "Thomas Carter on What Attracted Him to Directing," Thomas Carter interviewed by Stephen J. Abramson, November 18, 2013, Beverly Hills CA, https://www.youtube.com/watch?v=WJPBrU-XbqU.
50. Television Academy Foundation, The Interviews, "Thomas Carter on the Cast of 'The White Shadow,'" Thomas Carter interviewed by Stephen J. Abramson, November 18, 2013, Beverly Hills CA, https://www.youtube.com/watch?v=Fr6qNOSLNZU.
51. Television Academy Foundation, The Interviews, "Thomas Carter on the Legacy of 'The White Shadow,'" Thomas Carter interviewed by Stephen J. Abramson, November 18, 2013, Beverly Hills CA, https://www.youtube.com/watch?v=v3pdvUiiNkg.

52. "More than Basketball—The White Shadow: The Complete First Season DVD Extra," accessed April 17, 2024, https://www.youtube.com/watch?v= 0mPsmNMaIQk.
53. "More than Basketball—The White Shadow."
54. *St. Elsewhere*, season 3, episode 18, "Any Portrait in a Storm," aired January 30, 1985, on CBS.
55. "This Is *SportsCenter*: Don't Walk," aired on ESPN.
56. "This Is *SportsCenter*: Small World," aired on ESPN.
57. James A. Finefrock, "Aide: White 'a Wild Man,'" *San Francisco Examiner*, November 27, 1978, 1; "Feinstein Takes Over as Mayor," *San Francisco Examiner*, November 27, 1978, 1.

12. IT'S A BIRD . . .

1. *The Big Bang Theory*, season 1, episode 2, "The Big Bran Hypothesis," aired October 1, 2007, on CBS.
2. Bernard Drew, "'Superman' Plummets to Crash Landing," *Pensacola News Journal*, December 15, 1978, 7D; Charles Champlin, "Man of Steel, Feat of Clay," *Los Angeles Times*, December 15, 1978, C1.
3. Vincent Canby, "Screen: It's a Bird, It's a Plane, It's a Movie," *Los Angeles Times*, December 15, 1978, C15.
4. Scott Stump, "Christopher Reeve's Family Remembers 'Dad's Dearest Friend' Robin Williams," *Today*, NBC, August 12, 2014, https://www.today.com/popculture/robin-williams-remembered-christopher-reeves-family-dads-dearest-friend-1d80054349.
5. Dale Stevens, "'Superman' May Be Season's 'BIG' Movie," *Cincinnati Post*, December 4, 1978, 28.
6. *Saturday Night Live*, season 10, episode 17, "Superman Auditions," aired April 6, 1985, on NBC.
7. Gary Kroeger, email to author, January 25, 2024.
8. Laura Bradley, "Original Lois Lane Margot Kidder Explains Why the Original *Superman* Is Still the Best," *Vanity Fair*, September 2, 2016, https://www.vanityfair.com/hollywood/2016/09/margot-kidder-superman.
9. "Rose Meets with Pirates' Owner," *Cincinnati Post*, December 2, 1978, 9.
10. Earl Lawson, "These Offers Failed," *Cincinnati Post*, December 5, 1978, 26B.
11. Lawson, "These Offers Failed."
12. Lawson, "These Offers Failed"; Larry Eichel, "In the End, It Was Ball, Not Money," *Philadelphia Inquirer*, December 5, 1978, D1.
13. Bob Hertzel, "Rose, Phils Signing Took Some Doing," *Cincinnati Enquirer*, December 6, 1978, C1.
14. Larry Eichel, "Pete's Passage: An Uprooted Institution Linking His Future to Philly," *Philadelphia Inquirer*, December 5, 1978, D1.
15. Untitled article, United Press International, *Cincinnati Post*, December 8, 1978, 37.

16. Harry Levins, "The Big Romance of War," *St. Louis Post-Dispatch*, October 1, 1978, 4D.
17. Richard Allen Paul, "Wouk's Newest Is Really Two," *Sunday News Journal* (Wilmington DE), October 29, 1978, F6.
18. Floyd Logan, "'War and Remembrance' Is More Wouk Mastery," *Indianapolis News*, December 9, 1978, 22.
19. Rima L. Firrone, "Remembrance," *Jackson (TN) Sun*, November 5, 1978, 4A.
20. Herman Wouk, "War and Remembrance: The Paradox of Historical Fiction" (lecture, Library of Congress, Washington DC, October 29, 1979).
21. Herman Wouk, "War and Remembrance: Novel into Film" (lecture, Library of Congress, Washington DC, May 15, 1995).
22. Wouk, "War and Remembrance: The Paradox of Historical Fiction."
23. Herman Wouk, "Historical Fiction: A Workshop Glimpse" (lecture, Library of Congress, Washington DC, May 15, 1995).
24. Wouk, "Historical Fiction: A Workshop Glimpse."
25. Wouk, "War and Remembrance: The Paradox of Historical Fiction."
26. Herman Wouk, "War and Remembrance: Novel and Film" (lecture, Library of Congress, Washington DC, June 2, 1994).
27. Wouk, "War and Remembrance: Novel and Film."
28. Marjorie Hunter, "House Panel Reports a Conspiracy 'Probable' in the Kennedy Slaying," *New York Times*, December 31, 1978, 1; U.S. House of Representatives, findings and recommendations in *Report of the Select Committee on Assassinations*, 95th Congress, 2nd session, March 29, 1979.

BIBLIOGRAPHY

Anderson, Sparky, with Dan Ewald. *Sparky!* New York: Prentice Hall Press, 1990.
Appel, Marty. *Munson: The Life and Death of a Yankee Captain.* New York: Doubleday, 2009.
———. *Pinstripe Empire: The New York Yankees from Before the Babe to After the Boss.* New York: Bloomsbury, 2012.
Dark, Alvin, and John Underwood. *When in Doubt, Fire the Manager: My Life and Times in Baseball.* New York: E. P. Dutton, 1980.
Falkner, David. *The Last Yankee: The Turbulent Life of Billy Martin.* New York: Simon & Schuster, 1992.
Fallon, Michael. *Dodgerland: Decadent Los Angeles and the 1977–78 Dodgers.* Lincoln: University of Nebraska Press, 2016.
Guidry, Ron, and Andrew Beaton. *Gator: My Life in Pinstripes.* New York: Crown Archetype, 2018.
Hill, Doug, and Jeff Weingrad. *Saturday Night: A Backstage History of "Saturday Night Live."* New York: Beech Tree Books, 1986.
Jackson, Reggie, with Kevin Baker. *Becoming Mr. October.* New York: Doubleday, 2013.
Jacobs, Jim, and Warren Casey. *Grease: A New '50s Rock 'n' Roll Musical.* New York: Pocket Books, 1972.
Karp, Josh. *A Futile and Stupid Gesture: How Doug Kenney and "National Lampoon" Changed Comedy Forever.* Chicago: Chicago Review Press, 2006.
Kleiser, Randal. *"Grease": The Director's Notebook.* New York: Harper Design, 2019.
Lasorda, Tommy, and David Fisher. *The Artful Dodger.* New York: Arbor House, 1985.
Lyle, Sparky, and Peter Golenbock. *The Bronx Zoo.* New York: Crown, 1979.
Marshall, Garry. *Wake Me When It's Funny: How to Break into Show Business and Stay There.* Holbrook MA: Adams, 1995.
Martin, Billy, and Peter Golenbock. *Number 1.* New York: Delacorte Press, 1980.
McAdam, Sean. *Boston Red Sox: A Curated History of the Sox.* Chicago: Triumph Books, 2022.
Miller, Chris. *The Real Animal House: The Awesomely Depraved Saga of the Fraternity That Inspired the Movie.* New York: Little, Brown, 2006.
Moore, Tom, Adrienne Barbeau, and Ken Waissman. *"Grease": Tell Me More, Tell Me More—Stories from the Broadway Phenomenon That Started It All.* Chicago: Chicago Review Press, 2022.

Munson, Thurman, with Martin Appel. *Thurman Munson.* New York: Coward, McCann & Geoghegan, 1978.

Pennington, Bill. *Billy Martin: Baseball's Flawed Genius.* Boston: Houghton Mifflin Harcourt, 2015.

Simmons, Matty. *Fat, Drunk, and Stupid: The Inside Story behind the Making of "Animal House."* New York: St. Martin's Press, 2012.

Stout, Glenn. *The Dodgers: 120 Years of Dodgers Baseball.* Boston: Houghton Mifflin Harcourt, 2004.

Tiant, Luis, with Saul Wisnia. *Son of Havana: A Baseball Journey from Cuba to the Big Leagues and Back.* New York: Diversion Books, 2019.

Tiemann, Robert L. *Dodger Classics: Outstanding Games from Each of the Dodgers' 101 Seasons 1883–1983.* St. Louis: Baseball Histories, 1983.

Yastrzemski, Carl, and Gerald Eskenazi. *Yaz: Baseball, the Wall, and Me.* New York: Doubleday, 1990.

INDEX

Aaron, Hank, 13, 29, 60, 122
ABC, 25, 28–29, 122, 167, 169
Abel, Andy, 96, 148–49
Aker, Jack, 35
Albuquerque Dodgers, 73
Albuquerque Dukes, 38. *See also* Spokane Indians
Alexander, Gary, 95, 127, 128
Alomar, Sandy, 12
American Graffiti, 28
American Hot Wax, 63
Anderson, Sparky, 39, 71, 144–49
Animal House, 105–6, 107, 108, 159
Ann-Margret, 76
Asner, Ed, 152–53
Associated Press, 151
Atlanta Braves, 45, 71–72, 75–76, 95–96, 125, 163. *See also* Boston Braves
Atlantic City NJ, 60–62

The Bad News Bears, 86–88
The Bad News Bears Go to Japan, 86–87
The Bad News Bears in Breaking Training, 87
Baker, Dusty, 102, 103, 104, 129, 130, 131, 137, 138
Ball Four (Bouton), 143
Bally's, 62
Baltimore Orioles, 15, 40, 41, 67, 85, 96, 110, 119
Barber, Red, 8
Barfield, Jesse, 57
Barnes, Clive, 78
Bartholomay, Bill, 12

Baseball Writers' Association of America, 10
Bates, Alan, 90
Battle of Springfield, 62
Bauer, Hank, 84
Bavasi, Buzzie, 32, 33, 37
Bavasi, Peter, 68
Baylor, Don, 15, 67
BBC, 24–25
Beard, Henry, 106
The Beatles, 12
Beattie, Jim, 113, 137, 138
Beatty, Warren, 163
Bednarski, P. J., 123
Bell, Buddy, 127, 128
Belushi, John, 106
Bench, Johnny, 59, 71, 95, 145
Beníquez, Juan, 144
Bernstein, Elmer, 108–9
Berra, Yogi, 42, 84, 130
Berry, Chuck, 63
The Big Bang Theory, 158
Billboard, 77
Billingham, Jack, 145
Bixby, Bill, 141
Blair, Paul, 58–59, 82, 132, 134, 136, 137
blizzards: in New England, 21–22, 117; in New Jersey and New York, 17–20; in New York City (1947), 21
Blue, Vida, 14–15, 16, 40
Blyleven, Bert, 45, 85
Boccabella, John, 73
Bogart, Humphrey, 166, 168
Bonnell, Barry, 95, 96

Boone, Bob, 104
Borbón, Pedro, 71
Bostock, Lyman, 125
Boston Braves, 4, 10, 33–34. *See also* Atlanta Braves
Boston College, 149–50, 153
Boston Marathon bombing, 23
"Boston Massacre," 110–18
Boston Red Sox: and American League East playoff against Yankees, 128–29; and "Boston Massacre," 111–19; and last game of the season, 128; managed by Joe McCarthy, 4–5; and Mike Torrez, 42–43; Minor League teams of, 118; and New York Yankees, 96–98, 111–21; in 1972, 85; in 1977, 41; opinions of, on Catfish Hunter, 82; and pennant race (1978), 110–21, 125; and Rollie Fingers, 14; and spring training, 30–31, 85, 86; and World Series, 119, 144
Bouton, Jim, 73, 125, 143
Bowa, Larry, 104, 164
Bragan, Bobby, 12
Branca, Ralph, 35
Brando, Marlon, 158
Brett, George, 68, 80
Bristol, Dave, 146
Brohamer, Jack, 117
The Bronx Zoo (Lyle and Golenbock), 143–44
Brooklyn Dodgers, 8, 34, 72, 148. *See also* Los Angeles Dodgers
Brown, Willie, 155
Bruce, Bob, 12
Brusstar, Warren, 103
Buddy Holly and the Crickets, 64
The Buddy Holly Story, 63–64
Burgmeier, Tom, 97, 115
Burkel, Arthur, 3, 5
Burleson, Rick, 42, 82, 97, 98, 118, 120, 128
Burr, Harold C., 3
Burroughs, Jeff, 75–76, 95, 96

Busch, August, 163
Busey, Gary, 64, 65
Byrne, Brendan, 18, 61

Cabell, Enos, 38
Caesars Palace, 61
Cage, Wayne, 127
The Caine Mutiny (Wouk), 166, 168
Calhoun, Jim, 154
California Angels, 55, 66–67, 72, 74, 110, 145
California League, 72–73
Campanis, Al, 39, 100
Campbell, Bill, 112
Campbell, Jim, 85
Camp David Accords, 125–26
Canby, Vincent, 87, 159
Cannon Ball House, 62
Cape Cod Baseball League, 113
Capricorn One, 162
Carbo, Bernie, 31
Cardenal, José, 104
Caribbean World Series, 38
Carlton, Steve, 39, 66, 74, 75, 85, 103
Carlyle, Thomas, 169
Carr, Allan, 76
Carter, Bill, 124
Carter, Gary, 102
Carter, Thomas, 153–54
Carver, George Washington, 150
Casablanca Records, 91
The Castaways on Gilligan's Island, 142
Castro, Fidel, 170
CBS, 50–51, 53, 88, 121–23, 141, 149, 151, 169
Cedeño, César, 71
Central Park, 20
Cepeda, Orlando, 36
Cey, Ron, 36–37, 55, 102, 103, 105, 130, 132, 133, 134, 140
Chambliss, Chris: batting average of, 45; and "Boston Massacre," 111, 112, 113, 114, 115, 117, 118, 120, 121; on Reggie Jackson,

82–83; and regular season games, 58, 68, 80, 82, 97, 111; and World Series, 128, 131, 134
Champlin, Charles, 77, 159
Chaney, Darrel, 72
Channing, Stockard, 77
Chase, Chevy, 107
Chatham MA, 21
Chavez Ravine. *See* Dodger Stadium (Chavez Ravine)
Cheetah, 107
Chelsea Hotel, 133
Chicago Bulls, 149
Chicago Cubs, 2–3, 33, 48, 54, 57
Chicago Tribune, 77, 87, 124
Chicago White Sox, 4, 6–7, 39, 41, 45–46, 58, 68, 83, 99, 145
Cincinnati Enquirer, 96, 123, 144
Cincinnati Post, 144–45
Cincinnati Reds: and Don Sutton, 74; and Larry MacPhail, 8; and National League Championship Series, 116, 163–64; and National League West, 57, 76, 99, 105; and Opening Day, 71; and Pete Rose, 59–60, 95–96, 163–64; and Sparky Anderson, 39, 144–49; and Tom Seaver, 30, 55, 69–70; and Vida Blue, 14, 40; and World Series, 15, 44, 116
Claire, Fred, 74
Clark, Jack, 76
Clay, Ken, 112, 130–31
Clayburgh, Jill, 89–91
Clear Lake IA, 64, 65
Cleveland Indians, 4, 12, 29, 58, 85, 127–28, 130
Concepción, Dave, 70, 95, 96
Cooper, Gary, 169
Cooper, Jackie, 154
Coral Records, 64
Corbett, Brad, 86
Cornell University, 160

Corpus Christi Times, 77, 89
Correll, Vic, 96
Costello, Elvis, 19
Cowens, Al, 58, 68
Craig, Roger, 36
Craven, Wes, 88
Crawford, Shag, 36
Cromartie, Warren, 102, 103
Cronin, Joe, 5, 85
Crosley, Powel, Jr., 8
Crown Publishers, 143
Cruz, José, 71
Cunningham, Sean S., 88
Currier and Ives, 1
Curtis, Jamie Lee, 162
Curtis, Tony, 87
Cy Young Award, 39, 143, 144

Daily News (New York), 64, 143, 158
Dallas, 50–53
Dallas: J.R. Returns, 53
Dallas: The Early Years, 53
Dallas: War of the Ewings, 53
D'Amato, Tony, 78
Danner, Blythe, 6
Danza, Tony, 124
Dark, Alvin, 32–36
Darren, James, 19
Dartmouth College, 107, 113
Davalillo, Vic, 140
Davis, Dick, 99
Davis, Marvin, 30
Davis, Ron, 113
Davis, Tommy, 39
Davis, Willie, 36
Dawson, Andre, 102
Dayton OH, 123
D-Day, 167, 169
Deeb, Gary, 124
The Del Vikings, 63
Demas, Carole, 78
Denny, John, 70

INDEX • 197

Dent, Bucky: and American League East playoff, 128; and "Boston Massacre," 111, 112, 115; and regular season games, 46, 58, 68, 127; trade of, to Yankees, 99; and World Series, 130, 131, 134, 137, 138, 139, 140
Desert Inn, 124
Detroit Tigers, 13, 43, 69, 85, 110, 119, 149
Devane, William, 87
Dewey, Thomas, 8
Dey, Susan, 76
The Dick Van Dyke Show, 47
DiMaggio, Joe, 3, 164
Diners Club, 107
Diners Club Magazine, 107
disco music, 91–93
Disco Steppin', 92–93
Dodger Stadium (Chavez Ravine), 37, 56, 130
Doerr, Bobby, 119
Dowd, John, 165
Doyle, Brian, 128, 134, 138, 139, 140
Dragnet, 107
Drago, Dick, 112, 118
Driessen, Dan, 60, 70
Drysdale, Don, 39, 72, 74, 75, 122, 130
Dues, Hal, 105
Duffy, Frank, 115
Dukakis, Michael, 21
Durocher, Leo, 1, 34

Easterly, Jamie, 75
East Providence RI, 36
East River, 89
Eastwick, Rawly, 41–42
Eckersley, Dennis, 82, 114–15, 120
Eckert, William 14
Eddie Mathews Field, 10
Egan, Tom, 86
Eisenhower, Dwight, 62
Ellicott Creek Park, 1
Ellis, Dock, 41, 45

English, Reynold, 92–94
ESPN, 50, 155
Eugene OR, 107
Evans, Darrell, 76
Evans, Dwight, 57, 82, 97, 114
Evers, Medgar, 62

Feinstein, Dianne, 155–56
Fenway Park, 42, 69, 82, 110, 111–19, 128–29
Ferguson, Joe, 71, 102, 105
Ferrigno, Lou, 141
Figueroa, Ed, 45, 58, 82, 86, 117, 130, 131, 137, 140
Fingers, Rollie, 14–15, 16, 32
Finley, Charlie, 14, 15–16, 35, 40
Fisk, Carlton, 42, 71, 112–13, 118, 120, 129
Fitzgerald, Ray, 120–21
Foli, Tim, 101
Fontaine, Bob, 33
Ford, Gerald, 62
Ford, Whitey, 130
Forster, Terry, 101, 131, 132, 137
Fort Hood (Texas), 9
Fosse, Ray, 60
Foster, George, 57, 60, 72, 95, 145
Freed, Alan, 62–63
Freedman, Richard, 87
Frisch, Frankie, 164
Fulton County Stadium, 72, 75–76, 95

Gain, Charles, 155
Galbreath, John, 163
Game of the Week, 73
Garber, Gene, 95
Garvey, Steve: batting of, in 1977, 38; batting prowess of, 103, 132–33; and fight with Don Sutton, 99–100; junior high school named after, 39; performance of, in 1978, 101–2; praising Burt Hooton, 103; praising Jim Beattie, 138; and World Series, 136, 138
Gary IN, 125

Gaynor, Gloria, 91, 92
Gehrig, Lou, 3, 6, 40, 122, 137, 169
Gelmis, Joseph, 63
Gergen, Joe, 111
Germany, 166
Giamatti, A. Bartlett, 165
Giannoulas, Ted, 32
Gibson, Bob, 114
Gilbreath, Rod, 72, 96
Gilliam, Jim "Junior," 129, 131, 132
Gilligan's Island, 141
Glauberg, Joe, 25
Golenbock, Peter, 143
Gomez, Preston, 100, 101
Gossage, Goose, 41–42, 58, 68, 80, 81, 97, 117, 118, 119, 132, 137
Grammas, Alex, 145
Grease, 76–78, 159
Greene, Bob, 106
Green Monster, 128
Grich, Bobby, 57, 66, 68
Griffey, Ken, 95, 96
Grote, Jerry, 71, 104
Grotowski, Jerzy, 25
Gruber, Lisa (Katz), 49
Guidry, Ron: and American League East playoff against Red Sox, 128; and "Boston Massacre," 114–15; and crowd-standing tradition, 67; eighteen-strikeout game of, 66–68; and home opener (1978), 45–46, 115; nicknames of, 66, 68, 135; performance of, in 1978, 68, 98; trade proposals for, 67–68, 99; win-loss record of, 125; and World Series, 134, 135

Hagman, Larry, 52
Hall of Fame, 1, 5, 6, 10, 13, 34, 46, 75
Halloween, 162
Hancock, Garry, 113, 118
Happy Days: characters on, 22, 27–28; competition of, with *The Paper Chase*, 122; cultural references in, 22; and Fonzie as hero, 28; and *Laverne & Shirley* spinoff, 28–29, 124; and *Mork & Mindy* spinoff, 25, 123, 124; and *Potsie & Ralph* backdoor pilot, 29; premise of, 22; Robin Williams guest starring on, 23–25; shark episode of, 28; start of, on *Love, American Style*, 22; studio audience of, 24–28
Harlem Globetrotters, 50, 152, 155
The Harlem Globetrotters on Gilligan's Island, 142
Harrelson, Bud, 60, 104
Hartzell, Paul, 66
Harvard Lampoon, 106–7
Harvard Law School, 121
Hassler, Andy, 97, 111–12, 118, 128
"Hava Nagila," 28
Hawaii, 141, 166
Hawaii Islanders, 38
Heath, Mike, 80, 144
Heaven Can Wait, 163
Hecht, Henry, 131–32, 136
Held, Woodie, 84
Hendrick, George, 70
Henning, John, 21
Here Comes Mr. Jordan, 163
Here Come the Tigers, 88–89
Hernandez, Keith, 69
Herrmann, Edward, 6
Hertzel, Bob, 144
Herzog, Whitey, 58, 85
Hesseman, Howard, 123
High-Point Thomasville Hi-Toms, 11
Hillside Strangler, 100
Hill Street Blues, 153
Hilton: in Atlantic City, 62; in New York, 21; in Pikesville MD, 94
Hobson, Butch, 42, 82, 97, 111, 112, 120, 129
Hoffman, Robert, 106
Holly, Buddy, 63–65
Holmes, Johnny, 77, 90

Holocaust, 166, 167
Holocaust (miniseries), 169
Holtzman, Ken, 15
Hooks, Kevin, 153
Hooper, 162–63
Hooton, Burt, 16, 38, 45, 101, 102, 104, 132, 137
"Hopelessly Devoted to You," 77
Hopkins, Tom, 123
Horner, Bob, 96
Hough, Charlie, 16, 45, 103, 135, 138
Houseman, John, 26, 121–23, 160
House Select Committee on Assassinations, 170
Houston Astros, 12, 38, 45, 71–72, 74
Howard, Elston, 42
Howard, Ken, 149, 154, 155
Howard, Ron, 22
Howsam, Bob, 148
Howser, Dick, 79
Hrabosky, Al, 79, 80
Hunt, Ron, 73
Hunter, Catfish, 16, 45, 80, 81–82, 85, 112, 113, 127, 132, 140, 143
Hutton, Tom, 103

I Dream of Jeannie, 52
The Incredible Hulk, 141
Israel, 126
"It's So Easy," 65
Ivie, Mike, 33
"I Will Survive," 91

Jackson, Reggie: achievements of, 44, 132; as All-Star, 44; and American League East playoff against Red Sox, 128; assessment of Yankees by, 40; and Baltimore Orioles, 15, 44; and "Boston Massacre," 113, 115, 118, 119, 120; and candy bar, 46, 48, 68, 144; Catfish Hunter's opinion of, 144; collision of, with Paul Blair, 58–59; conflicts of, with Billy Martin, 41, 79–80; home run titles of, 44; and Minor Leagues, 44; and MVP Award, 44; and New York Yankees, 16, 41, 44–45, 143; and Oakland A's, 44; power of, 137, 164; and pressure, 48; and Ron Guidry's eighteen-strikeout game, 66; signing of, with New York Yankees, 143; slugging percentage title of, 44; Sparky Lyle's opinion of, 143; *Sport* interview of, 41; strikeouts of, 44; suspension of, 79, 81, 82–83; teammates' opinions of, 82–83; in World Series (1977), 16, 41, 45, 130; in World Series (1978), 131–32, 134, 135–36, 137, 138, 140; and World Series MVP Award, 83; and Yankees home opener (1978), 46, 60
Jacobs, David, 52
Janis, Conrad, 64
Jarry Park, 73
Jenkins, Ferguson, 85
John, Tommy, 38–39, 101, 103, 105, 130, 131, 135, 136, 137
Johnson, Cliff, 81, 86, 97
Johnson, Darrell, 98
Johnson, Tom, 45
Jolson Sings Again, 63, 64
The Jolson Story, 63
Jones, Edwin, 84
Jones, Randy, 32, 56
Jorgensen, Mike, 73
Joss, Adrian "Addie," 6–7
The Juilliard School, 26, 160
"jump the shark," 28
Junior World Series, 9

Kammeyer, Bob, 80
Kansas City A's, 23, 35, 47, 84. *See also* Oakland A's; Philadelphia A's
Kansas City Monarchs, 9
Kansas City Royals, 16, 32, 41, 79–81, 83, 110, 125, 129, 163

Katz, Allen, 48–49
Katz, Rhoda, 48–49
Keeler, Wee Willie, 95
Keneas, Alexander, 106
Kennedy, John F., 27, 62, 170
Kennedy, Junior, 96
Kennedy, Robert F., 27, 62
Kenney, Douglas, 105, 106–7
Kenvil NJ, 18
Kenvil Power Mower, 18
Kessinger, Don, 46
Kidder, Margot, 161
Kingman, Dave, 54–57
Kingston Mines Community Theater, 77–78
Kinney, Dennis, 75
Knight, Ray, 72
Knots Landing, 53
Koosman, Jerry, 165
Koufax, Sandy, 72, 74, 114, 122, 130
Kroc, Ray, 32, 33
Kroeger, Gary, 160–61
Krupnick, Jerry, 19
Krzyzewski, Mike, 154
Kucks, Johnny, 84
Kuhn, Bowie, 14–15, 40, 83, 125
Kuiper, Duane, 127

Lacy, Lee, 101, 104, 130, 131
La Guardia, Fiorello, 8
Lamp, Dennis, 55
Lancaster, Bill, 86, 87
Lancaster, Burt, 86
Landis, John, 107–8
Lasorda, Tommy: arguing with umpires, 101, 136; and Dodgers winning National League West, 125; as manager, 29–30, 36, 37–38; praising Graig Nettles, 135; praising Reggie Smith, 99; reaction of, to Dave Kingman's three-home-run game, 54–55, 60; reaction of, to death of Jim "Junior" Gilliam, 129–30; reaction of, to Don Sutton's Baseball Hall of Fame election, 75; and World Series, 134, 136, 137–38
"Last Dance," 91–92
Laugh-In, 25
Laverne & Shirley, 28–29, 122, 123, 124
Lee, Bill, 118
Lemmings, 107
Lemon, Bob, 46, 83, 99, 110–11, 127, 128, 132, 134, 140
Leonard, Harvey, 21
Lerch, Randy, 104
Levins, Harry, 166
Levitt, William J., 133
Lewis, Jerry, 60, 61
Lewis, Jerry Lee, 63
Library of Congress, 107, 167, 169
Lindblad, Paul, 127
Lindsay CA, 39
Lopes, Davey: batting prowess of, 103; describing fans, 104–5; as Dodgers captain, 36–37; and Minor Leagues, 37; opinion of, on Dodgers' performance, 125; praising Bob Welch, 132; praising Jim "Junior" Gilliam, 131; praising New York Yankees, 140; and regular season games, 55; and stolen bases, 132; and World Series, 130–32, 136, 137, 140
Los Angeles, 20, 27, 150
Los Angeles Dodgers: and Cincinnati Reds, 15; and Dave Kingman's three-home-run game, 54–55; and Gaylord Perry's 3,000th strikeout, 128; Minor League teams of, 72–73; move of, from Brooklyn, 8; and National League Championship Series, 129; National League pennants of, 163; and National League playoff (1962); and pennant race (1978), 110; performance of, in 1978, 99, 101–9; record of, in 1977, 30, 57; and spring training, 29–30, 38–39; strikeout record of, 72; and World Series (1974),

Los Angeles Dodgers (*cont.*)
  39; and World Series (1977), 39, 129, 131;
  and World Series (1978), 130–41. *See also* Brooklyn Dodgers
Los Angeles Rams, 163
Los Angeles River, 78
Los Angeles Times, 74, 77, 88, 99, 100, 151, 159
Lost in Space, 52
Louisville Colonels, 2, 9
"Love to Love You Baby," 91
Lubbock TX, 63
Ludtke, Melissa, 125
Luzinski, Greg "Bull," 104, 164
Lyle, Sparky, 42, 45, 67, 80, 81, 82, 86, 139, 143–44
Lynn, Fred, 82, 112, 113, 115, 118, 129

MacPhail, Andy, 10
MacPhail, Bill, 10
MacPhail, Larry, 3, 7–10, 133
MacPhail, Lee, 10, 125
MacPhail, Lee, IV, 10
Maddox, Garry, 104
Madlock, Bill, 76
Maloney, Jim, 70
Manning, Rick, 127, 128
Mantle, Mickey, 40, 44, 46–47, 48, 84, 101, 130, 137
Maris, Roger, 46–48
Marshall, Garry, 23, 25, 26
Marshall, Penny, 28
Marshall, Scott, 23
Martin, Billy: and conflict, 40, 84, 110; and Copacabana incident, 83–84; firings of, 85–86; playing for the Yankees, 83–84; Rawly Eastwick's opinion of, 41; resignation of, 83–84, 143; success of, as manager, 84–85; suspending Reggie Jackson, 79–80; trade of, to Kansas City A's, 84; using relief pitchers, 58, 68
Martin, Dean, 60, 61

Martínez, Ted, 103–4
Martyn, Bob, 84
Marvel Comics, 141
Maslin, Janet, 106
Mason, James, 163
Matheson, Tim, 105–6, 107–8
Mathews, Eddie: batting achievements of, 11, 12; and Boston Braves, 11; career home runs of, 10; childhood of, 10–11; and Cleveland Indians offer, 12; as coach, 13; comparison of, to Babe Ruth, 11; field named after, 10; 500th home run of, 12–13; and Hall of Fame, 10, 13; as manager, 13; as metaphor for power, 122; and Milwaukee Brewers, 13; in Minor Leagues, as instructor, 13; in Minor Leagues, as player, 13; and Oakland A's, 13; playing outfield, 12; playing third base, 12; rookie season of, in Major Leagues, 11; and Santa Barbara High School, 10; as scout, 13; on *Sports Illustrated*'s first cover, 11; and Texas Rangers, 13; trade of, to Detroit Tigers, 13; trade of, to Houston Astros, 12; and World Series, 12
Matthau, Walter, 86
Matthews, Gary, 72, 95
Mauch, Gene, 12
Mays, Willie, 60, 122, 146
Mazursky, Paul, 89, 90
Mazzilli, Lee, 101
McBride, Bake, 103, 104
McCall, Larry, 127, 144
McCarthy, Elizabeth, 3, 4
McCarthy, Joseph Vincent: and Boston Red Sox, 4; and Chicago Cubs, 2–3; death of, 1; and fan mail, 5; and Hall of Fame, 1, 5; leadership style of, 5–6; and Minor Leagues, 2; and New York Yankees, 2–3; and Niagara University, 2; retirement of, 4; wife of, 3, 4–5; and World Series, 2

McCovey, Willie, 75–76, 122
McDonald, John, 9–10
McEnaney, Will, 30
McGarr, Frank, 15
McGill, Bruce, 108
McGraw, Tug, 50, 103
McHale, John, 12
McIntire, Tim, 63
McKeever, Stephen, 8
McLain, Denny, 32, 114
McNamara, John, 32, 149
McRae, Hal, 80
McRaven, Dale, 25
McWilliams, Larry, 96
The Mercury Theatre on the Air, 122
Merrill, Durwood, 80
Messer, Frank, 40
Messersmith, Andy, 41–42
Milan, Clyde, 7
Milk, Harvey, 155–56
Miller, Chris, 105, 106–7
Miller, Gary, 155
Milner, John, 60, 165
Milwaukee Braves, 11, 29. *See also* Boston Braves
Milwaukee Brewers (Major League), 13, 16, 32, 45, 69, 85, 96, 98–99, 114
Milwaukee Brewers (Minor League), 11, 33
Milwaukee County Stadium, 98
Minnesota Twins, 68, 81, 82, 85
Mitchell, Paul, 15–16
Mogel, Len, 107
Monday, Rick, 103, 130, 131, 135, 137, 140
Montreal Expos, 30, 32, 41, 59–60, 73, 81, 102–3, 104–5, 165
Montreal Royals, 9
Moore, Junior, 46
Moore, Mary Tyler, 123
Mooresville Moors, 11
Morales, Jerry, 69
Morgan, Joe, 60, 149, 165
Mork & Mindy, 123, 124

Moscone, George, 155
Mota, Manny, 103
Mountainside NJ, 67
Mount Olivet Cemetery, 1
MTM Enterprises, 123, 153
Mumphrey, Jerry, 70
Muncie Star, 64
Munson, Thurman: batting prowess of, 45; and "Boston Massacre," 111, 112, 115, 118, 120; conflict of, with Reggie Jackson, 41; and effect of Yankees controversies, 86; and regular season games, 46, 58, 66, 79, 81, 97; and World Series, 128, 132, 134, 135, 136, 137, 138, 139, 140
Murcer, Bobby, 55
Murphy, Dale, 95, 96
Murphy, Michael, 90
Murray, Arch, 3
Murray, Eddie, 56
Murray, Jim 100
Murray, Larry, 41
Musial, Stan, 34, 60, 163

Nahorodny, Bill, 46
Naismith, James, 155
NASA, 52, 162
National Lampoon, 106–7
National Lampoon's Radio Hour, 107
NBA, 77, 149, 155
NBC, 25, 122, 141, 142
Negro Leagues, 8–9
Nettles, Graig: and American League East playoff, 128, 129; and "Boston Massacre," 112, 114, 115, 118, 120; and regular season games, 46, 58, 66, 80, 127; wanted by other teams, 29, 68; and World Series, 133, 134, 135, 138, 140
Newark NJ, 8, 18, 19, 27
New England, 17, 116–17
Newsday, 63, 106, 111
Newton-John, Olivia, 76, 77, 78
New York City, 17, 20–21, 61, 89, 91, 158

INDEX • 203

New York Giants, 2, 34–35. *See also* San Francisco Giants
New York Mets, 30, 39, 40, 57, 69, 85, 101, 147
New York Post, 3, 131–32, 138
New York Times, 5, 21, 78, 81, 87, 106, 151, 159
New York Yankees: and American League East (1976), 45; and American League East playoff against Red Sox, 128–29; and "Boston Massacre," 111–19; and Boston Red Sox, 97, 111–21, 128–29; and Brendan Byrne, 61; and Dave Winfield, 29; home opener of, in 1978, 45; homestand of, of seventeen games, 96–97; and Joe McCarthy, 3–5; and Kansas City Royals, 57–58, 163; and lawsuit by Melissa Ludtke, 125; logo of, on *Taxi*, 124; Minor League teams of, 113; owning ballparks other than Yankee Stadium, 8; and pennant race (1978), 110–21, 125; performance of, in 1977, 41; and Reggie Jackson's first season, 44–45; and Ron Guidry's eighteen-strikeout game, 66–68; slump of, 81; and spring training, 29; and World Series (1977), 41; and Yankee Stadium, 8, 45
Nicholson, Dave, 12
Nixon, Richard M., 27, 83
Nordhagen, Wayne, 46
Norris, Jim, 127
North, Bill, 105, 131, 138

Oakland A's, 13, 14–16, 30, 33, 41, 57, 68, 81, 110, 147. *See also* Kansas City A's; Philadelphia A's
Oakland Oaks, 84
Ocean County NJ, 18–19
Office, Rowland, 72, 96
Olden, Paul, 54
Osborn, John Jay, Jr., 121

Oswald, Lee Harvey, 170
Otis, Amos, 41, 57, 58–59, 68
Ozark, Danny, 103, 125

Pacific Coast League, 37, 38, 57, 84
Paltrow, Bruce, 151, 153
Pan Am Building, 158
The Paper Chase (Osborn), 121–23, 160
Paper Mill Playhouse, 19
Paramount Pictures, 86
Paramount Television, 27
Paramount Theater (Brooklyn), 63
Paris, Jerry, 24
Parks, Larry, 63
Parrish, Larry, 103
Parrott, Mike, 114
The Partridge Family, 76
Patek, Freddie, 80
Pattin, Marty, 58
Paul, Gabe, 68
Paul, Richard Allen, 166
Pearl Harbor, 166
"Peggy Sue," 65
Perez, Marty, 41
Perry, Gaylord, 85, 128, 134
Pesky, Johnny, 98, 119
Peters, Hank, 68
Peterson, Roger, 65
Petty, Norman, 64
Philadelphia A's, 2–3. *See also* Kansas City A's; Oakland A's
Philadelphia PA, 27, 49, 50, 61
Philadelphia Phillies, 2, 12, 48–49, 100, 103–4, 110, 125, 146, 163–64
Phillie Phanatic, 48–50
Phillips, Mike, 69
Phoenix Firebirds, 57
Piniella, Lou: and "Boston Massacre," 111, 112, 113, 115, 118, 119, 120; and regular season games, 80, 97; and World Series, 128, 129, 131, 133, 134, 136, 137, 138, 140
Pioneer League, 37

Pittsburgh Pirates, 34, 57, 110, 145, 163
Plum Island, 21
Polo Grounds, 35
Pope John Paul I, 117, 125
Pope Paul VI, 117
Poquette, Tom, 58
Porter, Darrell, 80
Potsie & Ralph, 29
Prager, Joshua, 35
Presley, Elvis, 76
The Pride of the Yankees, 169
Purdy, Mark, 145

Queen Mother, 52–53
Quinn, John, 11

Rajsich, Dave, 127, 144
Ramis, Harold, 105, 107
Ramos, Domingo, 144
Randle, Lenny, 30, 40
Randolph, Willie, 46, 58, 81, 111, 112, 113, 115, 118, 119, 120, 139
Rapp, Vern, 165
Rautzhan, Lance, 134, 135, 138
"Rave On," 65
Red Lion Elementary School, 49
Reed, Rex, 64, 158
Reed, Ron, 103
Reese, Pee Wee, 34, 36, 130
Reeve, Christopher, 158–61
Reitz, Ken, 69
Remy, Jerry, 82, 118, 120, 128, 129
Rescue from Gilligan's Island, 141–42
Resorts International, 61–62
Reynolds, Burt, 162–63
Rice, Jim, 42, 82, 97, 98, 113, 115, 118, 120, 128, 129
The Richard Pryor Show, 25
Richardson, J. P. "The Big Bopper," 64
Rickey, Branch, 7–8, 9
Rigney, Bill, 34, 35
Riverfront Stadium, 59, 74

Rivers, Mickey: and American League East playoff, 127, 128; batting prowess of, 45; and "Boston Massacre," 111, 112, 113, 115, 118, 120; and regular season games, 46, 58, 81, 97; and World Series, 134, 137, 138
Rizzuto, Phil, 34, 40
Robinson, Brooks, 135
Robinson, Jackie, 9, 129, 152
Robinson, Wilbert, 130
rock and roll music, 62–63
Rogers, Steve, 59
Roosevelt Hospital, 84
Rose, Pete: awards of, 145; banned from baseball, 165; batting achievements of, 164; as career leader in offensive categories, 165; collision of, with Ray Fosse, 60, 165; as everyday player, 164; fight of, with Bud Harrelson, 60, 165; as free agent, 144; getting 3,000th hit, 59–60; hitting streak of, 95–96; and Montreal Expos, 165; nickname of, 59, 70, 146; and Philadelphia Phillies, 163–66; praising Sparky Anderson, 146; retirement of, 165; self-assessment of, 164–65; suspension of, 165; and Tom Seaver's no-hitter, 69
Royster, Jerry, 95, 96
Ruppert, Jacob, 8
Russell, Bill, 38, 102, 103, 105, 130, 131, 134, 136, 137, 138, 139
Russo, Jim, 40
Ruth, Babe, 2, 13, 41, 44, 46–47, 115, 122, 137
Ryan, Nolan, 66–67, 85, 114

Saint Christopher Parish, 1
San Diego Chicken, 32, 49
San Diego Padres, 16, 29, 32, 38, 56, 69, 75, 128, 146
San Diego Stadium, 75
San Francisco Giants, 12, 30, 32–33, 35, 39, 55, 57, 76, 105, 110. *See also* New York Giants

Santa Barbara CA, 10–11
Santa Barbara Dodgers, 72
Santa Barbara High School, 10–11
Saturday Night Fever, 76, 91
Saturday Night Live, 53, 106, 107, 160–61
Schmidt, Mike, 103, 104
Schultz, Buddy, 70
Schunick, Howard, 92, 93–94
Schunick, Jory, 92–94
Schunick, Lacey, 92–94
Schunick, Sarla, 92–93
Schunick, Shelley, 92–94
Scott, George, 82, 111, 115, 117, 118, 120, 128, 129
Seattle Mariners, 68–69, 110, 114
Seaver, Tom: Don Werner on, 70–71; nicknames of, 69; nineteen-strikeout game of, 66, 69; no-hitter of, 69–70, 76; and Opening Day, 71–72; performance of, in 1977, 39; performance of, in 1978, 71–72; trade of, to Cincinnati Reds, 30, 55–56, 102
Sex Pistols, 133
Shea Stadium, 102
Short, Bob, 85
Shot Heard 'Round the World, 35
Showtime, 123
Siebert, Paul, 55
Sifford, Charlie, 152
Silver, Carol Ruth, 155
Silvestri, Joey, 84
Simmons, Matty, 107, 109
Siskel, Gene, 77, 87
*61**, 23, 47
Smith, Ballard, 33
Smith, Charley, 48
Smith, Reggie, 31, 38, 101, 103, 104, 105, 131, 132–33, 136, 137
Snellenburg's Department Store, 2
Snyder, Zack, 161
Soderholm, Eric, 46
Sosa, Elías, 16, 45

Southern Association, 11
Southmayd, William, 114
South Portland High School, 113
Speier, Chris, 103, 105
Spelling, Aaron, 124
Spencer, Jim, 86, 110–11, 128, 138, 140
Spokane Indians, 37, 38
Spokesman-Review, 91
Sport, 41
Sports Illustrated, 11, 32, 86, 135, 136
Springfield NJ, 17–18, 62
Sprowl, Bobby, 117–18
Spungen, Nancy Laura, 133
SS *Minnow*, 141
Standard Brands, 46
Stanley, Bob, 118, 120, 128
Star-Ledger, 19, 20
Star Trek, 52
Star Wars, 23, 88–89
Stearns, John, 101
Stearns Wharf, 10
Steinbrenner, George, 14, 16, 41, 44, 56, 81, 83, 84, 86, 129
Stengel, Casey, 1, 4, 84
Stevens, Howell, 11
Stewart, Byron, 154–55
St. Louis Cardinals, 3, 31, 41, 47, 48, 57, 69, 163
Sullivan, Niki, 64
Summer, Donna, 91–92, 94
"Summer Nights," 78
Summers, Champ, 72
Sunday News Journal (Wilmington DE), 106, 166
Superman, 64, 157–61
Surf Ballroom, 64, 65
Sutherland, Donald, 107
Sutton, Don: and Baseball Hall of Fame, 75; as career pitching leader of Los Angeles Dodgers, 72, 75; career statistics of, 75; fight of, with Steve Garvey, 99–100; and high school, 72; and

206 • INDEX

Minor Leagues, 72–73; outstanding games of, 73–74; performance of, in 1978, 101–2, 103; on pressure, 139; rookie season of, in Major Leagues, 73; 300th win of, 74; win-loss record of, in 1978, 134; and World Series, 134–35, 139

"Take Me Out to the Ball Game," 86
Tanana, Frank, 67
Tatum, Ken, 31
Taxi, 123, 124
Templeton, Garry, 70
Terry, Ralph, 84
Texarkana TX, 10
Texas League, 73
Texas Rangers, 13, 45, 67, 68, 74, 85–86, 143
"Thank God I'm a Country Boy," 86
"That'll Be the Day," 65
Themal, Harry F., 106
"This Is *SportsCenter*," 155
Thomasson, Gary, 66, 82, 121
Thompson, Fresco, 73
Thomson, Bobby, 35
Thornton, Andre, 127–28
Thornton, Billy Bob, 88
Tiant, Luis, 119, 120
Tidrow, Dick, 82, 97, 113, 127, 137
Tigres del Licey, 38
Toledo OH, 6
Topping, Dan, 8, 9–10
Toronto Blue Jays, 57, 58, 68, 81, 128
Torre, Joe, 102
Torrez, Mike, 16, 41–42, 111, 128
Travolta, John, 76–77, 91
"True Love Ways," 65
Turner, Ted, 163
21st Century Communications, 107
Twitchell, Wayne, 105

UCLA, 9
Ueberroth, Peter, 165
An Unmarried Woman, 89–91

Urich, Robert, 124
U.S. Court of Appeals, 16
U.S. District Court, 15
U.S. Open, 17–18
USS *Southard*, 168
USS *Zane*, 168

Valens, Ritchie, 64
Valentine, Bobby, 55
Van Bommel, Bill, 15
Van Patten, Timothy, 153–54
Veeck, Bill, 4
Vega$, 29, 124
Vero Beach FL, 37
Veryzer, Tom, 127
Vicious, Sid, 133
Vietnam War, 27, 62, 77, 162
Vincent, Fay, 48
Vincent, Jan-Michael, 163
Virdon, Bill, 86

Wagner, Dick, 145, 148
Wahlberg, Mark, 23
Waitkus, Eddie, 49
Waits, Rick, 127
War and Remembrance (Wouk), 166–70
Watergate scandal, 27, 162
Wathan, John, 80
Watson, Bob, 71
WCBS (TV), 19
WCVB (TV), 21
"We Are the World," 155
Webb, Del, 8, 10
Weight Watchers Magazine, 107
Welch, Bob, 101, 102, 131, 132, 137
Welcome Back, Kotter, 76
Welles, Orson, 122
Werner, Don, 69, 70–71
Wernik, Donald, 18
Westrum, Wes, 34
White, Bill, 40
White, Dan, 155–56

White, Frank, 58, 80–81
White, Roy: and "Boston Massacre," 111, 113, 115, 118, 121; and effect of Yankees controversies, 86; and regular season games, 46, 58, 66; and World Series, 128, 132, 134, 136, 137, 138, 139
White Night Riots, 156
The White Shadow, 149–55
Williams, Anson, 22, 23–24
Williams, Cindy, 28
Williams, Dick, 81
Williams, Robin, 23–27, 123, 160
Williams, Ted, 119, 164
Willkie Farr & Gallagher, 14
Wills, Maury, 36
Wilson, Hugh, 123
Wilson, Willie, 50, 58, 80, 81
The Winds of War (Wouk), 166, 167
Winfield, Dave, 29, 38, 57
Winkler, Henry, 24–25, 76
Winter Party '59 tour, 64–65
Wise, Rick, 30–31
WKRP in Cincinnati, 123–24, 149
Woodlawn Cemetery, 6
"Words of Love," 65
Works Progress Administration, 122
World Series: (1907–9), 7; (1916), 130; (1920), 130; (1926), 41; (1928), 41; (1929), 2; (1930), 3; (1932), 3; (1941), 130; (1946), 119; (1947), 9, 130; (1948), 4, 34; (1951), 35; (1952), 130; (1953), 130; (1954), 35; (1955), 130; (1956), 130; (1957), 12; (1958), 12; (1959), 132; (1960), 47; (1962), 16, 35; (1963), 16, 39, 130, 132; (1964), 16; (1965), 132; (1966), 132; (1967), 47, 119; (1968), 13; (1969), 57, 69, 85; (1970), 15, 135, 146; (1972), 15, 81, 85, 147; (1973), 15, 39, 81, 85; (1974), 15, 81, 85, 132; (1975), 15, 119; (1976), 15, 16, 44, 84–85, 143, 148; (1977), 16, 38, 41, 83, 84–85, 130, 132, 143; (1978), 130–41, 143; (1980), 50
World War I, 8, 23
World War II, 8, 166–70
Wouk, Herman, 166–70
WPIX (TV), 40, 67
Wrigley, William, Jr., 2
WXLO (radio), 133
Wygant, Bobbie, 90
Wynn, Jimmy, 45

Xavier University, 123

Yankee Stadium, 8, 45–46, 47, 96–98, 127, 133, 135
Yastrzemski, Carl, 42, 82, 97, 112, 115, 118, 119–20, 128, 129
Yeager, Steve, 130, 138–39

Zimmer, Don, 30–31, 82, 98, 111, 112, 115, 117, 119, 128